Hatred of Jews –
A Failure of Holocaust Education?

I dedicate this book to all the brave people who face evil, ask questions, search for answers, are willing to listen to other people, want to learn from experience and history and make an effort every day to make on all fronts the world a little better: academics, teachers, Holocaust educators, history enthusiasts, parents, family members, and friends. Stay strong.

Hatred of Jews

A FAILURE OF HOLOCAUST EDUCATION?

Melanie Carina Schmoll

Bibliografische Information der Deutschen Nationalbibliothek
Die Deutsche Nationalbibliothek verzeichnet diese Publikation in der
Deutschen Nationalbibliografie; detaillierte bibliografische Daten sind im
Internet über http://dnb.d-nb.de abrufbar.

Verlag: BoD · Books on Demand GmbH,
In de Tarpen 42, 22848 Norderstedt, bod@bod.de
Druck: Libri Plureos GmbH, Friedensallee 273, 22763 Hamburg

ISBN: 978-3-7693-3865-2

CONTENT

PREFACE

A few years ago, when I was teaching 9th grade history
at a Gymnasium in Hamburg, Germany,
I introduced the lesson with the words:
"And now we are starting a new chapter:
We are talking about National Socialism and the
Second World War and, of course, the Holocaust."
One pupil was writing something down, raised her head and asked:
"Holo...what?"
Based on the reaction, I asked the class if anyone
knew the term and what it was all about.
The students all shook their heads.
Students in grade 9 are around 15 years old.
They had never heard the term before.

The Holocaust is one of the main events in human history. It is the most terrible of all events in human history. It is the event that knows no pattern and no copy. The event that stands, indeed must stand, outside of all comparisons.

For me as a German, it is also part of the history of my country, of my society. The people who committed the greatest crime of all spoke my language, lived in my city, walked the streets I walk. They read the literature that I read, sang the same children's songs that I learnt and followed the same social norms and rules that I abide by. To many of the social norms and rules that I abide by. At some point, however, we parted ways.

When I speak of the greatest crime of all, I do so in the absence of words. I cannot think of any words to describe what people have done to people. And I do not think other words are needed, because *the greatest crime of all* is the maximum of what is possible – the absolute negative.

Why should the Holocaust be taught? Because families (both perpetrators and victims) do not talk about it and therefore state schools have to step in? Because it is simply part of history? Because we need to hear about it to make us realize that it does not necessarily remain a singular event? Because we can use the knowledge to make the present and future better? Because we can learn from history?

If Holocaust education was there to make the world a better, more peaceful place, then I do not understand the hatred we see these days.

But is that even possible? Turning absurd evil into something good?

Surely this is one of the reasons why people teach and engage with the Holocaust. In the course of the book, I list many reasons that can be given for why the Holocaust is taught, why people write about it, what they learnt and what the purpose of Holocaust education is. Each of these reasons probably has its justification and each purpose is desirable.

But my own personal reason, in addition to all the good ones, is this one: Because I cannot not do it.

And this has nothing to do with my passport in particular or a personal family history.

It has to do with the fact that I am human. It is as simple as that.

Or so complicated. Because it does not get any easier the more I deal with it–quite the opposite.

I have tried to put the issue to rest because it made me physically ill. There were years in my life when there was not a single day when the name Hitler did not come up. Simply because the subject was so dominant. And even if I did not bring it up myself–there is bound to be a report on German TV somewhere about Hitler, the Second World War or the Holocaust. It always seems to me that people cannot get enough. Hopefully, it is not about admiration, but much more about people wanting to understand. Basically, that is a very good start: when people want to understand when they have questions and are looking for answers.

I have found a way of not constantly poisoning myself with the topic–and still looking for answers. Then I also accept the fact that Hitler still seems to be omnipresent after all this time.

If it serves a good purpose.

Unfortunately, things seem to have changed since October 2023. And that is the reason for this book. To answer my own questions, as well as those of many colleagues, I sat down and wrote this book based on everything I had been working on for years. The book is intended to provide answers and show (new) ways forward. I did not write the book to defeat hatred of Jews through Holocaust education or because I think I have all the answers to all the questions. I wrote it because I was looking for answers myself–as an academic, historian, teacher, supporter, listener, friend, human being. Because simply being a human being makes me part of the story. As all of us.

ACKNOWLEDGEMENTS

I would like to take this opportunity to express my deep gratitude to:

Slawa Schwarz for his expertise about thousands of years of Jewish history,

Nancy Pearson Mackie for the proof-reading,

Henning Lau for the cover, which he designed exactly the way I wanted it,

Clarissa Schockemöhle (BoD) for support in publishing,

Judy Baumel–Schwartz for giving me an academic home when no one else did,

David Bercuson for his interest, and everything else he has done for me,

Jürgen Schiefer ... without words, because words are not enough.

1. INTRODUCTION

Many academics, politicians, teachers, and educators share the prominent idea that teaching and learning about the Holocaust is a primary bulwark against antisemitism. Teaching the Holocaust means to support political education. For some researchers, it is about nothing less than preventing genocides.[1] UNESCO mainly shaped this approach in which the Holocaust is part of a global education to build global citizens.[2] Global Citizenship Education (GCE) is defined as a response to challenges like human rights violations, inequality, and poverty and to prevent. It includes knowledge about human history and the greatest failures of humankind. More than this, teaching the Holocaust is mandatory. United Nations General Assembly Resolution 60/7 (2005) and UNESCO General Conference Resolution 34C/61 (2007) on Holocaust Remembrance emphasize the historical significance of the Holocaust and outline the importance of teaching this event as a contribution to the prevention of genocide and atrocity crimes. Holocaust education was present for years as *the answer* to the question of antisemitism.

Given the increase in antisemitic incidents worldwide, this answer should be reviewed.–Or, as Friedmann asked: *Why didn't all this help?*[3]

Increasing antisemitism worldwide

On October 7th, 2023, thousands of Iranian-backed Palestinian terrorists, namely Islamic Jihad and Hamas, attacked the State of Israel in a coordinated assault. Palestinian Islamist group Hamas fired a huge barrage of rockets across southern Israel, with alarm given also in Tel Aviv and Beersheba. Thousands of rockets had been fired on Israeli territory. The barrage served as a cover for an unprecedented, multi-pronged infiltration of terrorists into Israel. Most terrorists crossed through breaches in land security barriers separating Gaza and the State of Israel.[4] In total, some 1,200 people were murdered in Israel during the unprecedented assault, mostly civilians slaughtered in their homes or at an outdoor music festival, as well as soldiers on bases near the border. At least 224 people, including the elderly, women, and children, were abducted to Gaza, in the bloodiest and most deadly attack in Israeli history. UN indicated that rape and gang rape likely occurred during the October 7 Hamas onslaught against southern Israel, that *clear and convincing* evidence shows that hostages were raped while being held in Gaza, and that those currently [January 2025, note of the author] held captive are still facing such abuse.[5]

The terror attack must be mentioned since incomprehensibly and against humanity, this event leads to an explosion of antisemitic incidents worldwide. While Israel, the Jewish democratic state, started its defensive warfare, many people globally reacted with a hatred of Jews against the victims. The hatred of Jews, antisemitism, noticed a dramatic rise.

The 2023 *Antisemitism Report* by *Israel's Ministry of Diaspora and the Fight against Antisemitism*, in cooperation with the *World Zionist Organization* and the *Jewish Agency* states, that the year 2023 ended with a 235 percent increase in antisemitic incidents worldwide, as compared to the previous year. Forty-five percent of all antisemitic incidents monitored in 2023 took place in the United States; 39 percent occurred in Europe. Of equal concern was the 33 percent increase in violent antisemitic events as compared to those in 2022. Six Jews were murdered in the United States, Egypt, and Tunisia. According to the report, last year began with an approximate 10 percent increase in recorded incidents of antisemitism as compared to 2022. This trend was maintained throughout the first nine months of the year (January–September). The change came in the last quarter of 2023, when there were six times more antisemitic events as compared to the prior three quarters. According to the report, there was also a significant increase in Holocaust denial and distortion, with most (68 percent) of the content published between November and December 2023 appearing on the X social media platform, and the rest showing up on TikTok and Facebook, Instagram (both owned by Meta) and Telegram.[6]

The same is true for Germany, which seemed to be a *role model in handling the Holocaust* [7], because it is part of its very own history.[8] Germany seems to be the *World Champion of regeneration*.[9] Of course, the fear of a possible loss of prestige for Germany also plays a role here.[10] But it needs to be emphasized that although Germany was seen like this and saw itself this way, the German government's *Anti-Semitism Report* from 2017[11] showed already that the proportion of Germans who agree with antisemitic statements rose from 28 percent in 2014 to 40 percent in 2016. In absolute figures, this means that out of 83 million Germans, 33 million Germans agree with antisemitic statements. Additionally, *antisemitic incidents rose 320% in 2023 year-on-year compared to the same period in 2022*[12] in Germany. RIAS, the *Federal Association Promoting the Reporting and Support Network*, stressed during that period it looked at 994 verified cases—including three cases of extreme violence 29 attacks, 72 incidents of targeted property destruction, 32 threats, 4 antisemitic mass mailings and 854 cases of injurious behavior. The 854 cases of injurious behavior included 177 antisemitic gatherings.[13] Jews in Germany were advised to hide their identity, otherwise they would be in danger. *No other minority was ever given such advice.*[14]

These developments are not only Germany-related. On October 8, 2023 Jew hater sent out a *how-to* manual at universities across the US to tell students what to do, what to say, and even what placards to display, including a template of a Hamas terrorist on a paraglider with insert org name and organization logos at the bottom helpfully situated on the graphic. October 8 was the day after the Hamas massacres and atrocities and before Israel mounted its response.[15] And the campaign seems to have worked. A study, published by the *Maurice and Marilyn Cohen Center for Modern Jewish Studies* at Brandeis University, helps paint a clearer picture of the attitudes undergirding the widespread tensions over Israel and Gaza that spread across campuses since October 2023, leading to disruptive protests and university crackdowns. The survey put forward, 19% of non-Jewish students said that *Israel does not have the right to exist* and 24% agreed that *I wouldn't want to be friends with someone who supports the existence of Israel as a Jewish state*. Another statement, that *supporters of Israel control the media*, was endorsed by nearly 43% of non-Jewish students.[16]

In June 2024, the Executive Director of the American Jewish Committee (AJC) Deutch in Washington D. C. *declared a global state of emergency for the Jewish people*. This shows the pressure that Jews are currently under worldwide.[17] The Western fight against antisemitism was on the right side of history in the past. This stance is now being put to the test.[18] *Indeed, the entire apparatus of international human-rights advocacy and aid that was created in the wake of the Holocaust is now weaponized against the Jewish victims of Islamist attacks*.[19] Today it seems: Human rights for all, except Jews.

New initiatives are needed and since summer 2023 there is even a task force, called *J7* for the fight against antisemitism.[20] *The ease with which people have managed to portray the Jewish state as genocidal, a successor to Nazi Germany, marks a historic failure of Holocaust education in the West*, said Halevi in 2024. He also stated the end of the post-Holocaust era and even writes that *the Holocaust is back.*[21]

Watching this more than concerning developments, the question almost automatically occurs: Has Holocaust education failed?

To answer this question, a broader view is needed. If the main purpose of Holocaust education is the answer to the questions of antisemitism, it needs to make clear what Holocaust education is and what antisemitism is and how it looks like. Although some colleagues do not want to discuss the term itself[22], a discussion about terminology has to be done. As Pearce et al. write: *For if education, and specifically education about the Holocaust, is presented as 'the answer', it is important to consider what, exactly, is the nature of the 'problem'.*[23]

It seems like the usage of the term antisemitism needs some clarification. The fact that many people have difficulty recognizing antisemitism also speaks in favor of clarifying the term. Bernstein stresses that there is a pronounced defensive attitude regarding to the term antisemitism, which also manifests itself in trivialization.[24] Naturally, this means that antisemitism cannot be dealt with professionally. In the Arab world, for example, the term antisemitism is understood as a construct designed to silence the criticism of Israel. Antisemitism is conflated with political opposition, creating a moral and rhetorical maze that makes any meaningful discussion nearly impossible.[25]

Bernstein shows too, that antisemitism is not understood as a phenomenon in its own right. It is considered a sub-category of racism, xenophobia or misanthropy and is therefore misunderstood. In some cases, it is also considered a *fad*. The specific structure of the world view of antisemitism is just as little recognized as the underlying manifestations of its divergent forms. As a result, antisemitism is equated with racism and secondary antisemitism and Israel-related antisemitism are no longer given any attention. And even if there is a recognition of differences between antisemitism, racism, and other forms of misanthropy. Antisemitism is perceived as less important and pressing than other forms.[26] There seems to be an inherent distance between the term antisemitism and the meaning of the term hatred of Jews. Therefore, the term hatred of Jews seems way more constructive. To avoid misunderstandings, lacks of understanding or the misusage of the term antisemitism, the term **hatred of Jews** is better to use.

Holocaust education is always learning about the past–and this primarily takes place in a school context. It is initially irrelevant in which countries the topic is discussed in which subjects. Many of the insights into Holocaust education that are available today have therefore been acquired in a school context. For Germany in particular, public schools are the focal point for imparting knowledge and remembrance. Of course, hostility towards Jews or hatred of Jews are problems for society that need to be combated not only in the school environment. This also applies to many countries and societies and their schools. Many of the findings on which this book is based were acquired through research in Germany and North America. This is due to two things: First, Germany is the country of the perpetrators and, therefore, particularly in focus. Second, Holocaust education was invented in North America. Most of the studies used here therefore come from Germany and North America.

After these classifications, a closer look at what to expect it this study needs to be done: First, one needs to know what one is talking about when it comes to Holocaust education. After defining the concept of Holocaust education and tracing the history of hatred of Jews, the content and the current state of Holocaust education are examined. To find answers to complicated questions it is necessary to dive deeply into the research done within the last centuries before going on to make practical suggestions on how Holocaust education can be changed and how it can be used to confront hatred against Jews today and in the future. To give practical advice, suggestions are made for restructuring and possibly improving future Holocaust education. In the last part of the book, the connection between Holocaust education and hatred of Jews is shown, and it is made clear to what extent the two aspects are connected. It also shows how Holocaust education can perhaps be used in a modified and adapted form as a means of combating hatred of Jews.

2. HOLOCAUST EDUCATION – A CONFUSING TERM AND CONCEPT?

"The dying memory also increases the distance:
The experience-saturated, present survivors become a pure past
that the withdrawn from experience."[1]

School is often defined as a micro-level socialization agent, where political, religious, and social positions are further established. Teaching the Holocaust is one of the most demanding topics in schools and is highly difficult to teach. Besides the obvious challenge of teaching kids at the age of 14–16 about the *rupture of civilization* (Dan Diner) challenges teachers and educators are confronted with are numerous. As Totten stressed in 1999: The Holocaust is one of the most tortuously complex, not to mention *horrific subjects* an educator can tackle.[2] The Holocaust is viewed as a topic for experts with little bearing upon the lives of young people, or so it might seem–but not all teachers and educators are experts. Nevertheless, the Holocaust has to be taught.[3]

Certainly, the absolute negativity of the Holocaust is unsettling and discouraging. But a discussion on how the Holocaust is taught and whether moral impetus is allowed or even necessary must be held.

The word Holocaust comes from ancient Greek. The word Holocaust is derived from the Greek **holokauston,** a translation of the Hebrew word **'olah,** meaning a *burnt sacrifice offered whole to God.* This word was chosen, and gained wide usage, because, in the ultimate manifestation of the National Socialists killing program, the bodies of the victims were consumed whole in crematoria or open fires.[4] Since 1945, it has been synonymous with the murder of European Jews during the Second World War (1939–1945). Jews speak of the *Shoah*, which is the Hebrew word for *catastrophe.*

The Holocaust

The Holocaust was an unprecedented genocide, total and systematic, perpetrated by National Socialist Germany and its collaborators, with the aim of annihilating the Jewish people. The primary motivation was the national socialist anti-Semitic racist ideology. Between 1933 and 1941 Germany pursued a policy that dispossessed the Jews of their rights and their property, followed by the branding and the concentration of the Jewish population. This policy gained broad support in Germany and much of occupied Europe. In 1941, following the invasion of the Soviet Union, the National Socialists and their collaborators launched the systematic mass murder of the Jews. By 1945 nearly six million Jews had been murdered.[5]

Following this definition the term Holocaust is *used exclusively for the mass murder of Jews* and unlike the usage in other studies it is not applicable to other genocides or massacres in human history.[6] The Holocaust was a German initiative that took place throughout German- and Axis-controlled Europe. It affected nearly all of Europe's Jewish population, which in 1933 numbered 9 million people. By the end of the war, 6 million Jews and millions of other victims were dead.[7]

The time period of the Holocaust differs, here the years of the Holocaust are defined as 1933–1945. In 1933 the *Nationalsozialistische Deutsche Arbeiterpartei* (NSDAP) (National Socialist German Workers' Party) came to power in Germany. The Holocaust ended in May 1945, when the Allied Powers defeated Germany in the Second World War (1939–1945).

In order to better understand the background, it is necessary to take a closer look at the period of the Holocaust between 1933 and 1945. When the National Socialists came to power in Germany, they did not immediately start to carry out the mass murder of Jews. But they started quickly to exclude Jews from German society.

Adolf Hitler (1889–1945) was appointed Reichskanzler by President Paul von Hindenburg (1847–1934) on 30 January 1933. He and his party started immediately to rebuild the democratic system of the *Weimar Republic* by laying the foundations of the National Socialist state. One approach to Hitler's racist view of the world was the idea of the so-called *Volksgemeinschaft* (Volk Community). His idea was guided by racist and authoritarian principles. The National Socialists promoted a particularly virulent form of racial hatred of Jews. They believed that the world was divided into distinct races and that some of these races were superior to others. They considered Germans to be members of the supposedly superior race. They asserted that these so-called *Aryans* were locked in a struggle for existence with other, inferior races.

The National Socialists eliminated individual freedoms and a society which would, in theory, transcend class and religious differences. To reach this goal, Hitler and the National Socialists wanted to unite the German people politically and culturally. Thus, they said that Germans, German blood, and German culture were better than that of the rest of the world. Blood was especially important to the National Socialists for being part of the *Volk*, the nation. Hitler and other National Socialist thinkers were associating nationality with race. The connection between blood, race and nationality set up the qualifications for who was in and out of the *Volksgemeinschaft*. To them, the Germans were the perfect race and all others were inferior. They targeted Jews as the worst of all *races*. According to the National Socialists, Jews were a threat that needed to be removed from German society. Otherwise, Jews would permanently corrupt and destroy the German people–such was the thinking of the National Socialists.

The National Socialists used these ideas to promote an even bigger idea: that to improve the survival of the country, German blood should be preserved, or kept *pure*. The blood of so-called *weaker races* should have been eliminated.

Milestones on the way to mass murder were discriminatory laws and organized violence targeting Germany's Jews. The first anti-Jewish decrees were established in 1933. The persecution also started immediately for example by the public burning of books written by Jewish authors, random attacks on Jews and Jewish property and the police and the courts did no longer protect Jews. In 1934, Jewish students were excluded from exams in medicine, pharmacy, and law. 1935 another major step towards the Holocaust was taken, when the *Nürnberger Gesetze* (Nuremberg Laws) were established. These laws denied Jews many basic civil rights. One of them, the so-called *Law for 'The Protection of German Blood and German Honour'* forbade mixed marriages. In the fall of 1935, German Jews lost their citizenship according to the definitions posed in these new regulations. Only so-called *full* Germans were entitled to the full protection of the law.

This radicalization culminated in a plan that National Socialist leaders referred to as the so-called *Endlösung*, the Final Solution of the Jewish Question. By implementing these measures, the systematic mass murder of all Jews in Europe became a National Socialist policy. The *Final Solution* was the organized and systematic mass murder of European Jews and implemented by the National Socialists, their allies, and collaborators between 1941 and 1945. The policies varied from place to place. Thus, not all Jews experienced the Holocaust in the same way. But in all instances, millions of people were persecuted simply because they were identified as Jewish. The *Final Solution* was the last stage of the Holocaust and took place from 1941 to 1945. Though many Jews were killed before the vast majority of Jewish victims were murdered during this period.

As part of the *Final Solution*, Germany committed mass murder on an unprecedented scale. There were two main methods of killing. One method was mass shooting. German units carried out mass shootings on the outskirts of villages, towns, and cities throughout Eastern Europe. The other method was asphyxiation with poison gas. Gassing operations were conducted at killing centers and with mobile gas vans.[8]

The mass murder of Jews was very well planned and organized. Since the Germans did not see Jews as humans, they treated the mass murder as an *issue* that needed to be solved. In late 1941, the National Socialist regime began building specially designed, stationary killing centers in German-occupied Poland. In English, killing centers are sometimes called *extermination camps* or *death camps*. They built these killing centers for the sole purpose of efficiently murdering Jews on a mass scale. The primary means of murder at the killing centers was poisonous gas released into sealed gas chambers or vans. German authorities, with the help of their allies and collaborators, transported Jews from across Europe to these killing centers. They disguised their intentions by calling the transports to the killing centers *resettlement actions* or *evacuation transports*. In English, they are often referred to as *deportations*. Most of these deportations took place by train. The vast majority of Jews deported to killing centers were gassed almost immediately after their arrival. Some Jews whom German officials believed to be healthy and strong enough were selected for forced labor. At all five killing centers, German officials forced some Jewish prisoners to assist in the killing process. Among other tasks, these prisoners had to sort through victims' belongings and remove victims' bodies from the gas chambers. Special units disposed of the millions of corpses through mass burial, in burning pits, or by burning them in large, specially designed crematoria. Nearly 2,7 million Jewish men, women, and children were murdered at the five killing centers.[9]

Besides the killing in camps, areas of cities or towns occupied by Germans were developed into so-called *Ghettos*. In these areas, German occupiers forced Jews to live in overcrowded and unsanitary conditions. Ghettos were created first between 1939 and 1940 in occupied Poland. German authorities often enclosed these areas by building walls or other barriers. Guards prevented Jews from leaving without permission. Some ghettos existed for years, but others existed only for months, weeks, or even days as holding sites prior to deportation or murder. Beginning in June 1941, German officials also established them in newly conquered territories in eastern Europe following the German attack on the Soviet Union. German authorities and their allies and collaborators also established ghettos in other parts of Europe. Beginning in 1941–1942, Germans and their allies and collaborators murdered ghetto residents en masse and dissolved ghetto administrative structures. They called this process *liquidation*.[10]

Having said this, it becomes clear why the term Holocaust specifically refers to the systematic, state-sponsored persecution and murder of six million Jews. However, there were many other groups persecuted and murdered, too.[11]

Talking about these historical facts, it might be needed to mention the concept of *history* in general, since the question of the image of history also raises the question of the future. In this present, the struggle for the past, its contemplation, interpretation, and transmission, is a struggle for the future. History is politics. History exists in a field of tension. It is about the relationship between reflexive, rational remembrance on the one hand and identitarian, mostly emotionalized interpretation in order to achieve communitisation on the other. What is declared to be history does not depend on historical folds but on their interpretation. This is done by academia, the public, politics, and the media. Historical research means reinventing history. It is primarily about political questions.

The concept of *history* can be described as *sociologically amorphous* in the sense of Max Weber. Samuel Salzborn explains what he meant by this: History can be claimed in very different ways by many different political and social currents. Furthermore, it is characterized by the fact that it describes something *processual* in terms of content, but due to its singular *form* refers to something seemingly closed.[12] What is historically true is not what someone subjectively remembers, but what can actually be reconstructed historically as *history* on the basis of scientific analysis and supported by source material and contextual interpretations. In this respect, history is also pluralistic and contradictory. In democracies, history is interpreted, and people argue about their own interests, but **facts are not ignored** or reinterpreted. This also applies to the politics of remembrance.

In this sense, it is therefore important to strengthen political and historical education through factual knowledge. This is the only way to focus on the partial or general reinterpretation or denial of historical facts. Only in this way can historical revisionist positions be deciphered as such.

The Historical Development of Holocaust Education

In different countries and places of the world, different concepts of Holocaust education were developed for different reasons.[13] Holocaust education varies considerably from country to country. Teaching about the Holocaust is seen as linked to the history and society in which it is taught, with factors such as international politics, power relations, and religious and ideological perspectives. This connection is also understandable if one considers the concept of history just mentioned.

Since the entire concept of **Holocaust education was developed in North America**, concepts of Holocaust education and studies based in North America are important for this analysis. After 1945, the so-called *West* began to see the Holocaust as an important part of its own identity. The same applies to Germany, the country of the perpetrators. Germany was seen for centuries as a *gold standard* in Holocaust education.[14]

The term **Holocaust education** originates from the US educational debate of the 1980s. At the center of this very pragmatic discussion was the question of how the Holocaust as a singular historical event could itself become the subject of education. In this context, specific teaching materials, Holocaust curricula, were developed that focused on the historical subject, victims, perpetrators and bystanders and their choices and choice-less choices, for example, their respective historical scope for decision-making and action. This didactically prepared biographical source material was intended to make history concrete and bridge the gap between the learning subjects and the historical actors of the Holocaust.

Why did Holocaust education become so important and prominent in North America? More than one reason needs to be mentioned here. The circumstances were totally different than in Europe and especially in Germany, the country of the perpetrators. Right after the war social and cultural pluralism were observed as well as an increasing diversity within the societies. In Montreal and Toronto, Canada, for example, there were large size and vital survivor communities. In these areas, Holocaust education developed sooner, to a greater extent and faster than in other areas. Holocaust consciousness began to emerge in the 1970s. Before this time period, there was a lack of interest for example in the United States, mainly because of the ongoing *Cold War* and the fact, that the Jewish communities were preoccupied with re-establishing a sense of normalcy. The events that began to dislodge the Holocaust from the shadows were the *Eichmann trial* and Hanna Arendt's report.[15] Also, a number of other books about the mass murder of European Jewry were published during this time and helped to inform the American public about the Holocaust. Additionally, the events in the Middle East, the *Six-Day War of 1967*, acted as a powerful catalyst in defining the relationship of North American Jews to the Holocaust. In the weeks prior to the Six-Day War, Jews found themselves both ready and determined to face the perceived threat to their survival.[16] Holocaust consciousness had moved from the margins to the center.[17] But it is interesting to know that the term Holocaust was not commonly used before the end of the 1950s (for example there were school textbooks without mentioning the events).

1973 Holocaust commemoration was established by the *Canadian Jewish Congress* and since 1976 local remembrance committees have been active in 12 Canadian cities.[18] In Canada the term *Holocaust education* was included in the curricula of private Catholic schools as early as 1974, it became a mandatory part of the curriculum.

The TV series *Holocaust* from 1978 had a huge impact on North America. In Canada for example the *Toronto Remembrance Committee* started an education program including a summer teaching training institute, long-term collaboration with local school boards, production of Holocaust education curricula, professional development for teachers, lecture series and an annual student seminar day on the Holocaust.

Also, museums were created, like the *United States Holocaust Memorial Museum (USHMM)*. On 27 September 1979, the Commission presented its report to the President, recommending the establishment of a national Holocaust memorial museum in Washington, D. C., with three main components: a national museum/memorial, an educational foundation, and a *Committee on Conscience.* After a unanimous vote by the United States Congress in 1980 to establish the museum, the USHMM was founded.[19]

Also, *Holocaust Education Weeks* were established. *Holocaust Education Weeks* are annual events on the topic in which school classes are required to participate. They are organized in co-operation with universities or Jewish communities. The class groups meet academics who give short introductory talks and answer questions. Documentaries are shown and pupils are able to meet survivors or members of the second or third generation.

An educational program under the auspices of the *League for*

Human Rights of B´nai Brith to fight Holocaust denial was developed in 1986 in Canada.[20] This program included a three-week tour to Germany, Poland, and Israel. The goal was to confront teachers about history and become witnesses.[21] The program became necessary and was a response to the *Keegstra trial.* James Keegstra was a history teacher in a small town in Alberta, Canada. He had for years instructed his students that the Holocaust was an exaggeration perpetrated by the Jews. A non-Jewish parent filed a successful suit against Keegstra under Canada's anti-hate Laws.[22]

Another program is the *March of the Living Project* for Jewish students which is still active. 1998 the province of Ontario established a *Holocaust Remembrance Day*, and other provinces followed.

In 1982 a study by Glickmann/Bardikoff analyzed 72 textbooks. 50 percent of the reviewed books dealing with the modern world, had nothing or less than one paragraph on the topic.[23] After analyzing textbooks in 2004 again, Short/Reed came to the conclusion that the topic did not play a major role in Canadian public schools until 1990. Since 1990, it has been part of *History, English, world issues, citizenship, and human rights classes.*[24] Additionally, the *Ontario Jewish Federation* presented a study about the amount of Holocaust education in grade 9. The result: 5 hours of Holocaust education.

In today's USA Holocaust education is required in only 26 states (2024).[25] Taught at elementary, middle, and high schools throughout the country since the 1970s, it is been positioned for wide impact. The 2020 *Never Again Education Act*[26] was supported by conservatives and liberals alike. 85 Holocaust museums and memorials[27] exist in the USA today.

A fundamental difference between North American countries and Germany, for example, is that there is a binding and standardized curriculum that goes by the name of *Holocaust education*. The topic is effectively removed from the linear history lessons or social studies lessons and viewed as a separate unit. Teachers know when the unit has to take place so that the so-called *Holocaust Education Weeks* can take place afterwards.

Interestingly, the term *Holocaust Education* does not appear in classes in **Germany.** Within the main comprehensive understanding [Holocaust education, note of the author] means both history classes about the specific historical event and a way of systematic education about values and morals, starting in the kindergarten, applies to the entire education sector and conducts the [academic, note of the author] studies, in fact, each study.[28]

One problem in dealing with the topic is the semantic confusion over the meaning of the event as it is occurring in the education of teachers and educators. A glance at the international field of education about the Holocaust even reveals a lack of accord over the very name and purpose of this field. *Holocaust education, Holocaust studies, teaching about the Holocaust, education about the Holocaust, teaching from the Holocaust* and even simply *Holocaust* are among the various titles used.[29] Even the term *Holocaust* is only used to a small extent, namely a definition at the sidebar of a page in textbooks, so to say, as a lexicon article in the textbook for a better understanding.[30] Holocaust education is mainly part of German *history classes*[31], but not exclusively. Interestingly, Gautschi and Lücke prove in a study that pupils first and foremost come into contact with the Holocaust in history lessons. The pupils were given 10 options to choose from (e. g. TV documentaries, game files, parents/family, etc.). History lessons were clearly the front-runner. It was irrelevant whether history was a favorite subject or not. It is obvious, that history classes are the most important factor when it comes to Holocaust education in Germany.

The fact that history lessons are often no longer an independent subject in German state schools is problematic. Integrative concepts of several subject perspectives are often used. Unfortunately, it is also often the case that these subjects are primarily used as a cost-cutting program, leading to reduced learning time and a loss of content.[32] One can observe, that when it comes to university science and school subjects in general, science does not determine the definition and/ or the structure of subjects.[33] This seems to be a problem, as science could help to tailor these subjects and make clear what content and skills are needed.

Rathenow et al. stress, that there is currently a transition process ongoing: from *communicative memory*, which is based on recorded information and stories from one generation to another, to the *cultural memory* which is based on transfer by media.[34] However, this is not to be understood in the sense of a *collective history* in which a general lack of freedom of the individual is formed in the collective. Or, as Hilton and Patt put it, people hold a collective memory of the Holocaust, even if their understanding of it is cursory.[35]

As an important means of shaping and transmitting collective memory, Holocaust education in local classrooms is influenced by both national and personal factors. The national element is seen in the curriculum, teacher training and standardized tests, while the personal aspect is brought in by the beliefs and attitudes of students and teachers. However, teachers' personal connections, such as family history, can help students reflect on the human stories and the relevance of the Holocaust today.[36] Additionally, Germany has faced record immigration numbers in recent years, which has led to increased diversity within both the community and the classroom–this also contributes to a different kind of memory. Traditional approaches to teaching the Holocaust in German schools, often exclude those with migrant backgrounds who, despite possibly holding German citizenship, are not descendants of National Socialist perpetrators. Therefore, another predominant discourse focuses on what Holocaust education should look like in a migration society.

Following Adorno's postulate regarding *education after Auschwitz* (1966)[37] teaching and learning about the Holocaust in Germany, the country of perpetrators, still focuses on Adorno's suggestions. This postulate is based on the famous radio lecture, later also published as an essay. Adorno was referring to two aspects of education: Education in childhood, especially early childhood and a general enlightenment that creates a spiritual, cultural, and social climate that permits no repetition of such monstrous action, thus a climate in motives that have led to the horror become conscious to some degree.[38] In his essay Adorno addressed various aspects of learning and in particular the impetus of *not repeating Auschwitz.* Because: *All political education should ultimately be centered on the fact that Auschwitz should not be repeated.* It is clear from the research that young people rarely arrive in the classroom as *blank slates* with no knowledge, understanding or consciousness of the Holocaust.[39]

However, Adorno's postulate initially only applied to West Germany. Holocaust education developed along two separate trajectories in divided Germany. Education on the Holocaust was very different in both German countries. The Federal Republic of Germany (BRD) used the history of National Socialism to strengthen its new democratic order, the German Democratic Republic (GDR) was focused on combatting fascism through socialism.[40]

In West Germany, the Federal Republic of Germany, denazification attempted to re-orient the education system toward democracy by emphasizing German history prior to 1933, yet remaining silent on the Holocaust. Many students educated in the 1950s and 1960s do not recall learning about National Socialism, as teachers were mostly reluctant to deal with this time-period, even when it was included in the textbooks. Re-education policies, which confronted pupils, as well as adults in further education, with the Holocaust in the Allied occupation zones, focused primarily on the offenders, rather than on Jewish victims. Holocaust education was only slowly established following radical student movements in the late 1960s, which began to expose West Germany's silence. Between the 1960s and 1980s, discourse around the teaching of National Socialism focused on the concept of *Vergangenheitsbewältigung* (coming to terms with the past), with emphasis placed on German guilt, the responsibility to remember and prevent.[41]

Comparable to North America, the TV series *Holocaust* in 1978 left an impact on Germans and their view on the Holocaust. Finally, the German public started to discuss the issue. Silence and distortion prevailed for many years. The crimes against humanity committed during the National Socialist era were neither dealt with in school lessons nor were they part of the unofficial daily discourse.

By the late 1980s, the practice of Holocaust education in West Germany had become increasingly professionalized and encouraged new pedagogical techniques, such as the inclusion of first-person accounts and student visits to memorial sites. From the 1980s to the present day, discussion on Holocaust education has seen an increasing intensity of public, scholarly, and pedagogical interest.

In contrast to the developments in West Germany, the curriculum in East Germany (GDR/ German Democratic Republic) maintained a doctrine of anti-fascism, underscoring Soviet persecution and heroizing communist resistance fighters as a means to strengthen the official ideology of the state. This ritualized memorialization of the crimes of National Socialism in East Germany marginalized Jewish and other non-communist victims and ignored the involvement of the German population as perpetrators, thereby preventing the development of a commemorative culture like that in West Germany.[42]

These conflicting politics of memory and disparate approaches to history education blended together following German reunification in 1990. Compulsory Holocaust education was mandated throughout united Germany, as the transfer of Western Germany's memorial culture to East Germany (including textbooks, teacher training, and informal education at concentration camps, memorial sites, and museums). The reunification of Germany led to a convergence in the two divergent methods of addressing Holocaust education, the conversion of concentration camps into memorial sites, and the creation of laws against Holocaust denial.[43]

An official *Holocaust Remembrance Day* was declared in Germany in 1990 on 27 January–the day Auschwitz concentration camp was liberated by the Red Army in 1945.

Although Adorno is questioned[44], his statements still mark the baseline on which the topic Holocaust is taught in Germany. In

Germany, state schools serve as society's central location for memory and learning. Holocaust education is a mandatory part of the school curriculum in German history classes, the extent and depth to which it is presented, varies significantly between the states and educational levels.

As generations become further removed from the period of National Socialism, memories of the Holocaust are no longer constructed based on lived experiences or on the oral histories of witnesses. Today's students formulate memories that are primarily based on representations encountered in schools, films, literature, the Internet, and social media. With loosening generational ties and the transformation of Germany into an immigrant country, such memories are becoming increasingly deterritorialized as the traditional boundaries between perpetrators and victims are obscured. Second, third, fourth, and fifth-generation Germans wish to distance themselves from identification with the perpetrator generation.[45] New concerns are raised about how to make Holocaust education relevant for younger generations who no longer know family members who lived in the perpetrator society of the National Socialist era and may not find personal relevance in the topic, or share the same moral expectations as previous generations. Educators feel pressure to meet expectations that Holocaust education provides a transformative experience, and may fall short without a clear consensus on best practices.[46]

These blurred and sometimes new boundaries in the field of Holocaust education also encounter a heterogeneous school system in Germany. Germany is a federal state in which the jurisdiction over education belongs to the individual state. The German educational system offers a substantial amount of autonomy to the sixteen different states (*Länder*) in the creation and implementation of their curriculum. The states examine the school textbooks, which implies that each German state has its own textbook due to its own curriculum. Germany has no federal ministry of education but a *Kultusministerkonferenz (KMK)* a *Standing Conference of Ministries of Education and Cultural Affairs*, which should ensure that the requirements across states are comparable.

The Holocaust is usually firstly part of the curriculum in grades 9 or 10. In general, the German curricula focus on key skills rather than specific content. Therefore, teaching the Holocaust and the knowledge of the topic vary from state to state. In Bavaria for example it is mandatory to visit a camp, in Saarland it will become mandatory in 2025.[47] Gymnasien covers the topic at greater length, depth and with more detail, than e.g. the Hauptschule. In 2005 KMK made teaching the Holocaust a mandatory topic in history classes.

Teaching the Holocaust in German history classes is based on the concept of *Historischem Lernen* (Historical learning). Although the term *Historisches Lernen* is widely used without any precise definition, here it is used in the sense of Gautschi 2008. Gautschi explains the term as follows: *Historisches Lernen* happens in the meeting of the individual person with cuttings from the *universe of history*.[48] It starts if learners pay attention (e. g. because of a question, interest, or invitation) to the *universe of History* and perceive material from the past and history e. g. sources or portrayal. Learners deduce the perceived. They describe reconstructing facts from historical sources and clarify the historical circumstances. Following Jeismann the students work out an analysis of merits.[49] Pupils' knowledge, skills, attitudes, and approaches should change through historical learning. The main goal of *Historisches Lernen* is judgment. Rüsen underlines four different types of judgments of merits which can lead to value judgment: traditional, exemplary, critical, or genetic.

Today, learning is referred to as *competence*. In addition to subject-related knowledge and skills, these competencies also include subject-related interest and motivation.[50] German teachers use explicit and implicit theories of history for their teaching. In this regard, teaching is based on the one hand on parts and levels of history and the other hand on abilities and qualifications so-called *Lernziele* (learning objectives). Both sides, content, and methodology, are important to understand the educational theory as well as didactics of history.[51]

Borries asks on top of historical knowledge and competence, for the connection between human rights and history classes in Germany. He states that a redefinition of history classes in the sense of nation-building (after the German reunification) and because of the worldwide terror (in his view based on intercultural conflicts) is necessary. Borries underlines that this redefinition is only useful in an activity-based manner.[52] He also gives a warning to be precise when it comes to human rights. Borries does not want to mix up values education and social education with human rights education. Although human rights education plays a tremendous role in curricula in Germany, Borries sees a huge gap between claim and reality.[53] He comes to the conclusion that the youth –not only in Germany– decide about historical and political questions of conflict on the one hand based on their own interest, on the other hand, based on human and civil rights but without any information about details. Also, they are not able to analyze or appreciate conflicts or contradictions differentiated or nuanced.[54] This result is rooted in the teaching, which seems to be based on moral questions and not on a reflected historical orientation. He calls for a Holocaust education, in the original sense of the idea in Germany.[55]

It is not only against this background that teachers and educators have a profound responsibility that goes beyond the transmission of historical information. They have a role to play in conveying contemporary messages and values to their students and in fostering a deeper understanding of the significance of the Holocaust in the context of the present.[56] When taught well, the subject has the potential to help students to understand political power, particularly the role of the states in everyday lives.[57] The **personality of the teacher** is paramount when it comes to teaching the Holocaust in schools.[58] As studies stress: Teacher training had a limited impact on pedagogy, but teachers expressed a strong motivation to learn about Holocaust content and pedagogy.[59]

How to become a Holocaust educator?

Here, too, there are major global differences with regard to Holocaust education. As an example of the differences, the prerequisites and requirements for future teachers in Canada and Germany are presented here.

In **North America**, Alberta/Canada, all teachers require a minimum of four years of university education, inclusive of a recognized degree and pre-service teacher preparation program from an approved institution. Employment-based training programs are not recognized. The teacher preparation program must lead to teacher certification in the jurisdiction where the program was completed. It must also include:

- 48 semester hour credits of coursework in professional teacher education courses within a structured teacher preparation program and
- ten weeks of supervised student teaching (practicum) at the elementary or secondary level.

The *Alberta Certification of Teachers and Teacher Leaders Regulation* requires applicants to present evidence of language proficiency in at least one of the two official languages of Canada, English, or French. Proof of language proficiency ensures that teachers are able to communicate effectively in all modes (speaking, reading, listening and writing) in English or French prior to entering the classroom.[60] For teaching social studies it is not necessary to study history or any other subject related to the Holocaust or genocides.[61]

In **Germany**, Holocaust education has traditionally been seen as a national obligation, with students required to learn about the Holocaust because of their parents' and grandparents' involvement in the crimes.[62] The desire not to be labelled as a Jew-hater, if only to distance oneself from the history of National Socialist crimes, can be observed in both students and teachers.[63] How to become a history teacher at a Gymnasium in Germany? In Hamburg for example the first part of the studies at the University of Hamburg is the B.A. phase which is six semesters/three years.[64] During this period of time, so-called *LP* (Leistungspunkte) or *credits* have to be earned.

For teaching at a Gymnasium in Hamburg, three different partial programs are necessary to study during the B.A. phase. These parts are education including didactics (41 credits), the primary teaching subject (60 credits), the second teaching subject (60 credits), so-called free choice parts (*Freier Studienanteil*) (nine credits) and the finishing part (ten credits). The MA phase includes education and didactics (61 credits), the primary teaching subject (22 credits), the second subject (22 credits), and the finishing part (15 credits).

Usually, the combination of the teaching subjects is free. But for some subjects, the students need previous knowledge for example languages. Or they need to do a successful suitability test e.g. in sports, art, or music. Some combinations are not allowed, for example, history in combination with social studies, Greek or philosophy. For studying history to become a teacher the following criteria are required if history is the chosen primary teaching subject: proven knowledge of Latin so called *Kleines Latinum* or an *intermediate Latin certificate.*[65]

After finishing the studies and getting the state exam most teachers at public schools are appointed to a public service position and not employed. The appointment has several advantages for example private health insurance, permanent employment status and several benefits like exemption from vehicle tax, technically the position cannot be quit.[66]

Nägel et al. figured out that a lot of German Universities do not teach elementary knowledge about the Holocaust. The majority of courses in 2014–2016 about the Holocaust took place during the Historical seminar (196), German (80), cultural studies (45) and pedagogics and education (45). Only five of the analyzed Universities offered in 2014–2016 in each of the four semesters a course about the Holocaust. 29 Universities taught the topic during two or three semesters. 45 of 79 Universities offered one or no course during the four semesters. Nägel et al. emphasize that it is important to arouse interest among the students and to establish a solid basic knowledge.[67]

None of the German states requires courses that address Holocaust education in order to become a certified teacher, nor is there mandated professional development within schools on the topic.[68] It is also quite possible that, due to cost containment, a trained social studies teacher will teach history without ever having studied history. The same is true when it comes to contemporary Jewish research. It is virtually non-existent in the academic environment.[69]

In Hamburg, the teachers' further education and additional training after the exam (Staatsexamen/Master of Higher Education) is mainly organized by the *Institut für Lehrerfortbildung, LI* (Institute for Further Teachers Education). In 2024, for example, two additional trainings were offered for high school teachers: *Holocaust in film–What is useful for sustainable teaching? and The Warsaw Ghetto Uprising.*[70]

While the issue may be embedded within another course, the unique challenges that this subject entails, both the historical memory and the emotional responses it may elicit from the students, require a more focused and in-depth pedagogical framework for young teachers. Without this, many teachers are entering their classrooms pedagogically and methodologically unprepared to educate students about this complex topic. And this is not only true for the upper secondary classes, but also for the primary school, as Kriesten[71] writes.

Academics and societies worldwide believe that learning is lifelong. Therefore, educators and Holocaust educators must also engage in **lifelong learning.** The lifelong learning ecology is a complex and multi-layered concept that explores the development of learning resources and the relationship between beliefs and attitudes in different contexts.[72] But how to do lifelong learning, if training programs are very limited (see the German example)? Due to the lack of support on these fronts, many teachers and educators add informal learning, the so-called *learning in the wild* to their lifelong learning experience. According to Hutchins' book *Cognition in the Wild*, informal learning occurs when questions are asked, answers are given and knowledge is gained at the discretion of the learner and teacher.[73] This kind of learning takes place outside the classroom or in teacher-led instruction. It is particularly relevant in the context of teacher professional development, as it encompasses informal and non-formal learning processes that occur outside of traditional training programs.[74]

The Concept of Holocaust Education

If Holocaust education stands between this both sides, knowledge about the specific historical event and a way of systematic education about values and moral, the idea is obvious that Holocaust education is intended to immunize against racism, right-wing extremism, antisemitism, xenophobia and much more. While the actual events are pushed further and further into the background, teaching historical knowledge is not at the centre of this. But then the Holocaust cannot be reduced to a mere historical event. In addition to imparting cognitive knowledge, dealing with memory defence, and projections of guilt must be a central concern of school education.

Overall, the phenomenon of the globalization of Holocaust remembrance has also had a significant impact on Holocaust education over the last 30 years, fostering the emergence of a shared European cultural memory centred on teaching values such as empathy, human rights, and the rejection of discrimination. The connection between the Holocaust and human rights, both morally and politically, has extended beyond European states to influence other countries.[75]

Holocaust education must be **adapted to the changing life situations of each new generation**. To do so, an overwhelming number of materials and resources can be found to support teachers and educators. Following Manca et al. Holocaust education in our days covers study trips to Holocaust memorial sites, such as former concentration and extermination camps and have become increasingly important in creating high-impact learning experiences. Holocaust museums and memorials play an important role in providing educational opportunities for teacher training, lifelong learning and raising awareness about education and remembrance. In addition, popular media, including films, documentaries, and television series, serve as informal platforms for Holocaust education across generations. Finally, survivors and testimonies are recognized as valuable sources of information for teachers and students. They provide first-hand accounts of historical events, personal experiences and perspectives that can bring history to life in a unique and powerful way. Digital media, including interactive websites, social media, virtual reality applications and computer games, have attracted considerable interest from educators and teachers. Recognizing the potential of digital media to engage younger students, they are exploring new forms of digital Holocaust remembrance and education This includes using testimonies and presenting Holocaust survivors in novel ways. Projects in the United States and Europe are actively developing various digital Holocaust remembrance initiatives, such as interactive video testimonies, virtual reality films, augmented reality applications, museum installations and online exhibitions These efforts aim to convey the memory of the Holocaust through innovative and immersive approaches.[76]

Keeping all this in mind, **Holocaust education** remains a confusing term and concept. But is understood in the following as: Primarily the historical study of the systematic, bureaucratic, state-sponsored persecution and murder of six million Jews by National Socialist Germany and its collaborators. It also provides a starting point to examine warning signs that can indicate the potential for mass atrocity.[77] It illustrates the dangers of prejudice, discrimination, hatred of Jews, and dehumanization. Holocaust education also reveals the full range of human responses to the historical event as well as today's warning signs.

3. ANTISEMITISM OR HATRED OF JEWS?

When the Holocaust and Holocaust education are understood as a tool against antisemitism, it must be clarified what antisemitism is. To this end, it is necessary not only to explain the meaning of the word, but also to clarify the historical background and contexts.

The semantic question seems to be very important since the term *antisemitism* is often misunderstood or not understood at all. The term consists of the words *anti* and *semitism*. *Anti* means *against.* The Semites are a group of different peoples who are characterised by the fact that they speak a Semitic language. Semitic languages are, for example: Aramaic, Ethiopian, Arabic, and Hebrew. Antisemitism therefore means *against the Semites.*

Hebrew, or modern Ivrit (Hebrew in Hebrew) is spoken by Jews. *Antisemitism* refers to hatred of Jews or hostility towards Jews. Antisemitism is therefore hostility towards people who belong to Judaism. It does not, for example, mean hostility towards Arabs or Ethiopians. The term antisemitism was first employed in 1879 by the journalist Wilhelm Marr to distinguish a rejection of Jews understood to be scientifically motivated and secular from hostility based on religion. In Maar's text *The Victory of Judaism over Germanic Identity*, numerous conceptualizations find verbal expressions that were dominant in the 19th century.

Bauer emphasizes antisemitism was back then a *modern, scientific* term, hygienic, neutral, one that would not include the word, Jew.[1] Before the term was established in Germany for example, people spoke about *Judenhass.*

One of the headline findings of a 2016 study[2] was the startling proportion of students who appeared entirely unfamiliar with the term *antisemitism*. In an initial attempt to appreciate their understanding of key terms, students were asked in the questionnaire, *What does antisemitism mean?* They were then invited to select from five multiple-choice responses: *Prejudice against poor people; Prejudice against Jews; Prejudice against Hindus; Prejudice against homeless people; Not sure/ don't know.* Only 31.8 percent of students selected *Prejudice against Jews.* By the point of contrast, 89.5 percent and 87 percent of students identify the meanings of *racism* and *homophobia* as *Prejudice against people because of ethnicity* and *Prejudice against people because of their sexual orientation* respectively. Indeed, even more striking is that when A-level students aged 17 and 18 are excluded from the total, only 25.9 percent of students aged 11–16 selected the most appropriate response to the question on antisemitism. In order to understand how and why the vast majority of students of all ages (68.2 percent) did not appear to know about antisemitism—or certainly did not seem to recognize the term itself–a careful analysis of data from other survey questions and, more importantly, close scrutiny of interview responses from more than 244 students was undertaken.[3] In total over two-thirds of students (68 percent) were unaware of what *antisemitism* meant.

It is just comprehensible to ask: What is *antisemitism?* Who should be able to determine what constitutes *antisemitism* and how?

To talk about the term itself is important because of the risk of antisemitism being viewed by young people as discretely time-bound and interpreted as exclusively related to National Socialists, or of the murder of European Jewry being disconnected from anti–Jewish discrimination before and after the Holocaust, is real and palpable.

The term *antisemitism* is defined as follows: *Antisemitism is a certain perception of Jews, which may be expressed as hatred toward Jews. Rhetorical and physical manifestations of antisemitism are directed toward Jewish or non-Jewish individuals and/or their property, toward Jewish community institutions and religious facilities.*[4] But since this certain perception of Jews is a millennia-old concept one can find tons of different kinds of antisemitism, or as Lobo puts it: Hatred of Jews manages the almost unbelievable feat of simultaneously hiding everywhere and coming to light quite openly. New variants are constantly being added and age-old Jew-hating practices are being reinterpreted: Nazi antisemitism, Islamist antisemitism, right-wing antisemitism, left-wing antisemitism, Christian antisemitism, Muslim antisemitism, ethnic antisemitism, postcolonial antisemitism, bourgeois anti-semitism, woke antisemitism, conspiracy-theory antisemitism, vulgar anti-capitalist antisemitism, pseudo-anti-racist anti-semitism, intellectual antisemitism, accepting antisemitism, self-exonerating antisemitism and, among many others, the largest current at present: Israel-related anti-Semitism. Often enriched with a new, well-known anti-Semitism of annihilation.[5]

Antisemitism can manifest itself on different levels and in different ways. This might include the targeting of the State of Israel, conceived as a Jewish collectivity. However, criticism of Israel similar to that levelled against any other country cannot be regarded as antisemitic. Antisemitism frequently charges Jews with conspiring to harm humanity, and it is often used to blame Jews for why things go wrong.[6] It is expressed in speech, writing, visual forms and action, and employs sinister stereotypes and negative character traits. Contemporary examples of antisemitism in public life, the media, schools, the workplace, and in the religious sphere could, taking into account the overall context, include, but are not limited to:

- Calling for, aiding, or justifying the killing or harming of Jews in the name of a radical ideology or an extremist view of religion.
- Making mendacious, dehumanizing, demonizing, or stereotypical allegations about Jews as such or the power of Jews as a collective—such as, especially but not exclusively, the myth about a world Jewish conspiracy or of Jews controlling the media, economy, government or other societal institutions.
- Accusing Jews as a people of being responsible for real or imagined wrongdoing committed by a single Jewish person or group, or even for acts committed by non-Jews.
- Denying the fact, scope, mechanisms (e.g. gas chambers) or intentionality of the genocide of the Jewish people at the hands of National Socialist Germany and its supporters and accomplices during World War II (the Holocaust).
- Accusing the Jews as a people, or Israel as a state, of inventing or exaggerating the Holocaust.
- Accusing Jewish citizens of being more loyal to Israel, or to the alleged priorities of Jews worldwide, than to the interests of their own nations.
- Denying the Jewish people their right to self-determination, e.g., by claiming that the existence of a State of Israel is a racist endeavor.
- Applying double standards by requiring it is a behavior not expected or demanded of any other democratic nation.
- Using the symbols and images associated with classic antisemitism (e.g., claims of Jews killing Jesus or blood libel) to characterize Israel or Israelis.

- Drawing comparisons of contemporary Israeli policy to that of the Nazis.
- Holding Jews collectively responsible for the actions of the State of Israel.

Antisemitic acts are criminal when they are so defined by law (e.g., denial of the Holocaust or distribution of antisemitic materials in some countries).

Criminal acts are antisemitic when the targets of attacks, whether they are people or property–such as buildings, schools, places of worship and cemeteries–are selected because they are, or are perceived to be, Jewish or linked to Jews.

Antisemitic discrimination is the denial to Jews of opportunities or services available to others and is illegal in many countries.[7]

Following this definition, it has to be mentioned that there are other ideas on that define antisemitism, too. None of them is less complicated or confusing. Some tries of explanation lead in the wrong direction by–as the authors call it– *opening a room for debate*. The *Jerusalem Declaration*[8] is one example. By *opening the room for debate* the text becomes less precise and blurred. Even if the authors claim that *language would make a difference and be used differently*–the same goes for the authors of the *Nexus Definition*[9]–different languages and forms of expression cannot be contextual when it comes to hate. Whether it is hatred of Jews, hatred of women or hatred of indigenous people. The fact that the authors make a distinction here, i.e. evaluate antisemitism itself differently, namely in some assumed context, is in itself antisemitic.[10]

As of April 1, 2024, 1231 entities worldwide have adopted the former mentioned (IHRA) definition[11]. Therefore, criticising the State of Israel is also considered antisemitic. The State of Israel sees itself as the *nation-state of the Jewish people*. According to the Basic Law of the State of Israel, the Jewish people exercise their natural, cultural, historical, and religious right to self-determination. Criticising the State of Israel, its government and its people is fine as long as it is comparable to criticising other countries. However, if double standards are established, i.e. different standards are applied to the State of Israel than to other countries, then this behavior is also considered antisemitic.

Antisemitism is a global, yet disparate phenomenon. Antisemitic discourses and resentment structures are strongly characterized by regional characteristics, which are, however, intertwined transnationally. The nature of this relationship is often reduced quite mechanically to a relationship between imports and exports as if antisemitism were a commodity that could be shifted at will through the exchange of information or migration movements. This approach does not do justice to the dynamics of antisemitism. Hostility towards Jews adapts to the *requirements* of the present, changing its form as societies change. It is not an object that can be implanted in different societies but grows out of its own contradictions.[12]

Antisemitism is not merely the hatred of Jews as *others* but the symbolization of *the Jew*–that is, turning the Jews into the symbol for whatever a given civilization defines as its most loathsome qualities. For Christianity until the Holocaust, *the Jew* was Christ-killer; for Marxism, the ultimate capitalist; for Nazism, the defiler of race. And now, in the era of anti-racism, the Jewish state is the embodiment of racism.[13] But it is certainly the wrong answer to the respective conflicts of societies, which, however, interpenetrate each other in a globalized world.[14]

Additionally, especially in Germany, there might be a somewhat schematic distinction between anti-Judaism and antisemitism: Anti-Judaism, religiously based hostility towards Jews, is often declared to be a marginal phenomenon that has historically taken a back seat to modern antisemitism. The everyday discourse locates religious hatred of Jews primarily in Islamist antisemitism, which is fed both by the history of Islamic anti-Judaism and modern antisemitism. The perception that religious anti-Judaism is primarily to be found among Muslims corresponds to the secular self-image of modern societies, but even here the archaic religious hatred of Jews has by no means disappeared. It has been abolished in modern antisemitism, for example when the modern antisemitic belief in the Jews as sinister world rulers inherits the anti-Judaic belief in the devil. The boom in free churches and esotericism points to a need for re-sacralization[15], in the wake of which forms of anti-Judaism believed to be outdated is also being revived.[16] Just as the religious mentality can persist and even flourish alongside modernization, anti-Judaism also persists at the same time as antisemitism, both within and between societies.

Given these details, it seems like the usage of the term *antisemitism* leads to more confusion than clarity. Therefore, the term Jew-hatred or **hatred of Jews** seems way more constructive. There seems to be an inherent distance between the term *antisemitism* and the meaning of the term. As shown, younger people mostly miss the connection between the term antisemitism and *hatred of Jews*. To avoid misunderstandings, a lack of understanding or the misusage of the term antisemitism, the term *hatred of Jews* is better used to describe hostility toward Jews, which is not simply one prejudice among many but something unique.

Although it may almost seem like it, the hatred of Jews that can be observed at the moment is nothing new. On the contrary, it is the same old evil that has been known for thousands of years. What may be new is the shameless openness with which it is presented in public. This openness is part of a changing climate, but not just since October 2023. The fact that the social climate has changed is certainly due to historical distance on the one hand and ignorance on the other.

Hatred of Jews as an Ideology

Ernst Simmel wrote that hatred of Jews is a collective *delusional system*. In other words, a perception that is massively distorted by projections and contrary to reality. Inner, unbearable objects are shifted to the outside and then appear as hallucinatory, haunting monsters or voices. Moreover, as Simmel went on to explain, these projections are carried out in conformity with society. The object of projection, in this case, Jews, is attacked. The delusional Jew-hater then no longer feels paranoid powerlessness but feels justified when he exercises his power. This means that under these conditions, hatred of Jews can be understood as self-defense in order to oppose imagined persecution.[17] In this regard, Adorno and Horkheimer spoke about *pathical projection*. Although the term is borrowed from studies of delusional patients (pathological), it is intended here to show that these people are not considered ill, but that their views are even regarded as common sense and (group) identity-forming.[18] So it does not seem wonder, the uniqueness of hatred of Jews is based on the idea, that Jews are an *alleged evil in the world*.[19]

Paradoxically, global hatred of Jews these days forms a bridge ideology of regressive forces that are directed against globalization itself: A German neo-Nazi and an IS fighter in Syria may have little in common at first glance, but they can agree on their hostility towards Jews. In this ideology, Jews embody globalized modernity: they stand for the supposedly rootless, cosmopolitan, universal and individualism as well as against originality, autochthonous and collectivism. In this respect, too, the term hatred of Jews is cynically unifying and integrating.[20]

The use of the term **hatred of Jews** includes the inhuman ideology behind racist antisemitism. This is because the religious hatred, which had previously been based on religion or economics, was declared a racial issue. But antisemitism stayed as vague as concepts such as people, nation or German and Teutonism.[21] Elukin stresses, that antisemitism is unbounded by time or context, the idea is anachronistic. The term has come to be used to describe hatred of Jews through history, although the term has its origins in the 19th century.[22] This also supports the idea of using another, more appropriate word: hatred of Jews.

According to Benz, hatred of Jews is the prototype of social and political prejudice and is therefore an indicator of the state of a society. Jews are denied the right as citizens to criticize conditions in the state and society. They are regarded as guests, as foreigners. They are not part of the community.[23]

Maizels emphasizes the narrative of racism when it comes to hatred of Jews, which is very dominant for example in the US. Students are in many ways taught to look at all conflicts through that lens of racism, and that is a problem when they try to understand hatred of Jews. Differences are not been seen because education does not enable students to do so. In the US e.g., race relations are both literally and figuratively black and white and so people try to squeeze the Middle East conflict into that paradigm. This leads to all sorts of misunderstandings. Because within this prism there is only one victim and one oppressor. The idea that there are two people who have inflicted injustice and suffering on each other is extremely difficult to convey.[24]

Hostility toward Jews was and is an enduring component of Western patterns of thought and speech. Centuries of defamation and stigmatization of Jews have left deep traces in the collective memory and patterns of communicative language usage. Looking at history, one can discern not only the long tradition of thinking and feeling that is hostile toward Jews but also certain patterns of verbal stigmatization and defamation mirroring semantic and conceptual constants that have been preserved and passed down through the ages.[25]

To understand how deep the roots of stereotypes and emotional resentments of Jews go, one must delve into history. The historical and contemporary patterns of hostility toward Jews resemble each other strikingly. An unbroken continuity in Judeophobic thinking can be seen since the current forms in which (verbal) Jew-hatred appears can be accurately described and fully explained only if one becomes aware of the underlying traditional conceptualizations.

During the centuries many wise and educated people presented lots of explanations why non-Jews hate Jews. The idea of hating Jews is not only very adaptable but also very popular. Many Jews and non-Jews ask the same questions. Hate is an irrational feeling and perhaps that is why hate can only be *explained* with less rational approaches. In the end, hate is a moral failure. The emotional anchoring of the Jews as *evil* further emphasizes these irrational feelings.

To recognize that hatred of Jews is a millennia-old phenomenon, an overview of the history of hatred of Jews will be given below.

Israel and Early Jewish History

Around 1200 BCE, an Egyptian source named the people *Israel* for the first time. *Israel* means *one who struggles with God*. Previously, the nomadic people were known as the *Hebrews*. At that time, the people of Israel consisted of 12 tribes, which saw themselves as extended families or clan organisations. These tribes settled in the mountains of Judea and Galilee. Judea is located in modern-day Israel and the southern West Bank. Important villages such as Bethlehem and the city of Jerusalem are located here. Galilee is located in what is now northern Israel, near the Sea of Galilee. The 12 tribes differed from the other peoples in their belief in one single God. According to their belief, this God had made a covenant with the Israelites. His teachings, the basis for the faith and the believers' way of life were written down in a book. This book is the *Torah*. Around 1000 BCE, the 12 tribes united to form a kingdom. King David from the tribe of Judah (hence the name *Jew*) conquered Jerusalem.

Over the centuries, the kingdom split into two areas: the northern kingdom of Israel and the southern kingdom of Judea. The Northern Kingdom was an economically and politically growing buffer state that was able to flourish during a period of political weakness in Egypt and Mesopotamia. Only the rise of the Assyrian superpower put an end to this state of affairs. The northern kingdom of Israel was conquered by Assyria between 722 and 721 BCE and turned into a vassal state. Some of the inhabitants were forcibly resettled and replaced by deported inhabitants from other parts of the Assyrian empire. It is assumed that 10 tribes of the people of Israel were lost as a result of this resettlement.

After the destruction of the northern kingdom by the Assyrians, the state around Jerusalem, the southern kingdom of Judah, which had been spared by the Assyrians, was able to gain strength. The kings subsequently endeavoured to extend Judah's power to the northern territories and cities of the north. From the 4th century BCE, the Jews also settled outside of Judea. The best-known Jewish centre was in Egypt. Alexandria was a centre of Jewish science and culture.

After expulsion and war, the Jews returned to Jerusalem in 500 BCE and built a temple in honour of their God. This Second Temple was magnificently remodelled under King Herod shortly before the turn of time, in the year 0 CE.

Jews in Ancient times

The rejection of Jews is a centuries-old phenomenon. In addition to Christian anti-Judaism, a distinction can be made between racial antisemitism, secondary antisemitism, and anti-Zionism. What all forms have in common, however, is the irrational hatred of parts of the majority society towards a minority, the Jews.

The new Jewish concept of the monotheistic belief in an invisible God was something that separated Jews from Greeks, Romans, and Egyptians. It might have been a strange idea to these people who believed in many gods for centuries. Something, that made Jews in their eyes different from all the others. Monotheism upset society and its structures; household gods, for example, were suddenly no longer to have any function. They no longer existed.

The practice of Judaism was already seen in ancient Rome as a provocation. Hostility toward Jews arose after 500 BCE as a result of various Jewish emigrations after the destruction of the First Temple. The First Temple was constructed during the reign of Solomon and completed in 957 BCE. It was built as an abode for the *Ark of the Covenant.* In Judaism and Christianity, the Ark is the ornate, gold-plated wooden chest that in biblical times housed the two tablets of the Law given to Moses by God. The First Temple was also a place of assembly for the entire people. The Temple itself was not large, but the courtyard was extensive. The building faced eastward.

The Jewish minority is distinctly set apart from other groups in eating habits, clothing, living customs, and observance of the Sabbath. Jews resisted assimilation into the countries where they were living during that time and thereby attracted much attention, which sometimes took the form of admiration and conversions to Judaism but also resulted in much rejection. Fear and suspicion were attached to Jews, giving rise to the idea that they were out to undermine the existing society. This anxiety in turn bred the notion that Jews aimed to take over the world.[26]

Jews were seen as arrogant and stubborn because they refused to recognize the gods of the other faith communities. In 67 CE the Roman province the area the Jews were living in in the Eastern Mediterranean, became a battlefield of armed conflicts in the region. The Romans forced the Jews to perform forced labour. They dared to revolt against the Roman occupation, but after the destruction of their sanctuary, the Temple, the Roman troops took the temple treasures and Jewish prisoners of war to Rome. The Jewish temple was destroyed by the Romans in 70 CE. The last structural remnant of the temple is the former *Western Wall* of the building. It is also known as the so-called *Wailing Wall.*

Hatred of Jews: Turn of the Era and First Centuries

With the turn of the era around the year 0 and the associated process of separation of the early Christians from Judaism, hatred of Jews was raised to a new level. A bitter dispute broke out over the true faith. The separation between Christians and Jews took place over a longer period of time, which was not completed until around 150 CE. The *New Testament* with the texts on Jesus Christ became the Holy Book of the Christians. However, the Torah was also incorporated into the *Book of Books* by including large parts from the now-called *Old Testament*. Christianity saw itself as the true Israel. Its followers denied the Jews their covenant with God. They were accused of not recognizing Jesus as the *Messiah* and of believing a false doctrine. A negative image of the Jews was established, which was embellished with anti-Jewish clichés, myths and lies. This image shaped people's attitudes and penetrated deep into European societies.

Initially, Judaism remained legally a *religio licita* (permitted religion). The free Jews had Roman civil rights and lived as a minority among the peoples in the *Diaspora* (Greek: dispersion). Jewish communities developed around the Mediterranean as far as in today's Germany; there the first Jewish communities are documented in Cologne, Trier, Mainz, Worms, and Speyer. The rejection by the inhabitants of the European countries, who did not want the Jews to become integrated, was transformed by way of projection into a negative characteristic of the Jews. Since then, the stereotype of the Jews as *restless wanderers* has become commonplace; they are said to be unwilling to make themselves at home, preferring to remain foreign and therefore never developing solidarity with the majority society.[27]

However, the phenomenon of *Philo-Semitism*[28] must also be added to the overall picture. The relationship between Christians and Jews was and is far more than just rejection, hatred, and strict separation.

Nevertheless, it remains correct: Christian anti-Judaism refers to the religious, cultural, social, and/or economic form of resentment against Jews from the Middle Ages to modern times. Some of the current negative ideas applied to Jews and/or Israelis belong to the standard repertory used for centuries of people who reject Jews. Hostility toward and hatred of Jews have manifested themselves for two millennia both verbally and nonverbally, taking forms that include discrimination, intimidation, persecution, humiliation, and murder. This complex phenomenon involves religious, historical, economic, political, psychological, communicative, and philosophic aspects. All types and variants of hostility toward Jews grow out of specific, timeless conceptual patterns representative of non-Jews' mental constructs about Jews.[29] This approach was fueled by the split between Judaism and Christianity and by the notion of being the *chosen people.*

The accusation of the murder of God is just as persistent and was a Christian doctrine for centuries as the idea that Jews were followers of Satan because only Satan could kill God (in this case, the Son of God). Despite the fact, that this idea, that Jesus was killed by Jews and in conformity with Jewish law, is historically implausible in view of the existing political situation in Israel under Roman occupation and absolute rule, led to the establishment of the stereotype of Jews as the murderers of God.[30]

Christians were taught this view in pictures and images. Great Christian teachers and scholars, such as Martin Luther (1483–1546), contributed to the hatred of Jews in their texts. Christian theologians stressed that they represent the one true faith. They did not practice the tolerance Jesus preached. This tradition of hatred persists–in blood legends and hate-filled untrue stories. According to Benz, when accusing the Israeli military of allegedly murdering Palestinian children, the Bethlehemite infanticide of Herod must also be taken into account.[31]

Jews were also seen as deniers of the divine plan, as godless, as criminal, as Jesus is not the Messiah for Jews, as he is for Christians. Again, Jews were seen as arrogant and stubborn because they now refused to recognize the Christian God and his son. The profound hatred toward Jews arose after Christianity split off from Judaism, since then the hate started to go hand in hand with religiously motivated hostility and hatred. By making their belief absolute, the Christians excluded any possibility that they might be wrong. This momentum is considered the origin of the hatred of Jews that has persisted for more than two thousand years. Judaism came to be identified as the complete opposite of Christianity. Over the centuries a competition between Judaism and Christianity arose in which Christianity established itself as the one true religion. The former brothers in the faith become anti–Christians who reject the true faith; Judaism became a source of damnation.[32]

Then as now, the majority accused the minority of separating themselves, of exalting themselves out of a sense of *elitist chosenness*. In the course of the centuries a Christian theological concept, the Christian religious view becomes a system in which Jews and Judaism on principle come to figure as the negative dimension. The majority developed a system for determining the meaning of the world. The unfounded accusation that Jews are forced by their religion to despise other religions is just as much a part of this argument as other prejudices according to which Jews are unforgiving, greedy for money and addicted to power.

But the conflict between Christians and Jews was not only of a religious nature. It was also a very secular dispute about followers and support, as well as recognition by Rome. In the 4th century CE, Christianity prevailed in the Roman Empire and became the state religion. The practice of other religions was forbidden under penalty of punishment. The Jews were now considered *pagans* and *unbelievers*.

The prejudice that the minority marginalizes the majority because Jews see themselves as the *chosen ones* and are therefore hostile to integration is just as persistent as the idea that Jews always see themselves as having a special role. They would then claim this special role through special rights. This makes them unpopular. In the perception of people who reject Jews, however, this unpopularity is not only fed by the supposed special role but also by stereotypes that were already formed very early: Business acumen, wealth, self-centeredness, and political influence. The death of Jesus seems to have triggered a wave of retaliation that continues to this day and can be seen, for example, in the seizure, even theft, of Jewish property. There seems to be a kind of unconscious certainty in Christian anti-Judaism that is passed down through generations and centuries.[33]

While Judaism was initially still considered a *permitted religion* in the Roman Empire, after Christianity was recognized as the state religion, the legally protected space of the Jewish minority was significantly restricted. In the following centuries, the Christian church enacted laws that worked towards a strict separation of Jews and Christians. Jews were to be banned from public life. From the 5th century CE, they were also prohibited from building synagogues.[34]

Hatred of Jews during the Middle Ages

The Christian Church has been a constant through the centuries based on doctrines and rules. It influenced all spheres of life, including all social, cultural, and political structures. It was a powerful societal and ideological force, that dominated all literary and artistic forms, that accompanied or shaped all hegemonic structures (and to this day remains a factor in broad sectors of society). Therefore, it is not surprising that the image the Christian church created of the Jews as enemies survived. Hostility toward Jews belongs to a mentality with deep roots in Western culture, passed down from generation to generation as a fixed component of Christian tradition and identity. The Jews were conceptualized as murderers of Jesus, as murderers of the Messiah. This led to various negative views and concepts that stood the test of time. The hatred of Jews was inscribed in Western structures of thought and feeling in the conceptualization of the Christian model and the sense of its superiority.

During the Middle Ages, the Christian Church developed a different attitude towards the Jews. They now tried to *save* them by conversion. Officially the conversion to Christianity had to be voluntary, but reality was different. Conversion would have been the *victory of the church over the synagogue*.[35] Even if Jews were considered as the satanic influence in the world, Christianity would have the power to save their souls. Therefore, conversion was the ultimate goal that the Christians wanted to achieve with regard to the Jews. It was not just about converting them and ensuring that Christ was finally recognized as the Messiah by the Jews. It was also about making the Jews disappear. As John Roth points out, Christians and the later National Socialists are very similar in this respect. Moreover, it seems that Christianity urgently needed Judaism in order to distinguish itself and prove itself as the only true religion. Judaism, on the other hand, did not need Christianity; it was and is sufficient unto itself.[36]

Due to humiliation and setting apart from the Christian majority in societies, Jews wandered from place to place to find peace. In the Carolingian Frankish Empire, Jews received royal protection in the 8th and 9th centuries CE. They worked as doctors and traders. Their widespread communities served as trading centres between the continents. Under Charlemagne (747–814), Jews received privileges and recognition and achieved considerable prosperity. This earned them the envy of the Christian majority society and the Christian Church found an answer to the Jewish stubbornness not to convert and also to the economic success: *stigmatization.*

From the 9th and 10th centuries CE, Jews were forced into a special role by the Christian society and secular law. Jews were not allowed to own land or farm, they were excluded from the merchants' guilds and craft guilds, as only Christians were accepted. Their economic activity was limited to petty or junk trading, or they were allowed to engage in money transactions and trading. According to Christian belief, trading money was contrary to divine teaching and was forbidden to Christians under church law until the 15th century CE. Jews therefore became very successful as bankers and an important element in international commerce. This success was also envied by the Christians. Jews made a virtue out of the necessity. However, the envy of the Christian majority society led to ever new prejudices and stereotypes. These prejudices turned into enemy stereotypes, which incomprehensibly persist to this day. The resentment is fed by social envy, petty-bourgeois fear of foreign infiltration, the misguided feeling of being patronized by a supposedly massive media presence, and even the idea that Jewish masterminds manipulate media coverage at will.

With the First Crusade in 1096, the situation of the Jews deteriorated dramatically. The peasant army that initially set out and the crusading army murdered and plundered the Jewish communities in the Rhineland, Magdeburg, Regensburg, and Prague. This was only superficially about killing the Jews as enemies of Christ or forcibly baptising them. The crusaders were primarily concerned with the Jews' wealth, which they needed to finance their crusade. Major massacres occurred in the area of today's Germany e. g. in 1096 and in England in 1290.[37] In 1103, after the Crusade pogroms, Emperor Henry IV (1050–1106) placed the so-called *Jewish subjects* under his personal protection in the *Imperial Peace of Mainz*. However, Jews were no longer allowed to bear arms in the empire. They were, therefore, literally defenceless. Emperor Frederick II (1194–1250) finally declared the Jews to be so-called *chamber servants* and therefore, property of the emperor. However, in return for this protection and a certain degree of independence granted to the Jews, they had to pay special taxes. These protection payments were a welcome source of income for the emperor, but also for the electors and imperial princes.

While most Christians were to remain illiterate for centuries to come, Jewish boys learnt to read Hebrew more than a thousand years ago in order to fulfil the divine commandment to study the Torah. And while the society around them was characterised by immobility–most people spent their lives in the place of their birth or not far away–mobility had been familiar to the Jews for generations: They could read in the Torah that there was nothing special about crossing countries and deserts, being on the move and settling in among strangers; and reading the Talmud, with all its stories about settling disputes and breaking the law, about weights and measures, damages and overreaching, depreciation and compensation, not only taught them cosmopolitanism but also provided them with valuable knowledge of trade and commerce, science and administration. Both secular and spiritual rulers were happy to utilise this knowledge. Jews were valued as doctors as well as long-distance traders and seafarers, who in the 8th and 9th centuries held an almost monopoly position in the Mediterranean trade and supplied the royal palaces and Episcopal palaces with jewellery, spices, perfumes, and other luxury goods.[38]

Stigmatization had practical effects on the Jews. The measurements included: the ban on converting to Judaism, the ban on marriage between Christians and Jews, the ban on Christians and Jews eating together, the requirement for Jews to wear certain clothing and the requirement for Jews to live in certain neighborhoods. The clothing regulations were clearly reflected in the so-called *Jewish hat*, which became compulsory in 1180. In 1215, clothing was introduced to identify people of other faiths. Jews had to wear a yellow patch or ring of cloth on their clothing. The freedom of movement of Jews was also increasingly restricted, or they were expelled altogether. In Frankfurt am Main, for example, Jews had to live in sealed-off areas since 1462. Throughout Europe, there were forced baptisms in which Jews had to profess Christianity. Church institutions were also directly involved in the persecution of Jews. They contributed to keeping the negative image of Jews alive. Anti-Jewish prejudices, lies and myths were deeply imprinted in the consciousness of the Christian population of all social classes and formed the starting point for numerous violent riots and pogroms[39] against the Jewish population.

From the middle of the 12th century onwards, accusations of ritual murder were repeatedly made. Jews were accused of torturing

Christian children to death in order to obtain blood for their religious rituals. These conspiracy myths can still be found in church accounts today. When the plague spread to Central Europe in 1348, the transmission routes of the disease–lice in the fur of rats–were unknown. The Jews were therefore accused of poisoning the wells and thus being responsible for the plague. This lie led to violent pogroms. The emperor, pope and imperial estates tried to exercise their role as patrons of the Jews but were often unsuccessful. Too many people had an interest in murdering the Jews and enriching themselves with their property. At this time, Christian authorities also spread the stereotype of the *money-grubbing Jew* who would enrich himself at the expense of the Christians. The Jews had no choice but to find their own economic niche in order to ensure their survival.

The religious, social, and economic stigmatization of the Jews led to massive waves of persecution in the late 13th and 14th centuries CE. Most of the Jewish communities of the Middle Ages fell victim to them. In 1290, the Jews were expelled from England, and in the course of the 14th century, they were also expelled from France. They were also expelled from German cities and many other regions.

While the emperor of the Holy Roman Empire still had a duty to protect the Jews in Europe until the 13th and 14th centuries CE, this imperial right to protect the Jews diminished more and more over the centuries. It passed to smaller sovereigns and rulers. The idea of protection was increasingly characterized by financial interests and the protection taxes to be paid. In Rothenburg ob der Tauber, for example, tax rates for Jews were eight times higher than for Christians in the 14th century. In addition, taxes for defence facilities and town administration were extorted from them. As the Jews themselves were not allowed to bear arms or hold higher office, they had no choice but to pay whatever was demanded.

At the end of the 15th century CE, the Sephardic Jews of Spain and Portugal were also affected. In March 1492, the Catholic Monarchs of Spain, Isabella I of Castile and Ferdinand II of Aragon, issued the *Alhambra Edict*. This stated that all Jews had to leave the Iberian Peninsula if they were not forcibly baptised and converted to Christianity by the end of July 1492. It was claimed that the Jews were a constant threat to the Christians and that it would be impossible for them to live together. The edict allowed these Sephardic Jews to take their possessions with them, but no gold or money. Between 130,000 and 300,000 Jews are said to have left Spain.

Jewish life soon returned to the empire, but the Jews had lost their economic importance. As they now had to live almost exclusively in segregated neighborhoods, the *ghettos*, their marginalization and persecution only became easier. Poland became a new centre of Jewish life in Europe due to the influx of refugees and displaced persons.

Hatred of Jews: The German Empire

Over the centuries Jews were spread, thinly, all over the Mideast, Europe, England, and the New World. Numbering about 2,5 million, they functioned as middlemen in Gentile society, being neither very poor nor very rich but very visible. Although relationships with the Christian world were difficult and contradictory, between the periods of persecution long years of relative peace ensued, with socioeconomic ties developing between the Jews and their neighbors. In the 19th century, Jews achieved civic equality in many Christian European countries. However, Jews and non-Jews had some rather different perceptions of the meaning of emancipation. With the attainment of equal legal rights in Western and Central Europe, Jews in those countries thought, in general, the *Jewish problem* had been solved. But it soon became clear, that legal status did not convey equality in the non-Jewish social world. Hidden and open discrimination persisted and it became a social problem. The traditional hatred of Jews was based on Christian anti-Judaism but modern hatred of Jews has several components. The romantic movement excluded the Jews by emphazising the purity of the national tradition. Jew-hating *fantasies* are then also in terms of a gendering of Jew-hating resentment in the sense of an interweaving of Jew-hating argumentation patterns and anti-feminist discourses. The emancipation of Jews and women was thus interpreted as a counter-movement to the natural order, as unnatural and perverse.[40]

Although, there is certainly *no almost genetic German inclination toward Jew-hatred* as Goldenhagen[41] touted–historically there is a close connection between developments in German intellectual and power elites and radical and potentially lethal manifestations of hatred of Jews.[42] Religion is a key criterion for exclusion from Germany and other European mainstream societies.[43] Or, as Friedmann puts it: Hatred of Jews *is not a German invention. But Auschwitz is a German invention.*[44]

Even if one does not follow Goldenhagen here, Adorno already knew something like *collective narcissism*, which he associated with hatred of Jews. According to this, a collective ego ideal is established that experiences feelings of unity and shared strength. Communities that hate Jews function in this way–in terms of *mass psychology*. They feel superior to others, outsiders–

in this case the Jews.[45] It is important for mass psychological collectives to have an external enemy because this is the only way to keep their own community *pure*. Even if it is always said that people who join a Jew-hating or *foreign/hostile* (here better: misanthropic, because Jews are not foreign in German society) collective have certain fears that must be taken seriously, this is not true. Because these people do not use the collective to arm themselves against *foreign infiltration* (which is again a false term). They join people who reject Jews because then they are no longer alone and do not have to think for themselves. This is about *displacement* (fear of losing social integration: relegation or unrest, depending on the social position) and *projection* (fear of one's own superego and drive desires). As individuals, the enemies of Jews and foreigners [sic!] would have been afraid of many things, but as a collective, they would have gone on the attack against what they now believe they were *afraid* of.[46] During the German *Kaiserreich* (Empire) some developments came up which have contributed to the development of hatred of Jews a *collective narcissism*. And so, it seems that the Germans have an extra close connection to it.

One example is class antagonism which is another element of modern hatred of Jews. Socialist and anarchist thinkers such as Karl Marx (1818–1883) took an extreme anti-Jewish stand, accusing Jews of initiating capitalism and thus exaggerating out of all portions the important, though limited, contribution of Jewish traders and industrialists to the growth of industry and commerce.[47] The religious dimension of hostility toward Jews was displaced or overlaid with a secular form: in the 19th century, religious anti-Judaism was joined by a racist point of view that emphasized Jews' fundamental differentness as a race or people: the so-called *Aryan ideal* and the concept of human inequality moved into the foreground of the racial doctrine being promulgated as scientific and was used to justify the isolation and exclusion of Jews. Jews came to be described as an *alien race*, as foreign bodies, as *parasites* and corrosive elements within non-Jewish communities.[48] This hatred of Jews emphasized economic, social, and political differences. The term *antisemitism*, which refers to hostility toward Jews not necessarily as members of a different religion but of a different nation or even a particular race, became more and more accepted. Especially in Germany from the end of the 1870s and subsequently, the term spread to other countries. This new hatred of Jews merged with racist theories that had been widespread in Europe since the mid-nineteenth century.

Mainly the idea of social Darwinism supported the new view on hatred of Jews. In 1850 Herbert Spencer (1820–1903) developed in England the theory of constant struggle between humans, in which the strongest would win. In Spencer's day, social Darwinism was invoked to justify laissez-faire economics and the minimal state, which were thought to best promote unfettered competition between individuals and the gradual improvement of society through *the survival of the fittest*, a term that Spencer himself introduced.[49]

Another development must be taken into account to understand the new view on hatred of Jews in the 19th century. The progression of *antisemitism to racism* was accomplished with linguistic research.[50] A German linguist, Christian Lassen (1800–1876), promoted the idea, that *Semites* were egoistical and exclusive. *Indo-Europeans* were tolerant and altruistic. Count Arthur Joseph de Gobineau (1816–1882) mixed everything together when he referred to what he called the Aryan race (blond, tall, blue-eyed). For him, this race was superior and culture-bearing people in line with Social Darwinists' thoughts.[51]

This approach was closely linked to the symbol of *blood.* By doing so, the *biologization* of antisemitism was completed. As Bauer stresses: *To the imagery of the Jew as Satan was added the biologically oriented imagery of the parasite. Both images, that of the Devil and that of the parasite dehumanized the Jews and made theorizing about their physical destruction possible.*[52]

The now racially shaped hatred of Jews became a political connotation when the famous German historian, Heinrich von Treitschke (1834–1896), wrote an article in which he spoke out against what he feared would be mass immigration of East European Jews, and he charged the German Jews with an inadequate willingness to assimilate. In this work, Treitschke produced the sentence *The Jews are our misfortune!* This sentence, in which Treitschke expressed his conviction that the Jews were having a destructive influence on the cultural and economic life of the German state, mirrors the essential constants of hostility toward Jews: the unreal, hyperbolic, and demonizing fantasy of the Jews' negative role. The Jews accounted for barely one percent of the German population and were hardly in a position to be Germany's misfortune.[53]

In the German Empire (1871–1918), hatred of Jews led to the founding of anti-Jewish parties and anti-Jewish propaganda. The Jew-hater did not succeed in changing the civil status of German Jews until the First World War (1914–1918), but they did damage their reputation and social status.

Many Germans who did not identify with people who rejected Jews (including members of various elites of the German society) nevertheless resolutely avoided speaking out against it, as they too considered the Jews to be *different.*[54]

During the First World War (1914–1918), most German Jews enlisted to fight for their fatherland, hoping to prove their loyalty and thus put an end to hatred of Jews. Thousands gave their lives for their homeland. Nevertheless, the influence of hatred of Jews continued throughout the war and reached its peak when the German army carried out a census of Jewish soldiers at the front in 1916. Despite all this, the vast majority of German Jews remained loyal to their fatherland. Of 600 000 German Jews, fully 100 000 served in the German army, and 12 000 fell on the battlefield.[55]

As has become clear, hatred of Jews was already a problem in the German Empire. Modern hatred of Jews became socially acceptable in Germany at the latest with the doctrine of Social Darwinism in 1890. The apparent problem was based on the conviction that Jews were a different *race*. The racial characteristics assigned to Jews were consistently defined in negative terms.[56] Unfortunately, the end of the Kaiserreich was not also the end of hatred towards Jews.

Hatred of Jews between the Wars

The *Weimar Republic* (1919–1933) was an experiment in republican democracy in Germany. It emerged as a result of Germany's defeat and capitulation in the First World War (1914–1918), suffered from a lack of stability from the outset and had difficulty establishing a stable democracy. After months of bloody, bitter disputes, the National Assembly in Weimar[57] from February to September 1919 laid the foundations for the first German democracy and the Republicans prevailed. In this respect, Germany did not have to fight a war for democracy, it had to lose the war in order to become a democracy.

When the Weimar Republic was established in Germany in 1919, the new constitution also created the first democratic foundation in the *German Reich*. All sections of the population had equal political rights, including the Jewish part of the population. The basis of democracy, then as now, was the sovereignty of the people. The Kaiserreich before had already one of the most modern electoral laws of the time. Most citizens had the right to vote, unlike in the rest of Europe. And, of course, those who had gone to war for their fatherland could no longer be deprived of their civic rights.[58]

The revolutionary connotation of the term *democracy* became abundantly clear after 1918. The battle for the supposedly correct form of government was fought out bloodily and loudly. The call for social justice, and equality, to be able to fill the democratic principle with a life free from material worries and paternalism, resounded above all from the left-wing political spectrum. The society torn apart by the war, whose divisions had already become increasingly apparent during the war years, had to be reintegrated. The working class in particular, politically represented by the *Social Democratic Party* (SPD), was impatient and put pressure on the political elite through strikes (e.g. in 1917 with the elementary demand for peace) and protest actions (autumn 1915 against the poor food situation).

However, it was not only the working classes who renounced their loyalty to the Kaiserreich and blamed it for the lack of political and social modernisation. German society had been completely overwhelmed physically, militarily, economically and psychologically at the front and home during the World War. The war had to end immediately the monarchy had to disappear. Many in German society agreed on this. However, it was initially unclear exactly how to proceed. A kind of cooperation between the revolutionary government and the elites of the monarchy lasted until the new year 1919, but then the National Assembly was to decide on the future form of government and the constitution. In this window of time between November 1918 and February 1919, a fundamental course was set for the future republic. Above all, the signing of the *Treaty of Versailles* on 11 November 1918 by a democratic politician, Matthias Erzberger (1875–1921), and not by the military, left its mark on the Weimar Republic. The Weimar Republic was not only characterised by the propaganda lie that Germany had not been defeated at all, but had been brought down by a *stab in the back* in the course of the revolution, but also by the military's concealment of responsibility for the defeat. The rejection of the peace treaty thus served as a foundation for the feelings of German society.[59] On 6 February 1919, the National Assembly finally convened. The separation of powers, a balance of powers, territorial reorganisation, the freedom of the individual vis-à-vis the state, the relationship of the individual to the community, the rule of law, liberal fundamental rights including freedom of faith and conscience, as well as the ideal of the welfare state were enshrined in the constitutional text. The course was set for a successful parliamentary democracy in this respect. The greatest economic burden of the Weimar Republic was the reparations payments to the victorious powers stipulated in the *Treaty of Versailles*, as well as the switch from a wartime to a peacetime economy and the reintegration of soldiers (demobilisation).

When the first elections to the German National Assembly were held in January 1919, voting was based on proportional representation, the voting age was lowered to 20, women were given the right to vote and stand for election and soldiers were also allowed to vote for the first time. The government was now dependent on the approval of the *Reichstag* (the parliament), was elected by it and could be dismissed by it. In 1919, voter turnout was 83.0 percent of the 36.766 million eligible voters. The electorate was now younger, more female, and often first-time voters. Parties critical of the republic, such as the *Communist Party of Germany* (KPD), performed poorly. The political forces in favour of a new republican order had the majority of voters behind them. The trust placed in the German population proved to be correct and the normative foundation of democracy had thus also been proven.[60]

Demobilisation went far better than feared. Unemployment also fell rapidly. In 1922, there was full employment and a shortage of skilled labour. People achieved a modest level of prosperity. Community building was to be encouraged–and it was, at least to a certain extent. In 1923, the currency was also stabilised and credit restrictions for the state and private sector led to a further stabilisation of the overall situation. It seemed that the trust that the population had placed in the new system and the system of capitalism was paying off, at least for part of the population. In 1927, German industry as a whole and in many individual sectors reached pre-war production levels (in relation to the territory of the Weimar Republic) and ranked second among industrialised nations behind the USA. However, pre-war levels were not reached in every respect. In the white-collar sector, wages were consistently unsatisfactory. And the gap between them and the labour force, from which they had felt clearly set apart and therefore more privileged in the German Empire, was shrinking. In order to maintain their standard of living and satisfy their material and cultural needs, both men and women worked in the families. The modest prosperity came to an end at the latest in 1932 when unemployment among the population reached its peak. There were 6.1 million unemployed.[61]

Why are the details of the first German Republic so relevant?

Because it paved the way for the National Socialists and the Holocaust. Society in Weimar was full of contradictions. One part of the population saw their values and traditional ways of life disappearing, while another welcomed the new freedom. For example, there were major differences between the countryside and the city, between those who were stuck in tradition and those who dared to set out. The *we-feeling* of democracy in Weimar was therefore not anchored in all parts and anchored in all levels and areas of society. Public could not be decreed but had to be negotiated in public and the *Reichstag*.

In the countryside, it was above all the landowners and farmers that were particularly hostile to the Weimar Republic and their democracy. Although they were still privileged, they mourned the old system, especially in Prussia with its class suffrage. The new freedom, also culturally, was seen as a provocation, as a threat. The conflict between friends and opponents of modern mass culture was particularly evident in the assessment of the USA. While some praised the USA as a country of unlimited possibilities, for others it was a cesspool of sin full of decadence and hedonism.

As seen, the democratic system in Weimar came under pressure from the very beginning of its existence. Already during the First World War (1914–1918), many young men were torn out of their traditional, probably rather apolitical environment, the village, and rural surroundings, and were politicised by meeting other sections of the population. The young men were easily influenced politically and wanted to get involved.[62] In order to become politically involved, they voted for the *Deutscher Schutz-und Trutzbund* (German Protection and Defence League), for example, which primarily used propaganda to strengthen Jew-hatred and Jew-haters in Germany. In 1919, the *Bund* was the first right-wing radical mass organisation in Germany. It was mainly made up of disappointed young people who collectivised their personal disappointments.

The hatred of Jews fitted into the overall picture: Jews were excluded, demonized, marginalized, humiliated and virtually cut out of German society because, for the Germans, they embodied both: the rootlessness of modernity and the ultimate historical origins embedded in the Bible.[63] The number of members of the Jewish religious communities totalled 564,000, which was 0.9 percent of the entire population; they were concentrated in a few large cities such as Berlin or Frankfurt am Main. But even here they made up only a fraction of the population. Jews in Weimar were not a homogeneous class; there were differences in religious interpretation and cultural, social, and economic aspects.

The domain of the Jews in economic terms was trade and transport, especially goods and production trade. In 1925, 61.3 percent of the Jewish labour force worked in this sector. Most of the Jewish self-employed in the approximately 50,000 medium-sized businesses were small and medium-sized merchants, as well as craftsmen, doctors, and lawyers.

The fact that Jews were labelled as *scapegoats for the misery* after the World War was by no means due to their special position, because they were so particularly numerous or because they were economically better off than non-Jews. It was traditional hatred of Jews stereotypes and prejudices that the non-Jews harboured and which now found expression in the exaggeration of their own supposedly homogeneous mass. Even then, hostility towards Jews in the majority society was characterised by the fact that the marginalisation of the minority by the majority society arose and took effect without the minority's involvement.

The newly politicised young people in the Weimar Republic, who found themselves in a new environment in which they were easily influenced when they joined the army during the World War, also contributed to this. Within the fighting troops, they encountered German Jews who had allowed themselves to be infected by the wave of national enthusiasm and hoped to refute anti-Jewish resentment and overcome existing discrimination through self-sacrificing loyalty to the fatherland. Nevertheless, a great wave of Jew-hatred swept the country in 1917.[64] This culminated in the Weimar Republic being labelled a *Jewish republic*, as leading social and political figures such as Schacht (1877–1970), the author of the Weimar Constitution, were Jews. The extremists in Weimar used the term to express their rejection very clearly. Even non-Jews, whose politics did not suit those critical of the republic, were associated with Judaism, such as the Nobel Peace Prize winner Gustav Stresemann (1878–1929).

The Germans were particularly hostile towards the so-called *Eastern Jews*. Their appearance differed from the other Jews in the country, their habitus, their religious and cultural tradition, and often their language. Among them, especially among refugees from the Soviet Union, were many academics who also helped to shape cultural and scientific life in the Weimar Republic. However, it was not only the Eastern Jews who were the target of attacks due to their perceived otherness. The hatred of Jews in the Weimar Republic affected all Jews. Jewish Germans were subjected to insults and maltreatment. Jewish cemeteries were desecrated and Jewish property was damaged. Nevertheless, not all Germans of the Jewish faith left their homeland immediately.

The commitment of the Jewish communities to young people deserves special mention. Jewish schools were founded, especially in the larger cities. In 1930, there were 10 Jewish grammar schools in Germany, but the majority of German-Jewish children went to general schools. Jews were heavily overrepresented at secondary schools and among school leavers and students. Some of the young people were also preparing to emigrate to the Eastern Mediterranean, but by the end of the Weimar Republic, only 3,300 Jews had left Germany.[65]

Politically, most Jewish voters found themselves and their interests best represented by the *German Democratic Party* (DDP). This party was in favour of emancipation and equal rights. With the disintegration of the liberal parties as the Weimar Republic progressed, Jewish Germans often voted for the *Catholic Centre Party* (Zentrum).

For the Jews in Germany, the period of the Weimar Republic, even more than the times before it, was full of paradoxes. Despite its weakness and lack of stability, the Republic realised the principle of equal rights for Jews in practice for the first time: From then on, they were appointed to positions in the civil service, universities and the like. During this time, the creativity of Jews in Germany reached new heights in numerous areas of culture, philosophy and art, and this period was characterised by a Jewish cultural renaissance. But the signs of the crisis were recognisable above all in the rise of hatred of Jews, which at this time became more brutal than ever before.

The left-wing politicians in the Weimar Republic were divided on their attitude towards the Jews. While the SPD and *Independent Social Democratic Party of Germany* (USPD) strictly rejected hatred of Jews, the KPD also wanted to win over the middle class as voters and therefore allowed itself to be drawn into spreading petty-bourgeois Jew hatred prejudices. Nevertheless, leading Jewish politicians, such as Rosa Luxemburg (1871–1919), came to power. The left, above all the KPD, followed the argument that Jews were not part of the labour force. The hatred of Jews of the left became particularly conspicuous in 1923 during the *Ruhr War* when extreme anti-Jewish hostility and nationalist tones could be heard.

For the right-wingers in Weimar, the first mass organization for hatred of Jews, the *Deutscher Schutz- und Trutzbund*, was the association in which the later *Nationalsozialistische Deutsche Arbeiterpartei* (NSDAP) (National Socialist German Workers' Party)–members initially came together. Through their propaganda measures, leaflet campaigns, inflammatory speeches and publications, hatred of Jews became a threat to democracy. From 1924 at the latest, the economic livelihoods of the Jewish population collapsed due to calls for boycotts and the destruction of shops in rural areas of Germany.[66]

The anti-Jewish attacks on Jewish Germans reached a climax on the Jewish New Year in 1931 when 500 men of the *Sturmabteilung* (SA) (storm division or storm troops) in civilian clothes attacked Jews celebrating in Berlin's Kurfürstendamm. But it was not only the right-wing extremists' militant hostility towards Jews that contributed, large sections of the middle and upper classes made a point of emphasizing their dislike of Jews. Doctors and lawyers, for example, complained about the influx of Jews into their professions. Protestant theologians and churchmen also fuelled Jew-hatred with supposedly religious justifications.[67]

The widespread ideological basis for hatred of Jews in the right-wing spectrum, like the assumption that Jews were not part of the people and did not belong racially, could not be counteracted by joint efforts by Jews and non-Jews to live together. Adolf Hitler's (1889–1945) hostility towards Jews was rooted in this irrational assumption of *otherness*. This *otherness* led to what Confino calls a *war of identity*.[68] The essential motivations for this war were not practical. German and Jews had for example no conflict over territory, land, resources, borders, or political power.[69]

For Hitler, world history was a battle of fate between Jews and *Aryans*, with the Germans in the lead. Everything negative was attributed to the Jews.[70] The Jews possessed alleged positions of power in that they were supposed to dominate the world. The concept of international (financial) Jewry, which was much publicised by the National Socialists, reflected this perception. Hitler used all means at his disposal to satisfy the wishes and resentments of right-wing, (petty) bourgeois circles. His ideas were already in the nationalist repertoire long before Hitler, but Hitler used other means to spread them. Hitler and his NSDAP, founded in Munich in February 1920, were louder than others in the truest sense of the word. The NSDAP sold itself as a young, dynamic party and Hitler was a professional politician who was fully committed to his cause. Even a ban on his party in 1923 in response to the *Munich Putsch* of November, 9 could only stop him briefly. In his book *Mein Kampf* human existence is viewed as a struggle for existence between *Aryans* and Jews, who stand for good and evil in the world. Constructs of the enemy that combine racist and political elements give rise to fictional notions of conspiracies forged by the Jewish-Bolshevist *world enemy* to achieve universal hegemony.[71]

The actionism pursued by the party and Hitler was totally new. The main idea of the politically right was the proclamation of the so-called *Volksgemeinschaft* (national or peoples' community). The term *Volksgemeinschaft* in the true sense of the word did not have anti-Jewish connotations. *Volksgemeinschaft* had long been a social-democratic or bourgeois-liberal concept of democratic integration. All classes and groups should find a place in a democracy. According to Müller, the term was to be understood openly and optimistically, as a promise of democratic awakening and collective participation.[72]

However, the National Socialists used it to exclude the Jews and other population groups and to exalt themselves. The overemphasis on the national community on the one hand and the personal disappointments of the people in Weimar were collectivized on the other hand with the term. Their collective, their *national community* offered simple solutions to the big problems. For these people the *Volksgemeinschaft* was good and spread true assumptions, its members were friends and insiders and belonged to the elite. To strengthen the self and build an *emotional community* Germans acted publicly against the Jews.[73] By supporting Hitler, they hoped for salvation from their misery and eternal truth (providence). The actionism of the NSDAP supporters is another clear signal of the overemphasis on their own homogeneous masses.[74]

Society in Weimar was extremely charged. The rejection of democracy by the opposition was, of course, fuelled by Hitler. People were fascinated by Hitler and the so-called *Bewegung* (movement). They wanted to be a part of it and followed their natural urge to socialise and participate in communities. The fact that they mistrusted other communities, isolated, and marginalised them, was something they at least accepted. On the eve of the National Socialist Party's rise to power, there were around 500,000 Jews living in Germany, less than one percent (0.8 percent) of the total population. Despite all the difficulties and crises, most considered themselves loyal patriots, connected to the German way of life through their language and culture. There was a widespread belief among the Jewish public that, because of their role in trade and industry and their contribution to the German economy, the National Socialists would shy away from their total ousting.[75]

But this assessment was a misjudgement.

The clear election winner in 1930 was the NSDAP. It rose from 2.6 percent to 18.3 percent and was represented in the *Reichstag* with 107 Members of Parliament. In absolute terms, the NSDAP gained 6.4 million voters. The 6.4 million people who voted for the NSDAP in September 1930 were made up of former non-voters, whom the movement was able to mobilise, as well as the disintegration of the *German National People's Party* (DNVP). They capitalised most on the national and economic crisis of the late 1920s. When the NSDAP was also able to present an attractive economic policy program, it became an electable alternative for many. The conceptualization of Jews as global evil was the basis for the National Socialist eliminatory hatred, which led to the *Final Solution* within the framework of their closed ideological view of the world and an immanent *logic* that lacked any basis in reality. From the Nuremberg race laws, a straight unbroken line, ideologically homogeneous and bureaucratically perfected, led—by way of public stigmatization, exclusion from all realms of normal life, denial of all rights, and refusal to recognize Jews' humanity—to the gas chambers.[76]

Manifestations of hatred of Jews after the Holocaust

After 1945, once the dimensions of the crimes against the Jews became widely known and unmistakable, the transformation in the collective consciousness that this caesura in civilization should have brought about did not occur. To be sure, Judeophobic images and texts were officially banned, and their reproduction was publicly subjected to sanctions and taboos, but there was no truly probing reflection, no comprehensive critical analysis of the reasons and motives for the hatred and the extermination policy. Instead, the Holocaust was usually described as resulting from the obsessions of a few National Socialists, an explanation that led to decisive misinterpretation and a failure to take into account the extent to which Jews were hated. Neither the institutional elites nor the general population sufficiently explored the hatred of Jews that had existed in almost all parts of society as an integral part of the much-invoked Western way of thinking and had belonged for centuries to the general culture.[77] After six million Jews had been systematically and industrially murdered by the National Socialists and their allies, the shame and denial of guilt of the perpetrators and their descendants was so immense that resentment was mobilized again because of the Holocaust. *Hatred was never really and never structurally combated. And by whom? By the original National Socialists who had become democrats overnight?* asks Friedmann correctly.[78]

So-called *secondary antisemitism* (e.g., refusing Holocaust remembrance, advancing conspiracy theories, claiming Jews exploit the memory of the Holocaust, stating that Jews have too much economic power) broke out after the Holocaust. It is expressed also, in the call for a final line to be drawn: according to this, the Holocaust has been sufficiently dealt with, but *the Jews* never give up and constantly remind *the Germans* of their guilt.

This defence of memory and guilt finds its expression in the relativization of the Holocaust, the relativization of perpetration and also where family entanglements are made taboo. It can be seen in the accusation of a supposed instrumentalization of the Holocaust on the part of the Jews as well as in what is called (in Germany) the *perpetrator-victim reversal*. Post-Holocaust hatred of Jews culminates in the relativization or denial of the Holocaust.

Defense and self-appeasement, including the denial of historical facts, lead to a completely distorted–indeed, irrational, and insane–view of history. German national sentiment was offended and to this day the desire to correct this perspective persists. In line with this argument, the image of the *vengeful and powerful Jew* can also be kept alive. The mass murder was initially intended to get rid of the unwanted minority. When this did not succeed, guilt and shame turned into a discourse of justification that articulated itself out of feelings of guilt in hatred of the Jews.[79] In order to be freed from the nightmare of the murder of the Jews (or *redeemed*, as Benz calls it[80]), the perpetrators must not have been to blame. Others must have been to blame–preferably the Jews themselves. The Jews must not be victims and must not have a victim function. If Jews are perceived as perpetrators, then they cannot fulfill a victim function. Then the real perpetrators, the National Socialists and their allies are no longer real perpetrators, then the descendants, then the whole German nation no longer has to be ashamed. But how can one ensure that Jews no longer act as victims in order to feel better about themselves?

Friedman stresses that it was said behind closed doors: *"If there hadn't been any Jews, we wouldn't have had to build Auschwitz". They will never forgive us for having to build Auschwitz.*[81]

However, individual misconduct by individual Jews is not enough to feel better. One needs demonstrable reasons, a *collective guilt of the Jews* in which all enemy images and prejudices accumulate. The politics of the Jewish State of Israel, for example, are used to demonstrate the collective guilt of the Jews. Anti-Jewish emotions can be articulated through anti-Israeli attitudes. The construction of the collective guilt of Jews seemingly exonerates people from the suffering of their own history. The old insane ideas of the omnipotence of the Jews fit perfectly into their own cranky worldview of exclusion and negative attributions. Stereotypes unquestioningly underpin the belief in a threatening Jewish collective that must be countered with defense. This also includes publicly articulating accusations of guilt, such as that the Jews themselves are to blame if they are rejected. The behavior of the Jews is thus the breeding ground for rejection. Israeli security policy, compensation payments, the historical facts in German school lessons and one's own prejudices due to the assumed *arrogance of chosenness* are then thrown together in a completely unreflected and irrational manner and Jews are portrayed as arsonists, as disturbers of the peace.

This is where the idea of hatred of Jews based *on defense* comes into play again. At the latest since the *6-day war*, the relativization of the crimes committed by the National Socialists became legitimate in parts of the Federal Republic of Germany. Now, however, hatred of Jews was given a new name: *criticism of Israel*. This hatred of Jews also expressed itself in hostility towards Israel and Jews, who were now perceived as *privileged* and *white*.[82]

Since statements against Israel are not explicitly directed against Jews (in the view of the people who make them), they seem to have nothing to do with hatred of Jews. On the contrary–hostility towards Jews disguised as criticism of Israel even attempts to distinguish itself from the National Socialists, for example by threatening Israel not with annihilation but with prosecution before the International Criminal Court.[83] Howeverer, people who reject Jews, disguised as critics of Israel, do not refrain from engaging in making use of age-old stereotypes and narratives. Only now it is no longer the Jews, but Israel, which as a *nuclear power is endangering the already fragile world peace.*[84] It is no less than that: Israeli Jews endangering the entire world peace with nuclear weapons!

Alongside far-right organizations and populist radical right parties, groups in Europe which are commonly identified as demonstrating a proclivity to the articulation of contemporary forms of hatred of Jews include left-wing movements. They use stereotypes to attack the legitimacy of the State of Israel. The radical actions of individuals ascribing to Islamist ideologies have also been an area of major concern.[85]

With *anti-Zionism*, hatred of Jews became established above all in the DDR (GDR/*German Democratic Republic*) and is therefore part of the socialization of GDR citizens. This form of hatred of Jews has persisted even after reunification.[86] For example, Jews are expected to show charity towards the supposed losers of unification and to support the East Germans with money and influence, as a kind of compensation for the coexistence that was disrupted by the Jews. Ancient stereotypes of wealth, power and influence are also evident here.

In the political left-wing spectrum, hatred of Jews appears partly veiled, partly openly as criticism of Israel in the *anti-imperialist sphere*. This has ideological and organizational links to left-wing terrorism. All pluralistic, democratic characteristics of history are thus completely suppressed in favor of a monistic and anti-pluralistic worldview. This worldview then differs only in nuances from those of neo-Nazism.[87]

To this day in the united Federal Republic of Germany, the concept of the people (*Volkssouveränität*, the German people) is explicitly linked to the constitution, the Basic Law. People and nations are linked (Article 116, Basic Law). Therefore, the concept of the people makes it easy to understand certain groups as not belonging to the people. This applies in particular to people of the Jewish faith. The Jews are regarded as a foreign people that have infiltrated their own people and are destroying their unity from within.[88] This can also be observed when dichomization between *Jews* and *Germans*, which is still valid today, is applied. *Jews* are also excluded linguistically and regarded as *non-German*.[89] As Friedman puts it: *There are people [Germans, note of the author] who cannot bear their [the Jewish, note of the author] identity.*[90]

The following can be established: As an object of hatred, Israel occupies the central position in the current hatred of Jews. In the 21st century, the Middle East conflict provides the overarching pretext for the expression of Jews rejecting opinions and serves as a catalyst for hostility toward Jews. *Anti-Israelism* is communicated not only by extremists on the right or left but also by academics and intellectuals, as well as representatives of the mainstream since this attitude can pass for politically correct. This situation is not confined to one region but is globalized; hostility toward Israel appears all over the world, disseminated through the mass media. Verbal violence in everyday and public discourse on Israel has taken on a new cast; increasingly prominent in the mainstream communication realm are virulent forms of denigration.

Another new feature is the willingness manifested by more and more people the world over to agree with drastically pejorative statements about the Jewish State of Israel.[91] Additionally, there is unlimited access to and massive dissemination of verbal hatred of Jews, which in a virtual world and communication system has long since become an essential feature of the real world and contributes in a crucial way to transmitting hatred of Jews. This thinking is by no means restricted to right-wing-extremist, fundamentalist, or Islamist websites, but also appears in mainstream Internet forums and chat rooms, and on social network sites. As a result, hate can come to seem habitual and normal and become firmly established.

Once again, various public, political, and digital actors from different political camps and milieus and in different social arenas and media ecologies are interpreting Jews, a *tiny minority of less than 0.2% of the world's citizens*, as the *existential enemies of humanity*.

They thus meet with a broad response around the globe, while the boundaries of what is (seemingly legitimate) to say are currently eroding at an enormous rate in the global context.[92] Israel-related hatred of Jews applies special moral standards to the political actions of the State of Israel that are not applied to any other democracy. It can go so far as to deny Israel's right to exist. This form is also present when hater call on Jews as supposed representatives to justify Israel's policies or hold them responsible for them. This seems to make it possible to criticize Jews without being openly against them. In Germany, this phenomenon is referred to as *Umwegkommunikation* (detour communication).[93]

Tobin stresses that it is time for decent people of all backgrounds and faiths to understand that the *war on the Jews* did not end with the defeat of the National Socialists. It continues to this day under new slogans, flags and worse, with many of those who claim to stand for enlightened thought, allowing the enablers of Jew-hatred to pose as advocates for human rights and the oppressed. Those lies must not be allowed to stand. The only difference between then and now is that the Jewish people are not as vulnerable as they were in the world that existed without Jewish sovereignty and military power.[94] If one considers this millennia-old persecution and the mass murder of the Holocaust in the run-up to the founding of modern Israel, it can be assumed that the Israel Defense Forces (IDF) are a direct consequence of this.

Hatred of Jews is constructed in such a way that Jews are used as a projection surface, as imaginary enemies, and this hatred is irrationally anchored, it is so difficult to resolve by rational means.[95] Especially, because of *the essential trick of people hating Jews today: to present themselves as persecuted*,[96] to behave as if it is impossible to make statements in public that are against Jews or Israel and that they are therefore the victims in society. The idea is that there is no hatred of Jews. It is simply denied. People who reject Jews claim, that such accusations are made by *powerful Jews* and Israelis with hostile intentions. It is precisely this self-immunization and self-excuse mechanism–which includes making discussions about hatred of Jews a taboo, refusing to confront one's own prejudices and blaming the (Jewish) messenger–that supports hatred of Jews.[97]

Having said all that, the question remains: Why do non-Jews hate the Jews?

An attempt at an explanation
why non-Jews hate Jews

After all the millennia-old hatred that the morally failed have repeatedly adapted to situations so that they could continue to hate, the ideology of hatred of Jews can be viewed as follows:

In addition to well-known anti-Jewish images that Jews are omnipotent (and thus every event from the social sphere can be reinterpreted as an expression and proof of this) because, after all, they killed God and are thus the personification of an invisible power and the associated indirect approval of the idea of a *chosen people*, which produces deep envy and is thus much more than just a prejudice, there is another explanation. Of course, the expressions of hatred of Jews form ideological enemy images. Moreover, haters are not concerned with enemies who, for example, were regarded as such in a colonially subjugated population, but with citizens of their own country. People who are declared to be internal strangers and therefore enemies. The pronounced desire for destruction coupled with fantasies of annihilation can also be located here. Fantasies of omnipotence, also towards authority figures, are to be classified in this regard.

But on top of this, as Shore writes, one characterization of Jews is a drive for more, or for a better or different way to do things, from the secrets of the universe to better economic and political systems for mankind. The desire for change and improvement has manifested itself not only in religious matters but in all aspects of human endeavor. For thousands of years, Shore notes, the Jews may have been powerless militarily but possessed great strength in the world of ideas. One example: Jews have won 40% of all the Nobel Prizes in Economic Sciences, which includes 38 awards in the 56 years since that award's establishment. Shore stresses that the roots of hatred of Jews stem from Sinai. At Sinai, the Jewish people received the Ten Commandments and accepted the mission to bring morality, ethics, ethical monotheism, and light into the world. The Jews will be hated for it, and the world will protest and resist. That resistance, he says, is called hatred of Jews.[98] So the world would be better off without the Jews. Because without them, one would not always have to explain and justify own failures and the missing drive for more. The assessment, that the world would be better off without Jews then works as a *relief function*. The humiliation that some may feel because their prophet, their Messiah, is not recognized by the Jews, also plays a role here.

It all comes back to lower irrational human emotions.

4. HOLOCAUST EDUCATION IN PRACTICE

Why to teach the Holocaust? For many people, the answer to the question is clear: because Holocaust education combats hatred of Jews. This can be seen, for example, in a response to a parliamentary question in the German Bundestag on the topic of *Educating pupils about antisemitism and the Holocaust*[1] in 2019. The German government emphasized that knowledge about the Holocaust is central in the fight against hatred of Jews. They are inextricably linked, which is why knowledge of the National Socialist persecution policy is indispensable for dealing with current forms of the hatred of Jews. The same approach is evident when the former EU Justice Commissioner Vera Jourová stressed in 2018 that education is not only *the key to understanding the Shoah*, but also in the *fight against Jew hatred.*[2] And the approach can be seen also in North America. In Canada, for example Isha Chaudhuri, a spokesperson for the province of Ontarios' minister of education, states: *By mandating learning on the horrors of the Holocaust, we combat the scourge of antisemitism and denialism, and by doing so we help ensure 'Never Again' is our legacy to the next generation.*[3]

But: Is that the only reason?

When people ask why to teach the Holocaust, one answer is: Why not? Certainly, teaching the Holocaust represents a challenge. Especially in Germany, the relaying of the own historical abyss is awkward. Teachers and educators need to explain the morally and politically failure of grandparents or great-grandparents. Borries says that there might be good reasons to question the teaching of the Holocaust at all. Since it might not be the right topic for young people to establish a healthy mind without cynical contempt of the world or building a destabilizing fear for the world.[4] Novik argues, that *due to the extreme nature of the situation it would be almost impossible to extract lessons for our daily lives.*[5]

Contrary to these statements, there are number of reasons why the Holocaust should be taught. The following list is certainly not exhaustive, but gives an impression of why Holocaust education can or should take place. Having said that: What are the purposes to teach the Holocaust?

Purposes of Holocaust Education

One reason for Holocaust education is a **moral obligation** to murdered neighbors, friends, and families, to remember the victims and a precondition for rebuilding an own historical identity. Focusing on Europe, since the Holocaust happened here, teaching history in a rapidly changing world will demand rethinking the meaning of not only the most important social processes but also events that hold particular symbolism. The Holocaust is one such event which defines the contemporary culture of Europe and exerts a huge influence on the image of the social world. The Holocaust is often and rightly described as the most tragic moment in Europe's history, the culmination of what is worst in European civilization: intolerance, hatred of strangers, and genocide.[6] This is particularly true in Western Europe, although instances of hatred of Jews, which are often linked to radical right revivalism are also present in Eastern Europe and the Baltic states.[7]

Besides the moral obligation, some people do see a **spiritual reason:** The Holocaust was the mass killing of Jews, which cannot be forgotten, but that attempt to physically annihilate all of Jewish society was also an attack on the whole tradition and civilization of Europe. It was an attempt not only against the sum of human achievement but against God, without whom that culture certainly would not have taken shape. That is why the memory of the Holocaust is and should be the memory of the spiritual tradition from which the Western civilizations come, from which even secular Europe comes, however much it has treated that tradition as the distant past. The point is, that both of those totalitarian enterprises [National Socialism and Communism; note of the author] of the 20th century were aimed at disinheriting the new societies and the new people of memory and tradition so that they would become like a wave propelled by the leaders of their parties and activated by feelings hostile toward others.[8] The spiritual connection is also related to Jerusalem and the Land of Israel since the events fundamentally affected the attitudes of Jews. It sparked a determination to achieve Jewish sovereignty in the Land of Israel. What happens there impacts the world. Jerusalem is important to Christians and Muslims, too. Its current fate cannot be understood without some knowledge of the Holocaust, which left a deep, unhealed wound. More generally, the Jews played a special role in the history of Christianity. Judaism is the root. Thus, the attitude to the Jews is a component of the attitude toward one's own roots.[9]

Bearing witness to the truth about our life and experience is closely linked to moral obligation. It has a cleansing and healing effect. Demonstrating the community of suffering, conveying the message that there is no pain in the world that does not affect us. Genocide is the shared pain of all humanity, and it demands a global solution. Victims and perpetrators often spring from the very same root, suffering, despair, and humiliation.[10] Auschwitz and what it stands for is seen in a global view and therefore, because it is world history, people need to learn about it. Auschwitz has become a symbol clear to the whole world, probably to some extent because Western culture is omnipresent, and in this culture, much intellectual and emotional energy has been devoted to the Holocaust. To teach about the Holocaust means first of all to convey the truth about the events, and to give them an interpretation that incorporates on the one hand the state of people's consciousness at that point in history, and on the other hand our moral and social views today. Teaching the Holocaust means shaping the collective historical memory, recalling the role of Jews, and making clear the irreparable loss that the Holocaust inflicted on society, eliminating million citizens and their achievements.[11]

Conveying historical facts means also remembering. *Remembering* seems to be the ideal way of learning from and against dictatorship and the history of violence.[12]

If Holocaust education can be seen as conveying knowledge and values and if one can learn from history, this knowledge and education can be used to **develop more peaceful, tolerant, and understanding societies.** It can be used to sensitize children and youth, fostering their sensitivity to values such as the preciousness of human life and life in general, their tolerance toward the differentness of other people, their appreciation of all people's fundamental right to a free, decent and fulfilled life, their capacity for empathy with the suffering, and their sense of mutual dependence and connection with all living beings.[13] Navigating ways through this terrain is not easy–especially for classroom practitioners and others who do not work solely in the field of Holocaust education.[14] In particular, Gautschi stresses that judgement and the development of values through history classes need time. Democracies are based on passing main values and traditions and the new discussion from one generation to the next. However, the impact of history classes on the youth and their development regarding the main values are neither proven nor disproved.[15]

When it comes to peaceful societies, Galtung[16] emphasized, peace can be described as positive, warm peace and not as negative, cold peace; for example, there can be no question of peace if there is only non-violence, but only when all those involved also experience social justice and tolerance. In detail: By decreasing violence, Galtung does not only mean a decrease in physical violence such as visible destruction, injury, and damage. He also underlines a decrease in less visible psychological violence such as bullying, threatening, ostracising, blaming, and degrading. And even more: He also explains a decrease in structural violence such as surveillance, deprivation of liberty, overwork, and poverty. Finally, Galtung introduces the term *cultural violence*, which must decrease, such as harmful videos, music, caricatures, and computer games. According to Galtung, (peace) education therefore has the task of minimizing these four forms of violence: physical, psychological, structural, and cultural–on an ongoing basis.

This process has to happen in two respects: First, the addressees should be empowered to defend themselves against such forms of forms of violence; and second, they should stand up for others who suffer violence and intervene in a protesting manner. The call to reduce violence in its fourfold form is of course also a call for the prevention of hostility towards Jews in its physical, psychological, structural, and cultural forms. Jews were and are physically persecuted and destroyed, psychologically bullied and marginalized, structurally held responsible as scapegoats for political misery and culturally labelled. In terms of a positive, warm peace can be said: It is not enough to abolish all of this, rather, it is a matter of being respectful and tolerant towards everyone. Only then hatred of Jews will really be prevented. Given that, Holocaust education can be seen as a basis for knowledge and (peace) education. Although this may appear to be a pragmatic approach, it is much more of a psychological-intellectual challenge that both schools and society must face. But: *Without knowledge, there is no thinking, no grief, no insight.*[17]

Accepting the challenge Holocaust education can be understood as **a tool to fight hatred of Jews**, since Holocaust education is also used to work on myths, stereotypes, and prejudices, examining the myths and stereotypes about different nationalities involved in conflict, and how to neutralize them.[18] It is about *meeting the stranger in ourselves and others.*[19] To teach the Holocaust means to warn of a danger. To use Holocaust education as a tool to fight hatred of Jews, it is important to know about the history: true factories of death were organized. The best organizers and modern knowledge were employed to make the assembly line proceed with the greatest efficiency. The product was death. The Holocaust thus becomes a warning: This is what technological development without moral progress can lead to. Another historical fact points to the extent of the enterprise. The National Socialist Germans wanted to eliminate all Jews from the face of the earth. In one country after another a system was introduced, that would enable the capture of every Jew, old people, and babies as well. War aims were not the point. It is known that sometimes the killing of Jews interfered with the achievement of war aims because, for example, it required the use of means of transport that could have been of use to the soldiers. Additionally, the goal of the National Socialists has to be stressed: Their goal was to cleanse the world. Murdering Jews was not pleasant. It was understood, however, to be an essential step in the achievement of a grand ideological vision: Rule by a better race and the removal of the personification of evil, the Jews, according to Hitler, from humanity. These circumstances are worth studying because they say something important about our civilization. They also point to the fourth answer: it was not about just anyone, but about the Jews.[20]

Intolerance, xenophobia, and hatred of Jews have not died out. They are said to be intensifying. Also because of that, it is important to teach about the Holocaust, since it is to inculcate the **idea of a pluralistic society**. The history of the Holocaust also shows what intolerance and an ideology of racial purity can lead to, and to forge attitudes that encourage the building of a new, shared, pluralistic, open, and tolerant world of dealing with its legacy.[21] Teaching the Holocaust based on this reason, means, that (history) lessons always stand between two levels: On the one hand, the actual historical event that is to be analyzed and where it must be clarified what happened and why. On the other hand, there is the process in which students learn how people act and in which they should learn to evaluate, decide what is right or wrong and assess the consequences of their actions. Educating the population about the past in a way that is both historically accurate and conducive to reconciliation is important.[22] Fighting hatred of Jews, therefore, seems to be particularly important for society as a whole. Certainly, it would be naive to delude ourselves that a similar catastrophe like the Holocaust cannot be repeated in one or another region of Europe or outside. However, learning and understanding the sources of the Holocaust may give a chance to avert a similar tragedy in the future.[23]

If Holocaust education is supposed to fulfill all these claims, it is

clearly cited as the weapon in the fight against hatred of Jews–
but as seen actually not the only one. In any case, a closer look at
the content of Holocaust education is needed.

Content of Holocaust Education

Since the term *Holocaust education* was developed originally
in the English-speaking world, the meaning seems to be pretty
obvious. Following the Oxford Dictionary *to educate* means: *to
teach someone, especially using the formal system of school, college, or university (educate someone about something).*[24] So, the
original meaning of the term is basically *to teach.*

The term *to educate* in German *erziehen*, means *to form someone's (especially a child's) mind and character and encourage
their development or guide them to behave in a certain way.*[25] *To
educate someone* always includes values, behavior, and socialization in the German understanding of the term. Therefore,
Holocaust *Erziehung* (education) is way more than just learning
about the historical background and facts. It is way more than
to *know* about. It means to use knowledge to *form someone's
mind and character.* In this respect, the claim that Holocaust
education should be more than just factual knowledge is again
evident.

Keeping this in mind, the question occurs naturally: What is
the content of Holocaust education? The answer here must be:
It depends. It actually depends in which country Holocaust education takes place. And it is also important to ask who is doing
Holocaust education, who is going to be educated? What about
the sources and resources, how much time and scope is given to
education?

Even this short list of questions shows, that there is a lot to consider when it comes to the content of Holocaust education. Additionally, more aspects need to be included, since the Holocaust hat become institutionalized in formal institutions and structures. Its effects are no longer limited to perpetrator, bystander, and victim communities, but are experienced by national and international audiences. In this context narratives offered by political actors and the media are particularly significant.[26] The aspects of narratives and commemoration also play an important role. Since Holocaust education is based on historical knowledge, one part is always the historical background of the events.

Although Holocaust education was basically *invented* by **North Americans**, the topics requirements vary by state for example in the US. Illustrative the State of Colorado can be mentioned here, in which high school students are required to learn about Holocaust and genocide studies. The Colorado General Assembly gives the following information: *Concerning requiring the satisfactory completion of a course that includes Holocaust and genocide studies as a condition of high school graduation in public schools. [...] The act requires the state board to adopt standards related to Holocaust and genocide studies on or before July 1, 2021. [...] The act requires each school district board of education and charter school to incorporate the standards on Holocaust and genocide studies adopted by the state board into an existing course that is currently a condition of high school graduation for school years beginning on or after July 1, 2023, if the standards are adopted by the state board on or before July 1, 2023. The act requires the department of education to create and maintain a publicly available resource bank of materials pertaining to Holocaust and genocide courses and programs, which must be available for access by public schools no later than July 1, 2021.*[27]

Way more in-depth the State of North Carolina (NC) features Holocaust education.[28] The NC Council on the Holocaust supports on its website Holocaust Curriculum Resources for grades 6–12 developed by a team of North Carolina teachers and NCDPI as a result of the 2021 *Gizella Abramson Holocaust Education Act*. Holocaust education is part of English and Language Arts, as well as Social Studies and History. The *North Carolina Council on the Holocaust*, an agency of the N.C. Departments of Public Instruction, provides online and in-person programs and educational resources for teachers and the public across the state. Middle and high school resources are presented by the Council. *Educators will teach students the reasons why we must work to combat the rise in hatred, whether it be across the street or around the world.* This legislation expects English and Social Studies teachers in grades 6–12 to begin integrating teaching about the Holocaust, topics related to histories connecting to the Holocaust, and genocide, in their courses in August of 2023.[29] However, and this must be emphasized here, it is unclear, which material is used in the different US states and to what extent.

As mentioned before, the Holocaust is already a mandatory part of the curriculum in Roman Catholic Schools in Canada since 1974. Since 1990 the Holocaust has been part of History, English, world issues, citizenship, and human rights classes. In 2007 the governmentally initiated *Task Force for International Cooperation on Holocaust Education, Remembrance, and Research*, published a comparative study on Holocaust Education in Canada called: *Liaison Projects–Baseline Study*. The study's background was to provide a broad picture of the state of Holocaust education, remembrance, and research in Canada.[30] In four Canadian provinces, Holocaust education is mandatory or will be mandatory soon. These are the provinces of Ontario (grade 6 and 10[31]), Alberta (grade 11[32]), British Columbia (grade 10[33]), Manitoba (grade

11[34]), Saskatchewan and New Brunswick (grade 10[35]), but there is no concrete information about the content of the Social Studies curricula so far. That is why, the same curricula as well as the same old-dated school textbooks are in use. To name just one example: In Alberta/Canada Holocaust education is part of the topic on liberalism and nationalism (grade 11) and ultra-nationalism (grade 12) in Social Studies. Teachers chose the textbooks following their own estimation. The information about the Holocaust in all these books is very limited. Usually, half of a page is reserved for information about *Jews and other persecuted groups*. In one book a double page gives further information about *The Shoa–Mass Murder of the Jews*.[36]

Mostly, textbooks are still the leading mediums when it comes to teaching and learning. Therefore, textbooks represent national narratives and constructs about the past and support the collective memory as well as frame the societal discourse about interpretations of the past. This leads to orientation for the present and future. For the learners textbooks contribute to orientation, building of identities, gaining of knowledge and judgement about merits and values. It is absolutely necessary, therefore, to ensure high-quality textbooks, that convey balanced views as well as intellectual and unbiased approaches to the topics.

As for the precise content used for Holocaust education, one problem is the fact that there are materials and resources for teachers accessible (for example in preparation for a Holocaust education teaching event like the *Holocaust Education Symposium* in Calgary, Alberta[37] or the *Tour of Humanity* by the *Friends of Simon Wiesenthal Center* in Toronto[38])–but we do not know if and to what extend this material is used. Additionally, there is a lot of digital material offered online from different organizations.[39] But again: it is not clear why and to what occasion or subject this material is offered. This is also due to the fact that only very few studies were done about the content of Holocaust education in North America.[40]

The same is true for Germany: Although **Germany**, as the country of the perpetrators, has established itself over the years as a role model for Holocaust education in the international and domestic perception, there are only a few studies[41] dealing with the content of Holocaust education itself.[42]

Under the headline: *Teaching about the Holocaust and National Socialism* the KMK stresses: The topic of National Socialism and the Holocaust is firmly anchored in all federal states in the subject of history or–depending on federal state regulations–in social science subjects with a high proportion of history. It is a compulsory subject in year 9 or 10, and in some cases also in year 8. As a rule, no pupil leaves school without having learnt something about this chapter of German history. In addition, the topic is also discussed in other subjects at the lower secondary level, particularly in German and religion/ethics with a subject-specific focus.[43]

Since 2014 the focus has been more on a so-called *culture of remembrance*. The KMK underlines: A culture of remembrance is the result of complex interaction between many stakeholders, debates, and traditions. Both for individuals and groups, remembrance forms the respective basis for self-reassurance and for action that is directed toward the future. The contents and nature of remembrance may change over the course of time and need to be continuously remodelled in accordance with the system of values governing human rights and based on the Constitution. The area of conflict that arises as a result of various possible interpretations of history places an equal focus on the acquisition of historical awareness, knowledge, empathy, the development of a fundamental democratic attitude and on the promotion of judgement and competence to take action. Remembrance and a culture of remembrance form part of historical and political education and are therefore also an object of school-based learning. Many schools integrate memorial days or visits to places of commemoration, memorial sites, and museums into a long-term pedagogical concept of historical and political education. Numerous teaching subjects contain multiple points of reference and connection. Cooperation with non-school partners from memorial sites, museums, and archives and with further stakeholders from within civil society expand the leeway and horizons of historical and political education in schools.[44]

The following basic principles provide initial guidance for teaching in Germany: After dealing with the topic in grades 9 and 10, in the upper secondary level, National Socialism and the Holocaust are once again compulsory subject matter in a more in-depth and wider contextualizing way.

It should also be noted, that there is a differentiation between *Haupt– und Nebenfächer* (major and minor subjects) in Germany. History is often seen as a minor subject by pupils, parents, ministries, other teachers and unfortunately, by some history teachers themselves. This indifference has led to the fact that history classes are only 90 minutes per week, if at all.

One example of how Holocaust education takes place in a German history class is the following. In the state of Hamburg, the history curriculum for the Gymnasium stresses: In grades 9/10 the following questions regarding the Holocaust shall be answered: *Warum faszinierte der Nationalsozialismus so viele Menschen in Deutschland? Wie kam es zum Zweiten Weltkrieg und*

dem Zivilisationsbruch des Holocaust? (Why were so many people in Germany fascinated by the National Socialism? How did
the Second World War and the rupture in civilization Holocaust
happen?).[45] In grades 11/12 the curriculum says the goal to reach
is, that the pupils *verschiedene Formen der kollektiven Erinnerung
an die NS–Gewaltherrschaft und den Holocaust beurteilen* (judge
the different forms of collective memory about the NS tyranny
and the Holocaust resp. explain different perspectives on these
issues).

The level of knowledge and in-depth information depends on the
level of the history class. Pupils decide based on grades and interest between the *grundlegendes Niveau* (basic level) or *erweiter-
tes Niveau* (advanced level). One out of four semesters in grades
11/12 is called *Staat und Nation in der Deutschen Geschichte des
19. und 20. Jahrhunderts* (State and nation in the German history in the 19ᵗʰ and 20ᵗʰ century). Within this semester the
teacher is required to teach *Stationen, Phasen und Probleme der
deutschen Geschichte im 19. und 20. Jahrhundert im europäischen
Kontext (Deutsches Reich, Weimarer Republik, NS-Herrschaft, Holocaust, Grundgesetz und demokratischer Rechtstaat, SED-Diktat-
ur, Schritte zur Wiedervereinigung, Europäische Union* (Stations,
phases, and problems of German history in the 19ᵗʰ and 20ᵗʰ century in a European perspective).[46]

The Holocaust is part of the curriculum but subordinate. It depends on the teacher to which extent the Holocaust is taught in
history classes in Hamburg in the 9ᵗʰ– 12ᵗʰ grade. Even if these
surveys initially only apply to the city-state of Hamburg, they
can be transferred to other states.

Another example of Holocaust education in German history
classes is the area state of *Nordrhein Westphalen* (North Rhine

Westphalia NRW). The curriculum for NRW can serve as an additional test case.[47] German students learn about Jews, Judaism, and the Holocaust in history here, too.

Secondary education breaks down into *Sekundarstufe 1* (lower secondary level), which comprises the courses of education from grades 5 to 10 of school, and *Sekundarstufe II* (upper secondary level), which comprises all the courses of education that build on the foundations laid in the lower secondary level. The function of all the courses of education at the lower secondary level is to prepare pupils for courses of education at the upper secondary level, at the end of which a vocational qualification or the right to access higher education is acquired. Accordingly, lower secondary education is predominantly of a general nature whereas upper secondary level includes the general course of education at the *gymnasiale Oberstufe* as well as vocational courses of education.

As a rule, the lower secondary level is attended by pupils between 10 and 16 years of age and the upper secondary level by pupils between 16 and 19 years of age. Both age groups are required to attend school: the former full-time, the latter, 15–to 19-year-olds, generally part-time for three years or until they have reached the age of 18 unless they are attending a full-time school.

Secondary level educational institutions do differ in terms of duration and school leaving qualifications but largely constitute an open system allowing transfer from one type of course to the other. The same qualifications can, as a rule, also be obtained subsequently in vocational education and training institutions as well as adult education institutions or through an external examination.[48]

As seen, Holocaust education in Germany is taking place within the usual curriculum in public schools. Mostly, there is no extra topic or time frame like a project week or something similar. If teachers want to do a field trip they have to organize on their own and find time for it. Since a field trip to a learning location or camp is not required in 14 of the 16 states in Germany, many teachers do not organize such an excursion.[49] Also, one needs to take into account that even if the topic is part of the curriculum there is no proof that teachers really talk about the topic in classes, behind closed doors.

Studies have shown that the subject of history is actually primarily associated with learning about the 20th century, especially National Socialism. However, history consistently has little or nothing to do with the young people surveyed and their presence. For young people, history is school knowledge that is needed at school and not in daily life.[50]

When it comes to the used textbooks in Germany, the following applies: Some studies have indicated problematic content and misleading information about Jews, Judaism, the Holocaust, Israel, the Arab-Israeli conflict, and the Israeli-Palestinian conflict.[51] It is assumed that this misleading information supports hatred of Jews and Israel and often paints a wrong picture of current Israel and/or Jews in general.[52]

Textbooks in subjects with a dominant hermeneutic approach, such as history, can be regarded as media of school education that not only impart knowledge but also contribute to education. History books are therefore not only works of knowledge, but also media for the formation of meaning and social self-description. Jacobmeyer even describes them as *national autobiographies*.[53] They primarily deal with the history of the nation-state.

This also makes it clear who feels or should feel that they belong to this autobiography and who does not.

The development of teaching materials and teaching practice have changed considerably in recent years and, for example, include videotaped eyewitness interviews in the teaching of the subject.

To support teachers lots of additional teaching material is available. But as the following German example shows, additional material is also not always the solution, even if it comes from supposed experts:

In 2020, the *Institute for Teacher Training in Hamburg*, together with the partner organization in Schleswig–Holstein, published a brochure entitled *Holocaust/ Shoa in the classroom. Proven approaches–new paths in Hamburg and Schleswig-Holstein.*[54] In this booklet of just 84 pages, Holocaust education was described *as a new approach*. Under the heading *Holocaust education as a new approach* (p. 29), a concept is presented as *new* that has already been practiced for decades. The brochure goes on: The following is particularly suitable for biographical work sources that provide a subjective perspective on social and political events. The advantage of personal testimonies is the sovereign first-person perspective. Jews are narrators of their own history and not objects from a perpetrator's perspective. These authentic individual stories also help to break down stereotypes. Instead of repeatedly reproducing clichés, the narrators become visible within their own lives, with the identity they have chosen themselves. This subjective view enables an authentic picture of the respective time, as confusing, contradictory, complex or incomplete as it may be. So that this picture becomes comprehensive and *traces* of the context in certain situations can be grasped, the periodization of the sources not only covers the period during the Holocaust, but also the time before and after. – Placing the Holocaust in the context of Jewish life and hatred of Jews before and after the mass murder is really nothing new. The fact that the authors of the handout describe this as innovative and Holocaust education itself as *new* underlines the lack of knowledge–even among supposed experts who are supposed to train teachers. If not even the people who are supposed to educate others are aware of the current state of research, if they do not know the relevant concepts of Holocaust education, if the methods are new to them and if official bodies support this *work* financially–then Eckmann can only be agreed with: More than a *handling* of the Holocaust does not take place in German schools (here: in the states of Schleswig–Holstein and Hamburg). Eckmann pointed out already in 2017: It is clear that this development [Holocaust education and remembrance, note of the author] has been driven, to a considerable degree, by the need *to handle* the past so teachers follow at least the socially accepted—concept of a special German responsibility with a corresponding obligation to *handle* the past.[55]

What the example shows is that even additional materials do not necessarily have the goal of making teachers feel better prepared and pedagogically and methodically well-positioned to educate students about this complex topic– especially if the material is simply not up to date.

This background also underlines that there are no reliable findings as to whether and how engagement with the materials takes place and whether this leads to effective learning processes.[56] There is no information about what is taught in classes and which material is used to what extent.

It is also unclear how much time is spent on this topic in class or whether it is covered at all. An analysis by Möller 2015 states that the topic of National Socialism is taught in an average of nine lessons during history lessons in German classrooms.[57] One lesson is 45 minutes. How much time is actually spent on the topic of the Holocaust is an open question.

Given all that, the answer to the question *What is the content of Holocaust education?*–must be: It is unclear.

The *Organization for Security and Co-Operation in Europe* (OSCE) and the *Office for Democratic Institutions and Human Rights* (ODIHR) completed a report on *Education on the Holocaust and on Anti-Semitism: An Overview and Analysis of Educational Approaches*. The report surveyed 54 OSCE member states and found that 49 of these responded that the Holocaust was in some way incorporated into that country's curriculum. However, at the same time, many respondents admitted that there was inadequate teaching time and pedagogical materials devoted to the study of the Holocaust in schools. In countries such as Sweden, the UK, Lithuania, Romania and the USA, the Holocaust was taught more in-depth through extra-curricular or optional activities, often run by NGOs and charities.[58]

Although politicians, parents, stakeholders and even the students themselves want to do Holocaust education, it seems unclear what the content of Holocaust education looks like. There is a clear curriculum, teaching material and resources, but **it remains unclear what teachers and educators do in classrooms**.

Outcomes of Holocaust Education

Although the reasons for Holocaust education are so varied and unclear, and the content of Holocaust education is also obscure, it is surprising that there are so many studies on the outcomes of Holocaust education. The studies on this topic are diverse and cover a wide range of areas and topics. Since studies on Holocaust education focus mainly on the outcome due to all the former mentioned goals of Holocaust education, the study situation is more comprehensive.

Many of the studies address one of the reasons for Holocaust education: **a solid knowledge of historical facts.** Bernhardt emphasizes that in the public context, there is hardly ever any reflection on what is actually meant by historical knowledge, what should actually be known in order to understand the present. Most people are also unaware of the circumstances under which history is taught in schools. He points out that the few lessons can hardly live up to expectations. It must be emphasized that, according to Bernhardt, a frighteningly trivial level prevails when it comes to clarifying what should actually be learned in the classroom. The clarification is based on 1. In contrast to the past, people in the present basically know nothing about history. 2. However, such knowledge is absolutely necessary to understand the present. 3. History lessons have failed to impart this knowledge. The *principle of competencies*, the assumed second level of history, also contributes to the fact that content is no longer taught as comprehensively. In the Anglo-American world, this is referred to as the *second-order concept*. Here, the focus is on what he calls the *grammar of the subject* and less on the lexis.[59] Alavi/Barsch also stresses this aspect. In public discourse, the lack of knowledge of facts and events among pupils is lamented. The main issue would be a material-oriented and positivistic idea of history lessons. Studies also show that there are knowledge deficits among pupils. These could be traced back to a narrative-constructivist understanding of history, as competence models would have been developed on this basis, which would have led to an insufficiently clarified relationship between knowledge and skills.[60]

Existing studies about Holocaust education focus mostly on the **knowledge of pupils before and after teaching** the Holocaust in school.[61] There are numerous studies and investigations that have focused on various aspects of learning about the Holocaust, in the sense of gaining knowledge, not in the sense of *Erziehung*.

In the US and Canada, surveys dealing with Holocaust education are carried out at regular intervals. In the most recent study from 2019 entitled *Holocaust Knowledge and Awareness in Canada*, conducted by the Azrieli Foundation in cooperation with the Claims Conference, 22% of respondents said that they were not sure whether they had ever heard of the Holocaust and revealed other glaring gaps in their knowledge.[62] Various authors have shown that pupils' knowledge of the Holocaust was unsatisfactory due to the assumed outcome and the expectations of teachers and researchers. The knowledge among students is humble and the knowledge is not satisfactory.[63]

The same can be seen in Germany: A CNN study from 28 November 2018 on the topic of *Anti-Semitism in Europe* showed for example, that 40% of young adults in Germany had a lack of knowledge about the Holocaust.[64] Over the years, various areas have been analyzed in individual studies, some of which have produced very sobering results. A recent study from 2020 revealed an even more drastic lack of knowledge: *ZDF* (German television broadcasting company), in cooperation with the *Forschungs-*

gruppe Wahlen (Elections Research Group), a Germany-based research group, had been able to prove in a survey that 23% of Germans were not familiar with the term *Holocaust* at all. 26% said they knew little or nothing about the Holocaust. 47% of all respondents also stated that they were of the opinion that most Germans *were not so much or not at all to blame* for the extermination of the Jews.[65] In a study conducted by the German *Körber Foundation* in 2017, it became clear that only 71% of the pupils surveyed were able to correctly categorize the term *Auschwitz Birkenau*. In other words, 29% could not.[66]

To reproduce one study in detail: In 2018, the International *Central Institute for Youth and Educational Television* (IZI) presented the results of a study on the topic of *Knowledge about the Second World War and persecution during the National Socialist era*. A total of 840 children between the ages of six and 13 were surveyed. The evaluation of the study shows that around one in two primary school children is aware that Germany was involved in two major world wars: 40% of six to seven-year-olds (grade 1/2) know this, 64% of eight to nine-year-olds (grade 3/4) know this, 84% of ten to eleven-year-olds (grade 5/6) know this and this percentage even rises to 95% among 12 to 13-year-olds (grade 7/8). The fact that Germany lost the Second World War is known to 28% of six to seven-year-olds; this figure rises to 49% among eight to nine-year-olds. At the beginning of lower secondary school, between the ages of ten and eleven, 73% already know about it and 87% of 12 to 13-year-olds are already aware of it. This means that a quarter of primary school children who know that Germany was involved in two world wars do not know how the war ended, according to the study. It is concluded that this indicates that although the children have *inner images of the war* and a *sense of knowledge*, they lack even the minimal contextualization, e.g. Germany was defeated in the war.

The majority of pupils are only able to place the end of the war in chronological order from year seven onwards: 75% say that it was 70 years ago. The majority of children know the name Adolf Hitler: 52% of six to seven-year-olds, 64% of eight to nine-year-olds, 82% of ten to eleven-year-olds and 96% of 12 to 13-year-olds are familiar with the name and it has potentially negative connotations. When asked about victim groups at the time of National Socialism, a quarter of six to seven-year-old children were named *Jews*. As they got older, the percentage of this answer rose to 94% among 12 to 13-year-olds. However, the majority of children were unable to explain the term *Jew*. Also, only 12 to 13-year-olds knew that the group of Jews was extensively persecuted: 58% agreed with this statement. Overall, a superficial knowledge of terms is available. Terms were recognized in certain contexts, without these being able to be described as well-founded knowledge or even just as *islands of knowledge*. [67]

Fittingly, the results of Zülsdorf–Kersting who issues how students' prior understanding unfold in the classroom. He shows how German 9th and 10th-grade students' history education often falls short of politicians' or educators' expectations. Students tend to construct history based on the explanatory patterns that they bring with them to class. Subsequent formal instruction seems largely unable to overcome this deep-set mode of thinking.[68]

Why is a lack of knowledge about historical facts and their significance today so problematic? As Mohammed stresses: If people are uneducated, they are much more likely to be negatively influenced by information they receive because they cannot categorize it.[69]

Besides the lack of knowledge studies made on Holocaust education take care of other priorities: Some studies deal with the **usage of language and terms** in the classroom, e.g. dealing with pupils in Germany having a problem using the term *Jew*.[70] The term *Jew* generally seems to be a red rag. Bernstein speaks about a clear inhibition in the German language. She reports on a person who practiced saying the word *Jew* out loud and without inhibition in a workshop on hatred of Jews with the participants.[71] Winter refers to a study in which teachers and school social workers denied that the term *Jew* was used as a swearword at all–and if it was, then it would be a problem among *Muslim pupils*. The findings are interpreted to mean that one's own hatred of Jews is frowned upon and should be made invisible by blaming such an attitude on others. Hatred of Jews functions here as a cover for one's own enemy images and defense. This can be attributed to the complete defeat of National Socialist Germany and the so-called *communication latency*. This means that attitudes of hatred of Jews were henceforth frowned upon in the public sphere and excluded from communication. Hatred of Jews had disappeared from language, but not from thoughts and minds. This also applies to the anti-Israeli variant of hatred of Jews: all reasonably educated people know how to speak. This in turn shows that hatred of Jews does not always come from people who are *stupid* and *uneducated*.[72]

Another fact is important to mention here. Especially in German school classes anonymization is noticeable. The majority of the young people reference Jews, for example through pronouns (*sie, diese, mehrere*) and articles (*die, der*). Although it is clear from the context that Jews are the topic–the term *Jews* is only rarely used explicitly. Wagensommer says this may be due to language economy–in the frequency of the omissions in the data, however, also suggests the idea of a linguistic avoidance behavior that is tantamount to anonymization. Anonymization goes back to the time of National Socialism: people were labelled with numbers and thus de-individualized.[73]

Yet other studies focus on **remembering** in the context of Holocaust education. Since remembering seems to be the ideal way of learning from and against dictatorship and the history of violence. This applies although the direct, life-historical memory of National Socialism has been almost completely extinguished and that the omnipresent talk of remembrance has eroded the concept. Neither individual nor historical remembrance in society is automatically identical to critical, present-relevant learning from unacceptable history. Moreover, according to this understanding, remembering paradoxically denotes both the goal of learning–namely learning to remember, remembering learning–as well as the process of learning itself, insofar as remembering and learning are equated. Accordingly, remembering is as an adequate, quasi natural interweaving of knowledge about the past, cogent interpretation of the past and political and moral value formation. The different dimensions of memory–from the experience-bound micro-perspective life-historical to the more or less experienced forms of historical memory that are more or less experienced in society–are blurred.[74] In Germany, there is a certain trepidation and growing unease when it comes to the concept of a *culture of remembrance* and the supposed successes associated with it in the fight against hatred of Jews. Because talking about culture in Germany often involves hubris. Heyl describes this as ennobling the word *culture*.[75] This normative appraisal may lead to denial.

Questions of **identity and participation** were also studied to measure the success of Holocaust education especially in Germany. Borries warns about *aggressive reactions* and calls for *tactfulness* and *comfort*.[76] He underlines the necessity to mention the linkage but also the distance between present and past. As younger generations distance themselves from the perpetrator generation, today's educators also face the challenge of teaching the lessons of National Socialism within a changing social climate characterized by new dynamics of hatred of Jews. Despite Germany's memorial culture and official policies prohibiting hatred of Jews, it has continued to have a latent effect in the democratic society, where it is normalized in everyday social structures as linguistic distinctions between *the Germans* and *the Jews* implicitly classify Jews as non-German.[77]

However, research was not only done on Germans and Jews but also regarding pupils with an *immigration background*. In the group of migrants, the Holocaust is not a social frame of reference for young people. For them, traditional stories play a more significant role. The mass murder of the European Jews is therefore a historical event in *German* history. According to studies, the necessity of deriving and practising a broad and general assumption of responsibility from this is only undertaken on demand. Families do not feel obliged to do so either. The task of teaching or informing about the Holocaust falls to educational institutions. The Holocaust is only mentioned as a reference point when it comes to discrimination against Muslims and foreigners in Germany. The knowledge of supposed *Jewish characteristics* and the opportunity to defend oneself against them are experienced as *empowerment* in self-expression. They bring back the strength that people with an immigration background miss. Fighting back in this way helps to shape their own identity and position themselves in an uncertain world. In this way, they succeed in building a regulated worldview in which friends and foes can be clearly identified.[78]

The feeling of being unjustifiably attacked by Jews because of events in the past and hostility towards Israel can also be experienced as a unifying element. Defense against the supposed aggression of Jews is also seen as an opportunity to join a (school) community and no longer be excluded because one is of a different origin.[79] However, most young people in Germany are not familiar with the situation in the Middle East and/or the Middle East conflict from their own experience. They get their information from the media and what they hear about it on the street. The equation of Israel's policies with National Socialism is widespread. This equation can be made deliberately in order to express hatred of Israel (the Jews!)[80] or in the sense of a *perpetrator-victim reversal*. This complexity of the present German political and cultural landscape has raised several pedagogical questions concerning the teaching of National Socialism.

One very interesting result, when it comes to the outcome, is the finding, that studies verified that students give **socially desired answers** about the Holocaust or simply follow *social conventions*.[81] This applies above all to pupils from so-called *educationally disadvantaged backgrounds*. They have a rather traditionalist–positivist understanding of history, which is flanked by moralistic statements about National Socialism.[82] Students give socially desirable answers so that they follow social conventions. Radtke even claims that historical education is just about practicing socially desirable answers.[83] Therefore, Holocaust education also paves the way for practicing social conventions.[84] Winter presents some more results based on various studies, when he writes, that sensitive questions in recruitment surveys are often answered in a socially desirable way. He reports on a survey from 2002 which showed that 71% of Germans agree with the statement: *Many do not dare to express their real opinion about Jews.* He comes to the conclusion that there is a prevailing mood among the German population towards Jews that is difficult to capture by conventional attitude research.[85] This impression is also underlined when, contrary to social impressions and perceptions, a recent study on the subject of hatred of Jews states that *in the German population as a whole, pro-Palestinian attitudes are largely free of traditional anti-Semitism. And even if radical groups of activists with anti-Semitic slogans attract attention, this cannot be generalized for the left-wing academic milieu as a whole.*[86] Here too, the academically educated in particular seem to know exactly what to answer and the traditional survey techniques do not manage to compensate for and reflect this.

Kößler stresses due to these facts, that teaching the Holocaust is not the best way to fight the hatred of the Jews but it is part of general education, especially in Germany and the entire Europe.[87]

In this sense, the German word **Erziehung** also plays a role again with regard to the outcome. Learning about the Holocaust can be much more than just gaining knowledge, it can be used to *form a character*. Especially when it comes to the German term *Erziehung* the goal was set that Holocaust education shall *form someone's mind and character.* This affects learners, pupils, and students alike. Following the idea of fighting hatred of Jews by using Holocaust education the goal seems to be to stop hatred of Jews and form empathic morally stable and *rightly acting* people. For both sides, teachers and pupils, it is equally important that they understand the Holocaust as a collection of information that must be memorized. But more than this, it is a question of understanding as a mental task, as an intellectual challenge.[88] As Schmoll shows, many teachers feel not prepared enough to deal with the topic. It is precisely this feeling of a lack of preparation and their own lack of knowledge that leads teachers to deal with the topic inadequately or not at all.[89]

Holocaust education now has a long tradition. There can be various reasons why people deal with the Holocaust, and **only one of them is to combat hatred of Jews**. Teaching the Holocaust often has much more personal reasons than just the fact that the subject is compulsory in class. If one looks at the question of the results of Holocaust education, various studies have been presented that have come to different conclusions–depending on the question. However, knowledge of historical facts is often not very well developed.

5. HOLOCAUST EDUCATION TO CHANGE MINDS?

Even though academic studies have shown that historical and academic knowledge about the Holocaust is not available after Holocaust education to the extent that society, teachers, and historians would like it to be, the important question remains unanswered: Is Holocaust education able to change people's point of view at all? To answer this question, one must first consider the environment in which Holocaust education takes place today and what the limits are. In a further step, the study situation can then be taken as the basis for answering the question.

If Holocaust education is the assumed answer to the question of hatred of Jews, it can be seen as conveying knowledge and values. If one can learn from history, one can use this knowledge and education to develop more peaceful, tolerant, and understanding societies. Since Holocaust education is also used to work on myths, stereotypes, and prejudices, examining the myths and stereotypes about different nationalities involved in conflict, and how to neutralize them should be able to *change minds*.

Holocaust education offers a lot of opportunities and possibilities to make people think. Changing minds, or in other words *learning from history,* has been discussed for many years. The experience of National Socialism–and other dictatorships and crimes against humanity–makes it seem imperative to learn from history. Accordingly, Karl Jaspers spoke after 1945 of *self-illumination* in historical and personal terms. Erich Weniger (1946/49) called for historical experience *to be brought to consciousness and critically illuminated.* Felix Messerschmid (1963) understood remembrance to mean the reconnection of *historical consciousness to formative moral insights.* Theodor Litt (1948) set the task of *education for historical understanding* and *historical self-criticism.* The didactics of history that developed from the end of the 1960s onwards–led by Friedrich J. Lucas in 1966–freed historical learning from the spell of a supposedly value-neutral historicism, in particular its tendency to understand the past in its peculiarity and its normative stubbornness. Jean Améry, a resistance fighter and Auschwitz survivor emphatically opposed this in 1976. *In a humane sense, however, the more decisive demand is that the observation of history, no different from the historical processes themselves, must contain a morally evaluative element. The real is only rational as long as it is moral. And historicity becomes unnatural in the human sense as soon as it presents itself as value-neutral. Understood in this way, the myth of the [so-called, note of the author] Third Reich as a myth of radical evil is more accurate than a pretended objectivity that does not oppose evil and becomes an advocate of this evil through its indifference alone.* With the development of the *category of historical consciousness*, notions of historical learning that explicitly or implicitly linked descriptive representations of the past with the creation of meaning (if not the formation of attitudes) in conformity with the present lost their foundation. The focus now shifted to knowledge about and the understanding of the interweaving of past, present and future, of past experience and future expectation–in short: of historicity and the ability to think and judge historically.[1]

The Hostile Environment of Holocaust Education

When it comes to the current state of Holocaust education many aspects hinder Holocaust education and have an influence on it. At the level of society as a whole as well as in schools, certain hurdles in dealing with the topic can be identified which can have an impact on the results of Holocaust education and on possible change of minds.

The **lack of willingness** to deal with the topic is attributed to many people. The reasons for this are sometimes very different but sometimes actually very much the same, especially when it comes to teachers and students. Dealing with the behavior of (great–) grandparents are one of the main reasons for rejection as well as the lack of information.[2] Similar to society as a whole, many students are of the opinion that (great–) grandparents were no Jew haters; mostly students present stories about resistance fighters in their own families and especially German students demonize the National Socialists to keep acceptable (great–) grandparents and families by believing in and telling about the resistance fighters in their own families, no matter if this is true or not.[3] Also, many German students believe that Germans have suffered because of the National Socialists.

Another one is the fact, that the topic Holocaust does not seem to be important. This stand finds expression in resistance and surfeit.[4] Alike society as a whole, Borries observes an *overfeeding* or *surfeit*[5] in schools, too. Here in the sense of a feeling of having dealt with the topic too often, which leads to oversaturation. This is mainly due to the fact that Holocaust education comes at a too-early grade level in schools. Additionally, the teachers often deal with the topic outside of the history curriculum, which means that students feel they have to work on the topic *constantly and continuously*.[6] Additionally, 41% of people who were surveyed in 2019 in Germany come to the conclusion that *Jews talk too much about the Holocaust*.[7] Holocaust education can lead to the suppression of all topics that are perceived as stressful and lead to a confrontation with one's own emotional ambivalence.[8]

This ambivalence can lead to what is called (in Germany) **perpetrator-victim reversal.**

In order to demonize Israel and thus give free rein to one's own hatred of Jews (because this is not about Jews, but *only* about Israel) there is often a perpetrator-victim reversal or equation with National Socialism. The only explanation for this argumentation is the exoneration of one's own collective through the devaluation of Jews–or Israelis. Hatred of Jews can be said because it is *only* criticism of the State of Israel. This aspect is closely connected to questions of **guilt and guilt defense**. Psychological reasons include the feeling of being overwhelmed and stressed, the desire for easier and more tactful topics, as well as issues of guilt and oppression, insecurity, feelings of one's own superiority, nostalgia, and devaluation.[9] People can feel shame for crimes that they have not committed themselves. Attempts to memorialize past atrocities produce outcomes that range from formal apologies and financial compensation to vehement denials and intergroup tensions. Perpetrators and their compatriots have reacted to revelations of a violent past with defiance and anger, though they can also experience guilt and shame, becoming willing to rectify past wrongs and perceive ethnic others more favorably. Victims reminded of past traumas may feel threatened or experience the old traumas anew, which can increase their hostility and prejudice–against the original perpetrator group as well as against other groups.[10] Marks explains the lack of knowledge about the Holocaust in a similar way: Students react with resistance because of feeling ashamed.[11] Teachers and students alike are placed in a context of guilt when it comes to the National Socialist past and the Holocaust. Reflexively, they try to withdraw from it.[12]

Additionally, the assumption that great-grandparents or grandparents were no antisemites is widespread e.g. in Germany.[13]

Most students talk about resistance fighters in their own families. This impression is based on the memories inside German families and not on objective numbers. Many students are also convinced that the Germans suffered under the National Socialists and that they were not part of the system. Of course, this is by no means based on objective figures, but rather on family stories.[14] As we know: History is always family history. A culture is created through communicative memory, but this is inadequate when it comes to the organized mass murder of the National Socialists.[15] Almost one-third of Germans believe that their relatives explicitly resisted National Socialism by helping persecuted populations indicating a strong desire to distinguish parents and grandparents from the past. Beyond not wanting to face troublesome family biographies, many younger Germans exhibit *Holocaust fatigue*, asserting that they have heard enough about the topic. In 2020, over one-quarter of interviewed German adults agreed it is time to draw a final line (*Schlussstrich*) under German guilt instead of continuing to reflect on the past.[16]

The phenomenon **Hitlerism** —in the sense of the *Great Man* theory of history—is also a part of guilt defense. It has been proven in research for decades. It is documented in the reduction of National Socialism to the person of Adolf Hitler and in the fact that he is given an omnipotent position. Hitler is described as a man with convictions, visions, and powers of seduction–*Germans* (who are not explicitly named) are then innocently seduced. The mythologization and idealization of Adolf Hitler corresponds to the National Socialist world view and it can be asked to what extent a part of this ideology is restaged here. All those who supported Hitler and his followers and those who embraced National Socialism are not included. This also includes people with whom we are connected through family biography–great-grandparents or grandparents.[17] It seems to be a solution for many Germans to demonize the National Socialists and to keep acceptable grandparents and families by believing and talking about the resistance fighters in their own families, no matter if this is true or not.[18] Thereby, people apply the same simplistic interpretations that have circulated for decades. Hitlerism, which occurs throughout society and can be observed in the media and public opinion as well as in the family environment, can also be observed in the school context in the sense of **simplification**. Holocaust education is confronted with **simplicity.** Historical narratives that reduce historical explanation of the actions of top leaders appear as personalization in Holocaust education. There are cases, in which the broad complicity in the Holocaust is elided by focusing upon Hitler. Hitler, it seems as an omnipotent ruler and as such he also made the population compliant and instrumentalized them against the Jews. The Holocaust seems to have been personally and exclusively ordered and carried out by Hitler. Wagensommer quotes students who said: *he [Hitler, note of the author] persecuted/ he gassed/ he burned Jews.* As a reason for the mass murder, the young people cite Hitler's personal aversion to Jews. The statement of one pupil can serve as an example. Using National Socialist terminology, she says: that *Hitler saw the Jews as parasites.* Wagensommer emphasizes*: What is interesting about the formation of these [what he calls, note of the author] pairs is, that they emphasize an unequal degree which also indicates a negative symbiosis.* This is most pronounced in the contrasting pair of *Jews versus Hitler.*[19]

Simplicity can be observed already when it comes to kids in the primary school. Hitler is regarded by children as a key figure. He had the power to influence the German population, their thoughts, and actions. For their part, they were unable to escape this influence, even though the majority of them were against him and had also attempted to assassinate him. Ultimately, according to one analysis, the children were of the opinion that a refusal seemed impossible and that he had seduced the population. It seems to be an exculpatory function in the children's statements. This may also be important because the children are aware of the (world) domination efforts and name it as Hitler's overriding goal to persecute and murder all Jews and even more: They see him as the sole initiator, persecutor, and murderer. The children cite a religiously influenced antipathy as their main motive. Hitler seems to be solely responsible and his suicide also marks the end of the Second World War for the children. In other words, this is closely linked to the person of Hitler.[20] Simplicity also occurs when it comes to Hitler's idea of Jew-hatred and his *determination to remove Jews from Germany*. The latter formulation, of course, may reinforce the common but mistaken impression that most Jewish victims of the Holocaust lived in Germany, rather than in Poland and other Central and Eastern European countries.[21] Why Holocaust education is so simplified may also be due to the fact that students and teachers are spared having to memorize too many facts.

In dealing with the content of Holocaust education it is important to underline, that societies as a whole are changing its approach from a *communicative memory*, which is narrated and recorded, to a **cultural memory**, which concentrates on passing on information through the media. It should be noted that for today's people, the Holocaust is just as distant as the Roman Empire. The personal connection is completely missing. Also, it is often *old people* who talk about the past. This leads to a feeling of empathy but not developing an understanding of the topic. At best, people gain knowledge, but no awareness. This may also be due to the fact a so-called *empathy hype* in recent pedagogical discourse can be observed. Empathy is perceived as the most successful way to teach and educate about values and morality.

This new *empathy hype* follows decades in which for example Germans were socialized into a lack of empathetic consideration for Jewish perspectives on the Holocaust. Teaching about the Holocaust has tended to rely on documents from the perpetrator's perspective, thereby simultaneously normalizing the adoption of an unreflected perpetrator's viewpoint alongside an over-identification with the victims.[22]

Studies also show that the unimaginable and abstract number of victims leads to **downplaying the events**. When talking about six million murdered Jews, this number is hard to comprehend. Six million is an abstract number. The abstraction of victims is one reason for downplaying the Holocaust[23] or universalization of the Holocaust. The Holocaust then becomes just one event among many. The singularity of the event is called into question. In addition to the contradiction and disagreement as to whether and how the Holocaust happened, another aspect has been added in recent years, that of **comparison**. Instead of questioning the existence of the Holocaust altogether, people now like to make comparisons. These have led to the fact that a direct line is drawn between the colonial countries (from the time period of colonialism and imperialism), their responsibility and the Holocaust. But it should be borne in mind that no colonial power ever had a plan comparable to that pursued by the National Socialists. They wanted total, worldwide extermination–it was not *just* about exploitation, enslavement, and mass murder.[24] Confino stresses that t*he Holocaust was driven by a desire to extinguish an identity and to rewrite history, not by practical concerns. The motives and consequences went beyond contemporary historical circumstances: the genocide dictated a new history of Christianity and of European civilization.*[25] The ideology of comparison targets Jews and classifies them today as *white* oppressors, even though the conflict with the Palestinians has nothing to do with race.

The majority of Israeli Jews are themselves people of color since they trace their origins to the Middle East and North Africa.[26] In contrast to all other resentments against minorities, hatred of Jews imagines Jews not only as inferior (and supposedly physically weak) but also as *superior.* Jews are identified with cultural modernity, intellectuality, media power, and monetary power.[27] They are therefore often not considered in the development of post-colonialism theory or were themselves referred to as colonizers. Furthermore, critics of Jew-hatred were accused of not being sincere. They would only talk about hate in order to silence criticism of colonialism and Israel. The idea behind this is that Jews, by and large, have been very successful for example in American universities. They are actually overrepresented as students, as faculty and in the so-called *Ivy League* schools and are therefore perceived as part of this privileged white power structure. Rather, they are the ones who allegedly use their power to brand criticism of Israel as hating Jews (*antisemitic*) and thus silence it.[28] **Post-colonialism** ignores the long history of hatred of Jews. It ignores the fact that Israel, as a country, was established by the United Nations and has the same legitimate right to exist that all countries do. But in this dichotomy of oppressor and oppressed, Jews have been labelled oppressors without much thought to context or history.[29]

However, with all the comparisons and the search for similarities between mass murders and the Holocaust, the question arises as to why? There is no *Richter scale of suffering* (Dan Diner). So, what is actual the purpose? Is it, as Steinbacher rightly asks, to make the murders more bearable?[30] Or are Jews to be forbidden from being a special victim group that has arrogated to itself a hegemony in the discourse on victimization? That the Holocaust is something different from other mass murders is obviously perceived as an unbearable presumption. Or is it that only when the Holocaust is no longer special can the legitimacy of the State of Israel be questioned? If the Holocaust is a crime like others, then Israelis can be denigrated as colonial masters. Then there is no need for a Jewish state. Or is it about minimizing the Holocaust? If the Jewish experience is no longer a uniquely Jewish experience, what does it mean? If it is not unique, then it is acceptable? – Even if these questions remain unanswered or the answer is already in all the questions, the political intention is unmistakable. The denial of the uniqueness and the universalizing of the Holocaust, both in its memory and its experience, maybe a new form of a very old anti-Jewish effort.[31]

Mohammed offers a comparison albeit of a completely different kind. He points out that the terror organization Hamas had already geared its propaganda among young people. This can be seen, for example, in the way their propaganda clips resemble video games. They have also managed to make use of post-colonial research since Hamas terrorists are now labeled as *resistance fighters*. It is important to remember that Hamas is an offshoot of the Muslim Brotherhood, which is highly respected among post-colonial scholars. They even use the massacres of 7 October 2023, to stage themselves as *liberation fighters*.[32]

The environment in which Holocaust education is currently taking place, which makes it so difficult, unfortunately sometimes leads to the exact opposite of what Holocaust education should actually achieve. This opposite can also be called **counterproductivity.** There were warnings already in 1993 that an approach to Holocaust education in the sense of *changing minds* risks being counterproductive. Early on, Carole Ann Reed pointed out that a specific understanding of anti-racism could sometimes lead to hatred of Jews not being recognized as a problem. In her study of the large-scale US Holocaust education initiative *Facing His-*

tory and Ourselves, she mentions that it is the perception of *Jews as whites* that makes them seem privileged today and renders hatred of Jews invisible. Accordingly, it can be assumed that the current image of Jews and understanding of hatred of Jews also has an impact on the historical interpretation and teaching of the Holocaust (e.g. applying the Whiteness frame can lead to perceiving Jews as privileged and therefore not legitimate victims).[33]

The phenomenon of counterproductivity can also be observed with regard to *memorial sides*. For a long time, concentration camp memorials were relied upon to prevent hatred of Jews, but analyses of the defense against guilt show that this concept does not work. If people are fully informed about the National Socialist policy of extermination, they are not automatically armed against the hatred of Jews. Dealing with the crimes of the National Socialists does not necessarily lead to a self-critical reflection of one's own prejudices, but on the contrary, can motivate anti-Jewish ideas in a new way.[34] The same is true for *museums* as Dara Horn points out.[35]

Also, UNESCO emphasizes this risk of counterproductivity, but the principle to avoid genocides in future by using Holocaust education has nevertheless been embraced.[36] **Commemoration** of past atrocities is often viewed as a means to promote reconciliation, improve the treatment of ethnic and religious minorities, and prevent future violence. Memoralization and commemoration activities are particularly salient in regard to the Holocaust, the paradigmatic trauma of the 20th century. The explicit of *International Holocaust Remembrance Day* is to discredit political extremism and racial hatred, so that genocide never happens again. It is unclear, however, whether commemoration actually achieves these beneficial effects.[37]

In addition to the aspects already mentioned that affect society as a whole **and** schools, there are other issues that hinder Holocaust education, especially in a **school context**. These obstacles lie in the students, the teachers, the parents, the classmates, but also in the teaching material, the teaching structure, or the expectations themselves.

For both sides, teachers, and students, it is equally important that they understand the Holocaust as a collection of information that must be memorized. But besides the naked facts, it is a question of understanding the Holocaust as a mental task, as an intellectual challenge.[38] Schreier stresses that to remember the Holocaust in the context of education is less like a ritual and more like a sharing of dilemmas.[39] This assessment is also due to the fact that the evaluation of personal documents and the mental work on the Holocaust remains *insufficient* and partly *scandalous*.[40]

With regard to Holocaust education, the following obstacles can be identified on the **part of teachers**: Why do teachers deal with the topic inadequately or not at all?

On the one hand, studies show that teachers are embarrassed for their **lack of knowledge**. This is caused by the lack of studies on an academic level since the subject Holocaust is not embedded in the mandatory academic curricula.[41] There is still limited understanding of how teachers acquire holistic knowledge about the Holocaust and become professionally prepared to teach it. This refers to the learning dispositions and processes of individuals and the different factors that contribute to their understanding, such as their relationships, available resources, activities, and contextual elements. There is still a significant gap in the knowledge of how teachers and educators develop their learning ecologies about the Holocaust and acquire the skills necessary for effective teaching.[42]

Also, some teachers feel guilty about not teaching the Holocaust on their own and in their own classes or they do not want to visit a place of remembrance to neglect their own historical responsibility and therefore the teaching of the topic.[43] In general, the handling of the Holocaust is a problem for teachers.[44] As Schmoll[45] shows, many teachers feel not prepared enough to deal with the topic. It is precisely this feeling of a lack of preparation and their own lack of knowledge that leads teachers to deal with the topic inadequately or not at all.[46] Following Borries, the main reason for not teaching the Holocaust in schools lies in the fact that genocides are *unsavoury, disgusting* and an *imposition*. Genocides are an *insult as well as a provocation, an assault on the self-esteem of human beings*. Human beings are not rational or moral beings. Stupidity and sadism are boundless. To swallow this is difficult and a deep affront against self-confidence. This is true for the youth but also for teachers and educators. The absolute negativity of the Holocaust is unsettling and discouraging.[47] Also, teachers have high expectations of their own teaching and it is very easy to fail then.[48] So it might be better not to teach the subject at all.

Teachers are also critical about using emotions for teaching the Holocaust and do have a problem e.g. with meeting Holocaust survivors during class.[49] This behavior can be interpreted as a way to repress the remembrance of the own feeling of guilt or simply not to be confronted with the Holocaust. Here, a **lack of empathy** or even indifference towards the victims of the Holocaust can be observed among teachers. This attitude not only shows a lack of respect for the victims but is also an expression of a refusal to empathize and a rejection of memory and guilt.[50]

But then, talking about victims seems to be easier than talking about perpetrators.[51] Gerson asks: *How can teachers explain the charism of Adolf Hitler if he seems to be almost ridiculous for today's pupils?*[52]

Another influence that might hinder teaching the Holocaust is **Christian convictions**. Some teachers are afraid of upsetting pupils and their parents and avoid discussing the Christian roots of Jew-hatred and the long history of it; other teachers have a lack of understanding of Christian hostility to Jews themselves. Successful teaching of the Holocaust in a predominantly Christian society depends on students'– and, one might add, teachers' – perceptions of Jews and Judaism, and of the relationship between Judaism and Christianity.[53]

The same is true when it comes to the behavior of the **churches** during and after the Holocaust. Since there were members, including clergy and leading theologians, who openly supported the National Socialist regime. The general tactic by the leadership of both Protestant and Catholic churches in Germany for example was caution with respect to protest and compromise with the state leadership where possible. There was criticism within both churches of racialized ideology and movements emerged in both churches to defend church members. Yet throughout this period, there was virtually no public opposition to hatred of Jews or any readiness by church leaders to publicly oppose the regime on the issues of hatred of Jews and state-sanctioned violence against the Jews. There were individual Catholics and Protestants who spoke out on behalf of Jews, and small groups within both churches that became involved in rescue and resistance activities. After 1945, the silence of the church leadership and the widespread complicity of *ordinary Christians* compelled leaders of both churches to address issues of guilt and complicity during the Holocaust—a process that continues internationally to this day.[54] Some teachers want to prevent the teaching or do not want to know about it at all for the mentioned reasons.[55]

One more issue in avoiding Holocaust education is, that teachers expect **disinterest** from the students' side. Especially among students of minorities. Teachers misunderstand the feeling of not being part, because of the family background, as disinterest. The network of relationships is thus a kind of self-fulfilling prophecy–when teachers expect disinterest, they experience disinterest. Even though it does not exist.[56]

Short postulates, that teachers avoid teaching the Holocaust and also hatred of Jews because they believe it is not a current problem to discuss among their students or in general.[57] As mentioned before, teachers are sometimes *part of the problem*.[58] Since, as Berstein shows, some teachers themselves hate Jews. For example, they tell jokes about Jews (mockery), pick up on stereotypes or support conspiracy narratives.[59] In addition, they only perceive certain topics as a school obligation– and this includes the topic of the Holocaust and hatred of Jews. This view makes it impossible for them to draw a connection between the historical persecution and mass murder and today's hatred of Jews.[60] The hatred of Jews is often dealt with by teachers in educational discussions. When Jew-hating statements are made, teachers often only have limited time to respond and react. It is noticeable that abbreviated answers are often given.

Another issue is the often negative attitude of the teaching staff and parents and even attempts to put teachers under pressure and ban the topic from the classroom completely.[61] At first sight, the **parents** are an unexpected obstacle. But an enormous one: Some parents do not want their children to learn about the Holocaust for different reasons e.g. their own traumas and the question of guilt or because of their own lack of knowledge. Some parents want to talk in advance with the teachers or the principal of a school. In some cases, parents want to influence the selection of the used educational material. Parents also check the textbooks of their children to be prepared for questions or discussions.[62]

Besides the students, teachers and parents, **classmates** can hinder the teaching, too. This is especially true for classes with a large proportion of children with an immigrant background from the region of the Middle East, North Africa or partly Asia. Most young people are not familiar with the situation in the Middle East and/or conflicts in that region from their own experience, but they do have a strong opinion nevertheless. They get their information from the media and what they hear about it on the street.[63] They mix up knowledge and Holocaust education with current developments. They are unable to differentiate between what they learn about the Holocaust and their emotions about the Middle East conflict or the Israeli-Palestinian conflict. Also, students are not able to analyze or appreciate conflicts or contradictions differentiated or nuanced.[64] This result seems to be rooted in the teaching which seems to be based on moral questions and not about a reflected historical orientation, especially in the area of studying conflicts.[65]

Classmates are also an important obstacle, when it comes to visiting memorial sites because they are typically explored in groups and that processing occurs through interaction with one's peers, the importance of peer education in this field must be highlighted. Beyond the relationship between learners and a place, or that between pupils and teachers, the importance of educational processes within heterogeneous peer cohorts visiting memorial sites should not be underestimated.[66]

On a more structural level, the **outdated textbooks** and materials currently used in schools are causing problems, too. A distorted image of Jews, the State of Israel and/or conflicts in the Middle East can be found in school textbooks.[67] This is a serious problem, as the knowledge disseminated by textbooks is tested in exams, among other things, and is therefore not only learned but also repeatedly received.[68] Due to the Holocaust, this is not only about the victim's perspective but also about perpetrators and followers. It should be possible to discuss choices or the fact that there was no choice for perpetrators and bystanders. To provide a situation in which those topics can be discussed, suitable literature and teaching materials are required.

The outdated textbooks fit in with a further structural problem: Studies done in Germany showed, that there is **no** harmonized **overall concept** between the individual school levels and subjects. From primary school to upper secondary school, individual lesson plans in the context of Holocaust education are proposed in the subject curricula (some of which are compulsory) without any recognizable coherence or even a spiral curriculum structure for the sequences.[69] Similar problems can also be found in Israel, for example. The *Report on the State of Holocaust Studies in Research Universities and Colleges in Israel* reflects a fundamental disagreement in the Israel research community–between those who see the Holocaust as a unique and unprecedented event that should be studied as a separate field, and those who argue for incorporating into the broader field of genocide studies.[70] Here too, an overall concept is clearly lacking.

But it is not only all these hurdles and obstacles that make it difficult to combat or contain hatred of Jews through Holocaust education. There are also simply *limits* that Holocaust education in its current form, does not know how to overcome.

The Limits of Holocaust Education

The limit of Holocaust education is the false assumption, that Holocaust education is seen as promoting democracy in principle, which it is not. This is because historical orientations, especially at school, have to be normatively open and a wide variety of conclusions can be drawn. Insights can be adopted by learners, but they do not have to.[71] Although education can be used to promote, advocate, and emphasize the equality of all people in the sense of democracy, education does not always achieve this goal. The main reason for this is that many people today already have problems with the concept of democracy. The basic concept must be understood in order to use equivalence to break down prejudices that despise humanity. Unfortunately, this is often not the case. People who already have problems with the idea of democracy in the sense of equality do not manage to transfer existing values and norms to actual coexistence.[72] In addition, Holocaust education is seen as promoting democracy per se, human rights and democracy teaching needs to be precise. Although human rights education plays a tremendous role in curricula for example in Germany Borries sees a huge gap between claim and reality.[73] Studies show that abstract values like *democracy* are not as important as e.g. concrete rights like *freedom of speech*. The youth supports and defenses concrete rights passionate.[74] This is due to the fact that students decide about historical and political questions of conflict on the one hand based on their own interest and the other hand based on human and civil rights but without any information about details. Borries asks for the connection between human rights and history classes in Germany. He states that a redefinition of history classes in the sense of nation-building (after the German reunification) and because of the worldwide terror is necessary.[75]

Educational work is too often only concerned with **symptoms than with causes**: the defense of memory, the relativization of the Holocaust, and the hostility towards Israel. However, hatred of Jews has ideological and psychological causes that go back a long way.[76] It is therefore more than difficult to break down millennia-old ideas and change people. The hatred of Jews contains group constructions and judgmental attributions. It is important to emphasize that Jew-haters use constructions and these have nothing to do with the actual behavior of Jews. Anyone who speaks pejoratively about Jews is thereby valorizing and labeling themselves.

The whole idea that teaching about the Holocaust leads to a change in perspectives is based on the assumption **that teaching triggers a learning process**. This assumption has been relativized in history didactics for quite some time (1991!). The question is then also asked: What can trigger a learning process in pupils?[77] The aim is for students to be able to transfer and apply their own questions and interests in history.[78] As long as this hurdle has not been overcome, Holocaust education stays limited.

Do non-Jews hate Jews less because they are taught about the Holocaust?

Given the almost hostile environment in which Holocaust education must take place and the clear limits of what Holocaust education is capable of, the questions remain: Can Holocaust education in such an adverse environment, cause people to change their minds?

The answer to the questions is **not easy to give**, because the study situation is not clear. A review of the literature comes to the conclusion, that there is just a limited focus on the hatred of Jews in research on educational initiatives due to Holocaust education in general.[79]

Different studies show that there is a *changing mind* outcome through Holocaust education[80], but the information the research presented just focuses on the knowledge about Jews and Judaism or so-called *positive effects* [without further explanation of what positive effects mean, note of the author] due to these topics. Schäuble and Thoma emphasize that Holocaust education is essential for the learning of historical knowledge and the recognition of the Jewish experience of prosecution. Holocaust education can change perspectives, support empathy, and help to draw conclusions from the past.[81] A recent study was conducted in 2020 by the US Anti-Defamation League (ADL). According the study, it was shown that American students were more open to other points of view and statements after Holocaust education and that they held **more pluralistic** views than before. 48% of those surveyed state that Holocaust education helps them to draw a connection between the historical event of the Holocaust and current developments. 65% understand the importance of speaking out against stereotypes and prejudice. 71% understand how the Holocaust came about. However, these high percentages can only be achieved if the pupils were given the opportunity to listen to the statements and testimonies of survivors. This works best. It also makes no difference whether the students met the survivors in person or saw the person in the video. The values are lower for the group of respondents who had not experienced a personal testimony. Here, for example, only 31% states that they are able to draw a connection between historical events and current developments.[82] The study is a hopeful indication that education *can* make a difference.

However, Gautschi explains that the influence of history lessons on the development of core values could **neither be confirmed nor** rejected.[83]

But then, most of the studies present over the years in different countries came to the same, but here contradictory, conclusion: It is **impossible to change minds** through Holocaust education. Especially when it comes to a reduction in Jew-hatred views. Gordon et al. prove that knowledge about the Holocaust does not lead to a reduction in tendencies of hatred of Jews.[84] The same outcome is presented by Cowan.[85] Wagensommer stresses that learning about the Holocaust is an information transfer without any impact on personal development.[86] It is unclear how students and/or students' knowledge changes while learning about the Holocaust in school. One explanation is, that history classes come too late in the lives of young people to change their minds about National Socialism and too late to make relevant contributions.

Another finding supports the assumption that Holocaust education has very little impact on teaching values and ending hatred: Over the decades, Germany was not only considered the gold standard in Holocaust education around the world, but the Germans themselves developed a collective self-confidence, to be memory processing *world champions*. This view has arisen not despite, but because of Auschwitz, drawing a sense of moral superiority from the self-image of a successful remembrance culture.[87] Following the bare figures, Germany's role as a role model can therefore not endure. The German government's *Anti-Semitism Report* from 2017[88] shows that the proportion of Germans who agree with antisemitic statements rose from 28 percent in 2014 to 40 percent in 2016. In absolute figures, this means that out of 83 million Germans, 33 million Germans agree with antisemitic statements. Given that, have the Germans done too much too well? –If one follows Bernstein, then the answer must be: yes. She proves in her study that the oversupply of further training courses for teachers, including in the area of hatred of Jews, leads to one thing in particular: **Rejection**. People would have to admit that there is hatred of Jews in society. Unfortunately, this is not always the case, because it is considered unpleasant and dealing with hatred of Jews is seen as evidence of an undesirable problematization. Obviously, more education and training in Germany has not led to a decrease in hatred of Jews. [89]

Quite the contrary: In Germany, the so-called *Schlussstrichdebatte* (to draw a final line) has been gaining ground for some years now. This means that people are of the opinion that there must be a final line drawn under this chapter of history. Some even believe that the Germans have suffered enough from the actions of their ancestors and that *enough is enough.*

Another aspect supports the statement that Holocaust education has **no influence** *on hate.* And this can be clearly seen in the way the Jewish State of **Israel** is treated. *Changing minds* would also help to understand why the people of the State of Israel are handling situations the way they do. The situation today is different than back then when the Holocaust took place. Jews do have their own country, military, and society–but all of this is shaped by the trauma of the Holocaust. This statement can also be substantiated by surveys and study results. One example is a national survey of Holocaust education in Israeli state schools in which 307 principals, 519 teachers and 2,540 students in religious and general junior high and high schools throughout the country participated. Among the key findings of the study are: The Holocaust is a core theme within the Israeli state educational system. It is considered important by principals, teachers, and students. In fact, the Holocaust constitutes a common denominator among students of various backgrounds. 77% of the students and 96% of the teachers say the Holocaust affects their worldview. 94% of the students are committed to preserving the memory. 83% of the students are interested in learning more about the Holocaust. The importance attributed to this issue was articulated clearly in the interviews, focus groups and open questions. There is wide agreement among the principals and the teachers regarding the basic values and educational implications of Holocaust teaching. 85% of teachers see the Holocaust as a tragedy for all humanity, not only the Jewish People. The Jewish and universal implications of the Holocaust are considered important by principals and teachers: Strengthening commitment to the existence of an independent State of Israel is an important goal of Holocaust education for 100% of principals and 92% of teachers. Strengthening humanist-universal values is an important goal of Holocaust education for 97% of principals and 81% of teachers. Instilling a feeling of connection to the destiny of the Jewish people is an important goal of Holocaust education for 99% of principals and 93% of teachers.[90] Understanding *historical trauma* as a core component of state identity, which then in turn explains contemporary domestic and international behavior, is a relatively new approach. Subotic writes about the Holocaust memory in Germany, but the following applies also very much to the State of Israel: Memory is critical to state identity. Just as one's own individual memory constitutes identity, political memory is what constitutes state identities. International Relations research on political memory has demonstrated how memory helps create and sustain a particular state biography. Political memory is never about the past.[91] Memory can help to understand state identity and explain why politics is conducted the way it is: Why Israel is constantly in a state of struggle for survival and why it is fighting for the survival of the state with all its might and determination. Holocaust education against this background and with this understanding should also help to bring about a *change of mind*. But the reality is different. Today's hatred towards Jews is often hidden in criticizing the Jewish State of Israel as seen, especially due to the background of the Holocaust.[92]

Considering all this, the question must inevitably arise: Why do academic studies not give a clear picture? Because the studies refer to different expectations, areas, and subject areas. Why is it so difficult to measure the benefits of Holocaust education? Because methodologies are not clear and transparent. Even the term *benefit* itself is not binding.

Since academic studies cannot do it, reality has to do the job: If Holocaust education is understood as a means of combating hatred of Jews, then the reality seems to provide a clear answer. Looking at all the efforts that have been made over the decades in the field of Holocaust education and contrast them with current developments, Holocaust education does not seem to be the answer to hatred of Jews. Holocaust education has obviously not succeeded in fulfilling the expectations. Holocaust education weeks, compulsory lessons, technology, memorials, and peace education do not seem to have produced the desired results. Holocaust education is not a pill that can be given to people against hatred of humanity, in this case, hatred of Jews. To bring people to an event and hope they will hate Jews less after it is over, did not work.

Obviously, the basic assumption–that Holocaust education prevents and combats hatred of Jews–is wrong. Does that also mean that educators, teachers, and historians have failed? No, because the basic assumption is wrong. There are countless dedicated historians, teachers and educators who have made it their mission to teach about the Holocaust for all the reasons mentioned above. They give their all–working time, free time, and financial resources–to teach the subject. They rebel against all odds and teach against all obstacles. Nevertheless, Holocaust education in its current form does not always seem to be able to overcome hurdles, obstacles, and limits. Holocaust education apparently needs to be rethought and changed. The ADL study shows that Holocaust education can have an impact.[93] That gives hope. What was done differently in the case of these pupils? Where are new ideas and approaches that are promising? Promising and beneficial is understood here first of all in terms of historical knowledge. In addition, there should be an understanding of the connection between then and now, with all the problems and current challenges.

Only when teaching and knowledge become learning and understanding the current restrictions on Holocaust education can be broken: Then Holocaust education can make people think, and then they can learn from history and develop more peaceful, tolerant, and understanding societies. When Holocaust education is used to work on myths, stereotypes, and prejudices, examining the myths and stereotypes about different nationalities involved in conflict, and how to neutralize them, then Holocaust education should be able to *change minds*. But how can this be achieved? What should Holocaust education look like in the future?

6. THE FUTURE OF HOLOCAUST EDUCATION

As seen Holocaust education is not a panacea for hatred of Jews. However, to enable historical knowledge about the Holocaust and thus initiate a learning process, future Holocaust education should be changed in some areas. And perhaps it will then also be possible for education to build up understanding and to make people think. After all, that is what teachers and educators want to achieve. They want to make young people think, rethink established ideas and form their own opinions. One that they stand behind, that they defend and justify and that, in the best case, leads to them convincing others as well.

Having said that, the question of course remains, as to what Holocaust education can look like in the future to make people think. If it has not even been possible to impart knowledge with the existing means and methods, then new approaches are needed in Holocaust education.

Within the following passage, suggestions are made on how to reinvent Holocaust education. The goal of the following practical advice is to change Holocaust education to reach the minimum goal of a more satisfying outcome on the many levels mentioned before. Changes in the structure of Holocaust education are needed. Conditions must be created so that Holocaust education can take place adequately.

In the following, ideas and approaches are presented that can be used for a redesigning of Holocaust education:

More time

The introduction of **Holocaust project weeks** would be helpful, not only to give the topic more space but also to remove the topic from the curriculum and make it a *topic in its own right*. This would also do justice to the singularity of the event.[1] If there is a binding regulation that one week in grade nine for example would be dedicated to the topic, there would be enough time to prepare. Teachers and pupils would know about it. There would be a time slot, as well as sufficient space for the topic and, if necessary, time for project work.

In addition to the longer and therefore more favorable time factor, it is also important that the pupils also come into contact with other people on the topic. Teachers can assist here, but it is particularly useful to get to know each other personally and to work intensively on the topic, for example in a project. This could also involve choosing a topic that is not yet so familiar to the pupils so that the feeling of thematic oversaturation no longer arises.

Therefore, it is important to tailor the curricula, the topics, and the content to the environment (country, age group etc.) in which the Holocaust is taught. Most people are unaware of the circumstances under which history is taught in schools. Bernhardt points out, that the few lessons can hardly live up to expectations. The principle of competencies or skills the second level of history, also contributes to the fact that content is no longer taught as comprehensively. In the Anglo-American world, this is referred to as the *second-order concept*. Here, the focus is on what Bernhardt calls the *grammar of the subject* and less on the lexis.[2]

A multitude of aspects with which Holocaust education is burdened currently means, that the topic does not receive the attention it needs. Lessons at school are overloaded with external tasks. The focus on the acquisition of skills (For example: How to analyze a historical photo?), which needs to be reduced, contributes to this. If Holocaust education is intended to impart values as well as knowledge, then it must not be overloaded with the acquisition of skills. Skills can be learnt in other areas of lessons or acquired as part of a project in preparation for a Holocaust project week. The fact that history lessons are often no longer an independent subject in state schools is problematic, too. Integrative concepts of several subject perspectives are often used. Unfortunately, it is also the case that these subjects are primarily used as a cost-cutting program, leading to reduced learning time and a loss of content.[3]

All these structural weaknesses speak in favor of restructuring. Since the research shows that even in North America, where there are such outsourced *Holocaust* education symposia, this has not led to students acquiring more knowledge or to a decrease in hatred of Jews, other aspects of Holocaust education obviously need to be changed.

Another thing that needs to be changed is the **curricula** themselves. Some modifications of the curricula are necessary to provide misleading information that supports hatred of Jews and Israel and paints a wrong picture of current Israel and/or Jews in general. One example is the topic of Judaism, which in some places (e.g. Germany) occurs too late in the curriculum (Middle Ages). There is no introduction or approach to Jews and Judaism before the Middle Ages. Additionally, the topic of *Jews and Judaism* is mostly a victim perspective (Middle Ages, Holocaust).[4] Or, as Grünberg states: *Western opponents of hatred of Jews visit the murdered Jews in the museum, but they have a problem with* *the living ones.*[5] This needs to be changed. How the ambivalent relationship between Jews and the non-Jewish majority society should be dealt with is a contentious issue, too.

On the one hand, giving Judaism and thus also the persecution, exclusion, and murder of Jews a place in the curriculum, even before the pogroms in the Middle Ages, the permanence of hatred towards Jews becomes clear. To highlight the millennia-old hatred, all periods of history must, of course, be covered in class– as the example of some German states shows, this is not always the case. Here, the German *Kaiserreich (*Empire*)* (1871–1918) with its intensified hatred of Jews is no longer taught. Hence, it is no wonder that pupils are unaware of the longevity of this hatred or are unable to understand it.

On the other hand, the tendency of Holocaust education to reduce Jewish history and culture to the status of victims should be avoided. More comprehensive forms of teaching about Jewish history and culture are important in curricula.

In conclusion, it remains to be said that the following topics must be added as well in case they are not part of the current curricula: the Arab-Israeli conflict and the Israeli-Palestinian conflict. Even if these findings were made in the German context, discussion over new curricula due to the topics takes place in many countries.[6]

One textbook for all

Restructuring and rewriting of teaching material and resources is another practical advice for a better Holocaust education in future. Often **textbooks** are the leading mediums when it comes to teaching and learning. Therefore, textbooks represent national narratives and constructs about the past and support the collective memory as well as frame the societal discourse about interpretations of the past. This leads to orientation for the present and future. For the learners textbooks contribute to orientation, building of identities, gaining of knowledge and judgement about merits and values. Often textbooks are not very balanced and/or editors and authors are not aware of certain terms or stereotypes they are using which then gives a distorted or false picture.

To make textbooks more precise and less biased some easy changes and additions can be made: Mentioning the centrality of the Land of Israel for Judaism and the contributions to the Western civilization of Judaism e.g. the concept of a day of rest or the belief in the rule of law. Also, while explaining the time period of diaspora, stressing that Jews remained in the Land of Israel. The same applies when textbooks deal with religious titles. Texts need to clarify religious titles like Jesus Christ (Christ is a religious title) or the Prophet Mohammed as theological statements. It would also be important to explain, that hatred of Jews was not a new phenomenon in Europe beginning in 1933, but had a long history. The Jewish resistance during the period of National Socialism should be emphasized too. Another aspect that must be taken into account is the distorted image of Jews, the State of Israel and/or the Arab-Israel/ Palestinian-Israeli conflict in school textbooks.[7] The fact that the founding of modern Israel is often not discussed is a serious problem, as the knowledge disseminated by textbooks is tested in exams, among other things, and is therefore not only learned but also repeatedly received. If the founding of modern Israel is not even mentioned in school textbooks, then there is a huge lack of knowledge. The textbooks therefore need to be **reviewed and improved** if necessary.

Recommended literature and teaching material in lessons on these topics must also be reconsidered and replaced if necessary.[8]

Another option to make school textbooks better can used here, too. Paxton writes, that accomplished historians do take conspicuous note of the authors of historical texts and make judgments about the value of written documents as evidence. The presence of such a *visible author* appears to be of some help to adolescent students. If textbooks serve as strong representations of authentic historical discourse for adolescent students, then textbook writers must use this position of disciplinary authority to its best pedagogical advantage. One should bear in mind that the field of history, as it has evolved over the past few decades, is made up of multiple histories and competing narratives, and no single truths. Whether the textbook genre itself can provide a means to reflect this multifarious aspect of the discipline is an open question. Students learn more from textbooks than is contained in the words on the printed page. Professional historians, it seems, are not the only ones who read subtext. Adolescent history students also read between the lines, gleaning clues about epistemology and discourse practices. To ignore this prominent facet of textbook psychology by focusing exclusively on easy reading and retention is, in effect, turning a blind eye to a potent teaching tool.[9]

If Holocaust education is taken out of the usual curriculum and becomes an independent subject area, e.g. on project days or project weeks, then consideration should also be given to offering a textbook on this subject area alone, which can then be used by everyone. This applies to the different states or provinces of a country, as well as the differentiation in teaching level and class levels. If Holocaust education takes place in middle school, it can be assumed that all public school pupils can work on the topic at their respective performance levels (through differentiation in the textbook). To deal with the topic in more depth in the higher grades, the textbook could be supplemented with more sources and more demanding author texts at the appropriate point. Holocaust education must be a topic for all learners since it is an expression of society's need for self-realization and not a project for the elite. All the suggestions made above could then be integrated into this textbook. In addition, such a textbook could be written by proven experts, thus avoiding many of the mistakes and negligence that have been made to date.

Usage of technologies and online materials

Today, lots of material can be found online. However, the range of products on offer is now so diverse and the quantity so large that hardly anyone is likely to go to the trouble of searching and researching for themselves. *Recommendations* are needed to find material that is useful and technically correct in terms of didactics and content. These could come from ministries or relevant education providers. However, the material would then have to be adapted and scaled to the right level. It is not very helpful if teachers and Holocaust educators initially have to invest an excessive amount of unpaid time and effort in online research. Access to the offerings must be low-threshold and free of charge. It would be best if the ministries were to create a mandatory service that teachers have to use in addition to the above-mentioned textbook for all.

The radical **digital transformation** of societies can be seen in the *culture of remembrance*. For historical and political education, the question of what Holocaust education can look like without direct encounters with survivors is coming to the fore. There is also concern that future generations could lose interest in the topic. Accordingly, great hopes are pinned on the appeal of digital technologies. Direct encounters with contemporary witnesses are considered to be particularly impressive educational experiences, and this also applies in a similar way to *holograms*, for example. The connection between immersion and empathy is particularly challenging in relation to the portrayal of Holocaust survivors. Offers of historical-political education should not only aim to achieve emotional identification with the victims. Accordingly, distance and clarification of one's own physical and emotional location are central to critical reflection. Preparation and follow-up are crucial here, to link cognitive and affective elements. The use of immersive technologies in particular offers great potential for media education if it is accompanied and prepared accordingly.[10]

VR (virtual reality) and AR (augmented reality) are used in Holocaust education with the aim of making virtual representations as immersive as possible, and presenting artificial worlds as real as possible. At all events, these technologies must be handled with particular sensitivity. The subject-specific and didactic benefits of the technical means must be questioned.

If, for example, holograms and virtual reality are to be used, the conditions must be created. In addition to the technical possibilities in schools, teachers and educators must also be adequately trained.

Holocaust education can also be incorporated into lessons using other digital media. These include *computer games*[11] and *Instagram*.[12] This can also arouse pupils' interest, as values such as freedom of opinion no longer remain abstract, but become very concrete. The latest development can be seen again in North America. In Canada, an AI campaign aims to get mandatory Holocaust education in Canadian schools.[13]

Another area that forms an interface between digital space and history is *social media*. Today, institutions of historical culture use social media just as much as private individuals to tell history and to commemorate historical places, people, and events. Cultures of remembrance in social media on the history of the Holocaust are hybrid interfaces of diverse national, but above all transnational, discourses, and practices of remembrance. It is important to emphasize here, that they always involve a reduction in the complexity of the discourse. However, it is also characteristic of memory cultures in social media that patterns of memory and historical narratives are not necessarily continued, but are explicitly and implicitly broken through by certain actors. The great didactic potential of social media lies in the fact that controversial interpretations of history and perspectives on the past are often expressed in connection with current events or specific commemorative occasions. People can train their historical judgment skills in current debates with reference to historical contexts and they can engage with various interpretations of history not only in an abstract theoretical sense but also in a concrete, day-to-day political context.[14] Here too, social media can bring added value to Holocaust education when used consciously and sensitively in an accompanying manner. In addition, students can train their media and historical judgment skills through social media.

Leaving the classroom

One way of leaving the classroom can be to visit memorials. Memorials are intended to convey the history of the place.[15] Memorial site education takes place in a historically bound place, so it is difficult to establish a reference to the present. While, on the one hand, the increasing establishment of memorial sites enables them to be understood as powerful actors in the culture of history, it also leads to them being instrumentalized as passive projection surfaces. Memorial site education in particular runs the risk of losing its critical potential. Young people are taken to **museums and memorials** in the hope that they will come out less Jew-hating than when they went in. This hope is often in vain.[16] Therefore, it is important to provide incentives for self-reflection rather than simply affirming a community or group in which hatred of Jews is rejected. One's own possible resentments should be explored not just the hatred of Jews or others identified (which makes it easy to distance oneself). Such communication is certainly difficult to implement on a tour of a memorial. However, it should be possible to promote a discussion through self-reflection and reference to the present and not to curtail it through instructional communication. Memorial sites could thus become a *contact zone* in which participation and reflection would be possible. This requires the involvement of the participants and a reaction to the images of history they bring with them. It requires more space than is currently available.[17] What is particularly important in this work is, that learning about the Holocaust takes place in **connection with one's own environment**. This makes it easier to find access to the past. Concrete life stories, of both victims and perpetrators, enable a connection and reduce the distance that already exists due to the temporal distance.

As we have seen before one study (ADL) showed that changing

of minds could be achieved if the pupils were given the opportunity to listen to the statements and testimonies of survivors, if **biographies** were used. For students around the globe a combined educational approach that incorporates testimony and a variety of primary sources, locating and learning the history of an instance of mass atrocity with particular focus on the human story of genocide, can engage learning at the cognitive, moral, and affective levels. The impact is measurable not only through an increased interest in historical topics, but also through an increased capacity for critical thinking, being able to differentiate various forms of information and its sources and offer informed valuations, and an enhanced capacity to feel, think, and emote. This approach can thus provide students with the necessary tools to resist the *us versus them* paradigm identified by genocide scholars as necessary to bring about the social death of a group and other dehumanizing tactics often employed by extremists. And this is not only helpful for teaching the Holocaust but also when it comes to hatred of Jews. As a preventive practice, a combined approach accomplishes something that can be called *rehumanizing*[18] and which is exactly against the intent of the perpetrator who endeavors to take people and humanity out of it.[19]

The confrontation with different biographies of perpetrators and victims among students and teachers, as well as their own biographical backgrounds, can fulfill physical and social aspects as well as achieve a rethinking of one's own resentments and attitudes.[20] Teaching the human story also enables students to learn from allies and upstanders in history. Often testimony of individuals who survived or witnessed genocide can help make that connection and foster increased social-emotional engagement with difficult topics that may otherwise prompt learners to shut down. It is therefore strongly recommended to invite (contemporary) **witnesses** (if possible) to bring life stories to life and create access. As the ADL study shows, a video recording, a hologram or an audio recording *suffices* for this. Experts from educational institutions can help. It is not a weakness of the teacher to seek support! On the contrary: It shows a high level of responsibility and recognition of the importance of the topic.

Actually, leaving the classroom does not mean leaving the classroom physically. Today's digital opportunities allow you to visit a memorial or museum *virtually*. The technical implementation is not yet perfect but can be helpful in making historical learning sites whose topographical history is difficult to recognize perceptible. The didactic concept includes preparation and follow-up of the memorial site visit in the group. The focus here is not on an immersive or emotive, but on an analytical and media-educational approach to history, which takes great care to avoid emotional overwhelming. The most common form of VR currently used in educational work is 360° videos, which can be used to visit museums and memorials virtually. The 360° experience allows an interactive exploration of the previously filmed locations, but users remain tied to the camera's point of view and cannot interact with the physical world. As historical sites, concentration camp memorials commemorate both the suffering of the victims and the crimes and play an important role in learning about the Holocaust. In many cases, they were founded by survivors and are therefore closely linked to their testimony. The special feature of learning at these places of terror is the connection between their historical topography and the communication of historical knowledge. These special features are connected to real people and places and cannot be recreated in a virtual reality.[21] This also shows how sensitively the use of technology and virtual worlds must be handled. It would therefore be appropriate to leave this type of Holocaust education to experts and not to teachers.

Teaching modern Israel

As already mentioned in connection with the changes in the curricula and school textbooks, modern **Israel is often missing** from curricula and teaching materials. The equation of Israel's policies with National Socialism is widespread. Here too, more information and clarity are needed. It should be mentioned that in these conversations there is often a need to deflect blame and exonerate.[22] This can be explained psychologically, but it must be named. Here, too, it seems helpful to address individual fates and not remain on an abstract level in the discussion. Then the educational effects are possible. This equation can be made deliberately to express hatred of Israel and the Jews. Questions about the causes of the widespread hostility towards the State of Israel should always be asked and discussed on the basis of facts. These *facts* can be, for example, that 20% of people in Israel, the supposed Jews, are Arab Israelis and 16% are Muslim. Also, the Hamas Charter can be read to shake and question a pro-Palestinian stance. It can also be pointed out that at the time of the War of Independence in 1948, there were not only Palestinian refugees, which many people have heard of[23], but Jews had to flee from Arab states because the social and governmental pressure became too great.[24] However, to counteract mechanisms of guilt defense, it is important to perceive feelings of guilt as such. In groups, there should be a climate in which participants can express themselves openly and talk to each other sensitively in an appropriate environment and discussion framework.[25]

Education with regard to Israel and the **conflicts** in the Middle East should be treated for what they are: Conflicts. Developments and actors should be presented, but not everything here falls under the term hatred of Jews and the fight against it. It would be important to use approaches and results of peace and conflict research in the school environment. Knowledge about current conflicts, self-reflection on the part of teachers and pupils and the dissolution of thought patterns all play a role here.[26]

Support the teachers and educators

Since the personality of the teacher is paramount,[27] teachers and educators need special support. Teachers must feel **confident** about Holocaust education and hatred of Jews. More research would lead to more support of teachers by implementing activities aimed at fostering scholarly research on a high level, from the point of view of both content and method, along with in-depth academic teaching in the field. This applies not only to the Holocaust but also to issues of contemporary Judaism, especially in Germany. Only very few academics conduct consistent research in this area, mostly in disciplines that are not perceived as *locations of contemporary Jewish research* in this regard. This is because the denominations of their chairs are different: They simply do not read *professorship for contemporary Jewish research*. This means that a huge wealth of knowledge cannot be built up or passed on to the next generation of academics. The almost exclusive focus on Jewish history or philology means that even interested students can hardly quench their thirst for knowledge about contemporary Jewish life. In addition, Jews are *frozen in time*, often in the period before the Holocaust, or reduced to their pre-war material cultural heritage. This creates simplified ideas about Jews, with the dead overshadowing the living.[28] Helping teachers to become more confident with these topics, and to overcome obstacles and hurdles would make them better Holocaust educators. Holocaust education must be adequately funded and this also applies to teachers; greater resources and opportunities are needed.[29] These days, project funding is moderate, with the focus mostly on hatred of Jews, which can be called *damage limitation*. There is no structural funding for contemporary Jewish research with a social science and cultural anthropological focus.[30]

More conditions must be fulfilled in advance. In particular, the **preparation** of teachers during their studies is fundamental here. Teachers can leave universities and go into the classroom without having dealt with the Holocaust at an academic level. There is an urgent need to make improvements here and adapt the academic curricula. It should become compulsory to study the Holocaust to be able to work in education. This would certainly help teachers to deal with the topic more competently in the classroom and to feel more prepared themselves. **Suggestions** for better academic education of future Holocaust educators are: Imparting the skills, tools, and methods–disciplinary, linguistic, regional expertise, etc.–that future Holocaust educators will need to contend with the complex challenges of the subject at the highest level; and strengthening the infrastructure required for research and instruction in fields essential. Establishing an advisory system for students planning to engage in Holocaust research and education, so as to offer them a structured program of specialization (including suitable courses in different departments) and allocating the requisite resources. Establishing an inter-university program to enable students to take advantage of the various strengths (in programs, methodologies, and geographical specializations) of the different academic institutions. Leveraging agreements between academies around the world for exchanges of students, researchers, and lecturers in the field; and mobilizing research institutes that host leading scholars, to expose the academic community to a range of opinions and the latest research methods.[31]

There is an additional factor here: At present, teachers are overwhelmed by the need to attend courses, internalize, and ultimately apply all the desired courses in the classroom. As explained this leads often to rejection of the topic. To make this easier for teachers, schools, and education ministries would have to establish a **fixed structure**. There should be fixed elements, not only in studies but also in the context of further training, which are mandatory and generally valid. It would be relatively easy to implement a definition of mandatory content in the degree course and compulsory further training in this area in later professional life, and would relieve teachers of a great deal of stress and ignorance. They would also certainly be in a better position to recognize the dynamics of hatred of Jews or Israel-related hatred of Jews more easily and react appropriately.[32] The same applies to the Middle East conflicts and how to deal with them. Here too, due to the complexity of the topic, references would be necessary during the course of study, but at the latest when it comes to mandatory further training, structures would have to be established that help teachers maintain the required (and in Germany also mandatory![33]) neutrality in dealing with the topic.

In addition to better training and further training of teachers to provide support, the **school management and the principal's office** should also be mentioned. The school management is the backbone of the teaching staff. The school management is the institution that not only formulates, concretizes, specifies, and/or implements the structural guidelines for the respective school, but also acts as a link to other (external) actors. Unfortunately, the key issue for dealing with Holocaust education as well as hatred of Jews at the school management level is often a suppression of the problem. Just as every head teacher knows that there are problems with violence, bullying and drugs at their school, but far too rarely addresses this offensively and proactively before criticism or fundamental problems in everyday school life arise publicly (e.g. from parents), hatred of Jews in schools is not actively addressed enough. In this respect, the question for school administrators is not so much whether they have a problem with hatred of Jews at their school, but rather how they deal with it. Proactive options include, for example, offering theme days or project weeks on the topic, explicitly listing hatred of Jews as undesirable in school regulations, and not having school subjects in which the topic of the Holocaust could come up taught by non-specialists, but by designated experts. If there have been incidents in connection with Holocaust education and hatred of Jews, it is often up to the school management to decide how to deal with them. In the event of threats or even assault, the police and public prosecutor's office may need to be called in. The school supervisory authorities should also be informed. This is not only essential for statistical reasons, but also to be able to effectively identify problem areas at the city and regional level.[34]

Turning teaching into learning

A very important factor, especially when it comes to **knowledge** is the goal to turn teaching into learning. But as shown before the assumption that teaching leads necessarily to learning must be relativized. The question is asked: What can trigger a learning process in students?[35] Often teaching goes hand in hand with lessons in which teachers do too much and students do too little. Students should be involved on a *meta-level*. This could take the form of disclosing the lesson plan in advance or communicating longer-term lesson plans to the students. In this way, they feel involved and are able to understand and reflect on technical thought processes as a whole and individual steps of knowledge. The aim is for students to be able to transfer and apply their own questions and **interests** in history.[36] It is important to encourage teachers to move away from forms of Holocaust education that are framed by simplistic moral lessons but not substantive knowledge, to a mode of education that is built on rigorous historical knowledge which also includes critical reflection on the past and how it shapes young peoples' attitudes towards present-day social and cultural issues.[37] To keep the interest, it is necessary to ask about **what students want**. Calmbach et al. show that despite students' otherwise rather low level of historical interest, there is greater interest in the topic of National Socialism. The person of Adolf Hitler is of particular interest here. It would therefore be an opportunity to respond more to the students' expectations on the topic and to ask them about them. This would possibly increase interest in the topic. Of course, there should be no personality cult and a very differentiated approach to Hitler is certainly necessary, but this could still be a key to increasing interest in the topic in general.[38] It is crucial that students understand not only Hitler but also the changing function of hatred of Jews in different historical and cultural contexts and by doing so, understand the Holocaust better. Knowing the nuances helps young people to comprehend and critically reflect upon how hatred of Jews takes different forms in the present. Some students will be able to make these connections independently, while others may require teachers to facilitate initial discussions.[39]

The lessons should revolve around an **explicit key question**. In the case of the Holocaust, it is probably necessary for the teacher to specify the question due to its sensitivity. In this way, a conversation, a dialogue, can develop because everyone is dealing with the same question. The question should be open and allow for different answers. This means that the students can not only give their own answers but also have to tolerate other points of view. In addition, the pupils, as people who are already steeped in history and culture, have to represent views that can be questioned, compared and changed.[40]

The teacher or educator should not only present a question, additionally, it is important to communicate the **goals** they have set for the explanation to the learners. Many studies have shown that pupils learn better when they know what they are supposed to learn from the outset. Learners can engage better with an explanation if they know exactly how the explanation is structured, how long it will take and why they are supposed to learn something. The best way to start a complicated presentation is therefore with an informative introduction, in which the teacher explains the topic in a way that everyone can understand, formulates clear learning objectives, explains the process, and expresses positive expectations. In general, the opening is a key part of every presentation. If one manages to attract attention right from the start with an anecdote, a provocation, a contradiction, or an image, one will do a lot to ensure that students follow the explanation. As with the narrative, it is also important to pay attention to comprehensibility in other forms of presentation. New technical and foreign terms must be explained, attention must be paid to a clear presentation, and the presenters should limit themselves to the essentials and encourage the listeners to follow the explanation with stimulating impulses. Each explanation should also be graphically supported and visualized. Information is absorbed well when several senses are involved. For this reason, it is important to appeal to the learner's eyes. A single concise colored image or a clear mind map is best.[41] When questions are asked and worked on, the students must also be given **time** to present their answers and **results**. Only then can they be evaluated and validated. An exchange between teachers and students must take place. The results can be further developed and reflected on together. At the end of the process, there should be a joint result. To be able to achieve all of this, the time factor must also be mentioned here. Learning takes time.[42]

German studies have shown that the subject of history is actually primarily associated with learning about the 20th century, especially National Socialism. History means National Socialism. Sandkühler/ Lenkeit emphasize that there can be no question of oversaturation by National Socialism. The majority of pupils surveyed find the topic interesting and important.[43] But, history consistently has little or nothing to do with the young people surveyed and their presence. For them, history is school knowledge that is needed at school and not in daily life.[44] A connection to themselves is made with social studies or politics, but not with history. Keeping this in mind, another approach to teaching the Holocaust can be to make an immediate **connection** between a concrete value the students are interested in and the Holocaust. It is important to keep distance between present and past but to show the connection. Students often memorize a lesson, regurgitate it on a test, and then discard it from their brains. So, focusing on insights and skills is needed, which tend to be stickier. Building up inert knowledge alone is not enough; students must always be given the opportunity to apply their historical, theological, and ethical knowledge to the perception, analysis and solution of current challenges and problems. An understanding of how democracies function and malfunction, for example, can stay with children and adolescents for life, sharpening their worldview and lending them a moral compass. Critical thinking, fact-finding, and active listening can boost empathy and productive civic discourse, enabling students to better navigate the present, past, and future. Students need to be encouraged to come up with their own guiding questions and seek the truth and its implications for themselves.[45] One more thing is important: Holocaust education needs the idea of prevention since otherwise the topic would be frustrating and morally overstraining. Here too, a direct link to concrete values that interest the pupils is crucial. It is important that not only the abstract value of democracy is taught, but that concrete values and the connection to human rights become apparent to the students. Then they want to *engage* with the topic.[46]

Holocaust Education as a societal issue

Since the Holocaust is human history, it and the memory of it do not only affect the school environment. Therefore, schools should no longer be the central and, in some cases, the sole place of social learning and remembrance. Even if there are projects such as the *Stumbling Stones*[47] or joint commemoration ceremonies (e.g. in parliaments) on the *Night of Broken Glass*, these are clearly not enough. Even flying flags at half-mast is not enough. It will be necessary for students to take the topic back to their **families**–and ask questions. Cultural memory and the communication of **values** cannot only be achieved by schools but must be a task for the whole society. One way to reduce the immense task teachers are burdened with, is to let experts have their say on the subject. Studies show that students engage with a topic in greater depth and their level of knowledge increases when this is the case. And this is about **society as a whole**. This potential can be utilized if national identity formation no longer only encompasses the majority society, but also includes minorities with other family backgrounds, thus leading to participation in questions of shared values and ultimately to the communication of values. This also enables a change of perspective and the thematization of perpetration and followership. The suggestion to work more with the concept of *responsibility* (Messerschmidt) also fits in here. This offers the opportunity to relate to the Holocaust in different ways and not to declare the criterion of national origin to be the only relevant one. Responsibility then refers not only to the past but above all to the present. People with a migrant background, teachers, students, and families–also have a duty to get involved here.

If the aforementioned changes were to be incorporated into future Holocaust education, then Holocaust education might reach the minimum goal of a more satisfying outcome on the many levels mentioned before. The future of Holocaust education could be based on the suggestions made in order to facilitate learning. If knowledge is available and the learning process has begun, then Holocaust education can possibly lead to an understanding and change in thinking.

7. TURNING EDUCATION INTO AN EXPERIENCE

If all the suggestions made are implemented and knowledge and a learning effect occur, is that enough to make people think? To hate less?

Of course, it can be simply said that history cannot act as an instructor, history has happened and the present has its own challenges to bear, but this view does not fit in at all with how people learn. But the way human beings learn is to try and error, gain insights, and learn from prior experiences and mistakes. The study of the Holocaust helps to look back and see where warning signs were missed, and where unintended consequences were ignored. It is a question of respect to look back and see who was lost. Remembrance is a must to see what the world lost in the Holocaust. Looking back serves to understand the present and building a future. But, as we have seen, it takes more than just education to combat the hatred of Jews. Michalski comes to the same conclusion when he writes, that *something more is needed*. Knowledge of the Holocaust must become one element of a broader education grounded in an interdisciplinary context of historical knowledge, psychological techniques of conflict resolution, and sociological knowledge about stereotypes.[1] According to Mendel/Messerschmidt hatred of Jews is anchored in the center of society and is used and articulated from very different social positions. In addition to imparting knowledge about history, ideology and forms of expression, educational work is concerned with the functions of hatred of Jews, which account for its longevity and flexibility.[2] When just Holocaust education is used to fight hatred of Jews, it is too limited. Dealing with hatred of Jews does not mean only studying the Holocaust. The complexities of an understanding of hatred of Jews cannot be limited to the Holocaust. Hatred towards Jews is *incredibly adaptable*.[3] The flexibility makes it a persistent and dangerous form of hatred. To fight the questioning of Jewish identity and life or the delegitimizing of the Jewish state, it needs more than Holocaust education. Especially because it is the demonization which has been present for decades, also in academic settings, now spilled into public discourse and protests.[4] In such a hateful environment, communication and finding the most factually convincing argument is important. Helping people to carry out reality checks that stand up to communication is equally important.

Pure narrative knowledge is obviously not enough to change people's thinking and views. Nor is historical knowledge about the Holocaust enough, as has been shown. According to this, knowledge must take place in the sense of a process that enables people to have their own **educational experiences**. In this way, knowledge can be put into context and one's own perceptions can be recognized and reflected upon. This reflection can take place through independently formulated reasons so that statements based on hate can be recognized. In contrast to reproductive knowledge or historical knowledge, there is no right or wrong here.[5] The promotion of **critical reflection** and the resulting facilitation of a change in behavior is urgently needed. It takes courage and open-mindedness on the part of all those involved and, in addition to knowledge and understanding of the historical event of the Holocaust, an understanding of hatred of Jews. Historically and currently. **Education thus becomes an experience.**

To achieve this, it is important that stereotypes are broken down. The following approaches can be used to **break down stereotypes**: The emphasis here is on factual discussion and communication geared towards mutual understanding. Of course, teachers' and educators' perceptions are also already pre-structured and their own perceptions then also shape their reaction to hatred of Jews and communication. But to illustrate the irrelevance and unreality of a stereotype, it is essential that teachers succeed in establishing a connection to the everyday practice of young people. To dissolve the construction of the myth, it is inevitable to include a meta-level in the communication. To establish practical relevance, teachers and educators should not primarily refer to factual knowledge but allow everyday practical and real-life experiences to flow into the conversation. Radvan emphasizes that only limited information in the sense of true knowledge should be passed on to young people in communication. Rather, it should be about questioning what is said and creating a counter-horizon of statements or everyday practical experiences, which can then show the **contradiction of statements** or actions.[6] This could also help when it comes to teachers and pupils not having to memorize too many facts. Instead of simplifying, a binding selection of facts made by experts would be helpful.[7]

By confronting someone contradictions in the thinking and perception of hatred of Jews should be pointed out, then contradictions could be reflected upon and brought into the context of enemy image constructions. Such an approach can have an **educational effect**. Especially when it comes to completely unrealistic and irrational assumptions that Jews have *invisible powers* at their disposal. Discussions on content only make sense if the assumptions and functions of conspiracy narratives, for example, are pointed out and talked about. Then they can be refuted as unfounded by argument.[8] The confrontation with different biographies of perpetrators and victims, as well as people's own biographical backgrounds, can fulfill physical and social aspects as well as achieve a rethinking of one's own resentments and attitudes.[9] Empathy can be a step in the right direction, despite the formerly mentioned *empathy hype* in teaching. By using biographies for example empathetic learning is about students recognizing and reflecting on their own reactions rather than having particular emotions forced upon them as a goal of pedagogy.[10] It is also important to note that not every statement made in a school context immediately expresses deep-rooted hatred of Jews. Children and young people in particular use the greatest possible provocation for precisely this reason: to provoke. But even if hostility is used for this reason, it must be clear that this is not acceptable! Violations of this kind must always be clearly identified and sanctioned. At the latest when violence is justified, there should be an end to explanations–this is when boundaries are crossed and this must also be clearly stated.

The **functions of stereotypes** with regard to hatred of Jews must be worked out. Only when the students become clear about the functions can they place them in their world model. This reduces the risk of them misunderstanding hatred of Jews as secondary or dismissing it as a *quirky* worldview. In addition, students should not constantly be confronted with stereotypes, but rather have **positive images** in mind. In this way, it is not the stereotype that sticks, but an image of humanity that does not correspond to the traditional stereotypes. This in turn ties in with the idea of a cosmopolitan approach, which also plays a role in the UNESO's GCE.[11]

In this respect, education must address the hatred of Jews in its respective function in a historical longitudinal section, and the different forms must be explained. The personal approach should be taken, but also the recognition of hatred of Jews as a social power relationship, as a social and structural phenomenon. Just as hatred of Jews was not the only reason for the mass murder of the Holocaust, Holocaust education cannot be the only way to combat hatred of Jews. There is no mono causality in either realm.[12] Neither the one nor the other serves as a full explanation, neither for the Holocaust nor for the still-existing hatred of Jews. Both, the mass murder, and the hatred of Jews are multidimensional. Therefore, the relevant period and places must be included, and contextualized within broader historical trends. The actors involved must be identified, by name and in the scale of their involvement, with an understanding of their motivations and experiences. The passive voice, which disguises responsibility, must be avoided. False simplicity and singular causality must be prevented; treatments of the multiple causes of the Holocaust are necessary.[13]

To achieve these goals, the economy and capitalism can be explained as an economic system in which there are always experiences of alienation (e.g. winners/losers). The hatred of Jews supposedly provides a much too abbreviated answer to much more complex issues that have nothing to do with religious affiliation. The division of the world into good and evil is also a division that does not exist at all in reality. Examples can be given here that illustrate the ambivalence and the naivety of such a worldview, too.[14]

If the question is, how hatred of Jews can be combatted today, one must first of all recognize that the existing framework is inefficient, despite its many actors. But to declare a *war* (Mor) does not seem the right way to fight the hate. There are special emissaries at the foreign offices of several countries, such as the United States, Germany, the United Kingdom, France, and the European Union (EU). There are hundreds of NGOs whose task is to combat hatred of Jews, among them the *Combat Antisemitism Movement* with 850 member organizations. In the US, Israel, and Europe there are several academic centers for the research of hatred of Jews.[15] There are strategic plans in place for combating hatred of Jews, such as in the US and France, as well as in the European Union. There is an impressive number of influential active actors involved.

But there is still hate.

There must of course be **a fundamental willingness to act** on the part of all stakeholders. In July 2024 concerned states, special envoys, national coordinators, and representatives tasked by their governments to counter hatred of Jews, in cooperation with international bodies, offer best practices, which have proven to be effective guidelines in formulating public policy. These legally non-binding guidelines, adopted in Buenos Aires, Argentina, include policies to monitor and combat hatred of Jews that can be implemented and adapted to a wide variety of national, regional, and cultural contexts. Following these guidelines education is central. The text says: *Education is vital for identifying and countering antisemitism, including Holocaust remembrance and countering Holocaust denial and distortion, an especially pernicious form of antisemitism. It has also proven effective in sensitizing law enforcement. Education about Jewish culture and contributions to society demystifies Jews and Judaism.* Many countries and intergovernmental organizations have linked their efforts against hatred of Jews to broadening appreciation of Jewish heritage[16] and fostering Jewish life.

But efforts stay unfocused, scattered and without central leadership.

It seems that many of the attempts of states and officials to get to grips with the hatred of Jews are not very helpful so far. This is because, in addition to the problems listed above, there are often no suggestions for practical implementation of measures against hatred of Jews. Hatred of Jews remains academic, a problem that is not recognized as such in real life. Therefore, the most important step is to practically counter the hatred of Jews, to recognize the problem. The hatred of Jews must first be **recognized as a problem** so that it can be combated. Why do people do not see the problem? Different reasons can be mentioned here, for example, a trust in democracy related to carelessness and simply egoism. Another reason why people do not see hatred of Jews as a problem is shown by Bernstein in the school environment: Attacks on Jewish pupils are often perceived as an interpersonal conflict situation among children or young people[17], and the same applies to society as a whole. The hatred of Jews is not recognized for what it is.

That is why it is important to help people acknowledge their hatred of Jews. This includes, for example, making people aware of certain dates, such as 20 April, which is still firmly anchored in (German) society as the *Führer's birthday*. If conflict situations occur on this date and a person of Jewish faith is affected, an attack based on hatred of Jews is the obvious choice.[18] Especially when it comes to Israel-related hatred, many people lack **awareness**. Further training, e.g. for teachers or the police, is urgently needed. Even if there are more and more offers, it must be emphasized that these are not always accepted–precisely because hatred of Jews is not recognized as a pressing problem. It must also be mentioned that the police or teachers would first have to admit that there is hatred of Jews in society. Unfortunately, this is not always the case either, because it is considered unpleasant and dealing with hatred of Jews is seen as evidence of an undesirable problematization.[19]

Closely linked to the lack of recognition of hatred of Jews is the fact that even when it occurs and is recognized, it is often fought by reducing it. Reducing is a wrong concept. **Delegitimization** would be more helpful and actually, the right way to fight hate. The concept of reducing hatred of Jews is erroneous, as *reduction* leads to constantly accepting an unspecified measure of hate. Instead, it has to declared that hatred of Jews is fully unacceptable and therefore totally delegitimized, as has been done with delegitimizing terror.[20]

In order to delegitimize hate, it is important to react immediately when it is encountered. **Reacting quickly** to hatred of Jews is important. Sanctions must be imposed, hatred of Jews must be named and must have consequences. It is not a joke, not a provocation, not a *slip of the tongue*, not stupidity, not a lack of knowledge, no *blowing off steam*, not a desire for recognition by insecure young adults or part of any kind of group dynamic and it is certainly not oversensitivity on the Jewish side. It is also often said that there is no time to deal with the hatred of Jews appropriately and then it is better not to contradict it at all. This statement should be seen as a purely protective assertion. People who make hateful comments must be confronted directly. Of course, only if it does not endanger their own safety! The reaction is also allowed to break through current norms; it is allowed to be loud in defense of overriding values. Clear language should also be used. A *Jew-hater* can be called a *Jew-hater*. The fact that many people see themselves neither as Jew-haters nor as anti-Semites means that clear, unambiguous language can have an educational effect.[21]

It is also important to create **publicity**. Perpetrators must be clearly named for what they are. Moreover, this publicity can also contribute to clarification. Anonymity only protects the perpetrators and plays into their hands, because it creates insecurity among those affected.

It needs to be stressed, that the fight against hate does not end with a religion called Judaism–it has to go further. Since Israel is the only Jewish state, **Israel** is an elementary part when it comes to hatred of Jews. Jews have been facing hatred for as long as they have been a people and a religion. *From the ashes of the Holocaust, a new generation found strength in the Jewish state called Israel.*[22] Over the decades, the memory of the Holocaust has been seen as a domestic issue. As mentioned, only recently has remembrance been approached from the perspective of international relations and international politics. Questions of values and power must also refer to Israel. Only if we understand the Holocaust, as far as possible, and learn about the historical facts we can understand the politics and reactions of the government and the people of the State of Israel. Jews can fight and they do. It is a Jewish answer to the horror of the Holocaust.

If it is possible to tear down the stereotypes and turn education into experience, then hatred becomes less. Then the journey will hopefully be getting closer to what is urgently needed: More peaceful societies and an end to the hatred of Jews for lower irrational human emotions and motifs.

8. CONCLUSION

After 7 October 2023, hatred of Jews has increased worldwide. Holocaust educators and historians are not only asking themselves whether Holocaust education has failed: The question is also being put to them from outside.

To answer the question of a connection between Holocaust education and hatred of Jews, the presented study first shows that the concept of Holocaust education is still confusing. It should be noted that it is not just a matter of imparting bare factual knowledge, but that, in the sense of the German word *Erziehung*, it is also about a learning process, indeed a *changing of minds*.

Holocaust education now has a long tradition. There can be various reasons why people deal with the Holocaust, and only one of them is to combat hatred of Jews. Teaching the Holocaust often has much more personal reasons than just the fact that the subject is compulsory in class.

The study situation has shown that the current state of Holocaust education does not meet the demands placed on it. There are large gaps in knowledge, particularly in the areas of factual knowledge and historical contexts. Furthermore, Holocaust education itself takes place in a hostile environment, if it takes place at all. The supposed goal, that Holocaust education promotes democratic goals in principle, is not correct. The basic assumption that Holocaust education alone can combat hatred of Jews is therefore wrong–as both the studies and the current reality show. To make Holocaust education more effective at all levels in the future, e.g. when it comes to historical knowledge, but also if Holocaust education is to serve as a means of combating the hatred of Jews, it must be redesigned.

Learning and understanding must be added so that Holocaust education can have an impact beyond mere factual knowledge. To extend the benefits of Holocaust education necessary ideas for restructuring and improving Holocaust education are presented. They are not only intended to serve authors, editors, and publishers as a pool of ideas and pointers but also to help practitioners in the school and extracurricular environment. By implementing these ideas teaching will be turned into learning. Learning will be turned into understanding and will pave the way for *changing minds*. To reach the goal and enable Holocaust education to become an effective tool among others to fight hatred of Jews, more is needed. Learners need critical reflection, the breakdown of stereotypes and contradiction. To reach educational effects, positive images should stick, with no stereotypes. If this is achieved, then education can become an experience.

Education must address the hatred of Jews in its respective function in a historical longitudinal section, and the different forms must be explained. The personal approach should be taken, but also the recognition of hatred of Jews as a social power relationship, as a social and structural phenomenon. Just as hatred of Jews was not the only reason for the mass murder of the Holocaust, Holocaust education cannot be the only way to combat hatred of Jews. There is no mono causality in either realm.[1] Neither the one nor the other serves as a full explanation, neither for the Holocaust nor for the still-existing hatred of Jews. Both, the mass murder, and the hatred of Jews are multidimensional. Therefore, the relevant period and places must be included, and contextualized within broader historical trends.

It must be emphasized that action programs such as *Words to Action* are laudable, but probably do not get to the heart of the matter.[2] After all, why should young Jewish people have to fight hatred of Jews and Israel hatred? The problem lies with the non-Jews. They hate. Prejudice and hate against Jews is their moral failing. It does not mean that Jews are not allowed to fight. Certainly! However, they are not responsible for people's hate.

Compassion is needed. Not only compassion for the victims of the Holocaust but also for the victims of today's hatred of Jews. Here, too, people must recognize–or admit–that hatred of Jews is not a historical problem that has long been overcome. It is highly topical–and those affected are victims: They do not exaggerate, are not too sensitive or too biased.

For an education against hatred of Jews, it is necessary to counter-act popular personalization. The hatred of Jews was not brought into the world by Adolf Hitler. The long history of anti-Judaism and hostility towards Jews must be mentioned. Everyday hatred of Jews in the present day must also be addressed.[3] Meeting living Jews can bring about a change in the perception of the Holocaust and the current hatred of Jews, too.

It must be made clear that there can be no final line, no *Schlussstrich*, and **no end** of Holocaust education and talking about the Holocaust. Not only because the Holocaust is part of shared history but also because hatred still exists. And if education is to be used as a means of making people think and perhaps putting an end to hatred, then there can be no end as long as there is hatred. Nor can it be said that the culture of remembrance has done its job and that it is now time to make room for something new to provide a comprehensive view of the global history of violence over the past centuries. Violence cannot be played off against each other.

As mentioned before, Holocaust education can be used in the sense of **identity** and support the fight against hatred of Jews when it demonstrates that standing against oppression aligns with deeply held values. Framing Holocaust education in this way also offers an opportunity to address modern challenges. Highlighting the dangers of unchecked hate and bigotry through the lens of the Holocaust can help combat contemporary hatred of Jews. Again: The fight against hatred is not just a Jewish struggle. This fight is a collective one for the values of justice, tolerance, and mutual respect. Against this background, a historical judgment can be made, perspectives can be changed, and external attributions can be reconsidered, but feelings of belonging also culminate in the question of: How do we want to be seen?[4] Holocaust education can be used here in the context of teaching values and asking questions about identity. But less in the sense of identity-reflecting but identity-building. It should not use questions like: How has history shaped us? Rather, the topic can be viewed in a way that reflects identity, under the impression of: How do we want to be perceived?

Furthermore, teaching, knowing, and learning about the Holocaust means **having a mission**: to become part of a greater whole. Holocaust education is at its best when it conveys not only cautionary tales but also positive moral messages. Holocaust education then contributes to sharpening and understanding the meaning of a pluralistic society in which ethnicity, skin color, gender, language, religion, political or another opinion, national or social origin, property, birth, or other status play no role. In other words: a society in which everyone can and wants to live.

BIBLIOGRAPHY

Adorno, Theodor (1959/1997): Theorie der Halbbildung (Theory of semi-education), Bd. 8, Frankfurt, pp. 93–121.

Adorno, Theodor (1962/1977): Zur Bekämpfung des Antisemitismus heute (On the fight against antisemitism today), in: Gesammelte Schriften, Bd. 20/1, pp. 363–383.

Adorno, Theodor (1967): Erziehung nach Auschwitz (Education after Auschwitz), in: Heinz–Joachim et al. (1967): Zum Bildungsbegriff der Gegenwart (About the term education in present time), Frankfurt/M, 1967, pp. 111–123.

Alavi, Bettina/ Barsch, Sebastian (2018): Geschichtsunterricht zwischen Subjektorientierung und Standardisierung (History lessons between subject orientation and standardization), in: Sandkühler et al. (2018): Geschichtsunterricht im 21. Jahrhundert (History lessons in the 21st century), Bonn, pp. 189 –209.

Allwork, Larissa (2019): Holocaust education and contemporary anti-Semitism, in: Policy Papers, https://www.historyandpolicy.org/policy-papers/papers/holocaust-education-and-contemporary-anti-semitism, 02.10.2024.

Arendt, Hannah (1963): Eichmann in Jerusalem, New York.

Axelrod, Toby (2022): Antisemitic crimes in Germany increased by 29% in 2021 – gov't report, in: https://www.jpost.com/diaspora/antisemitism/article-709079 , 13.07.2022.

Backes, Uwe (2017): Demokratie (Democracy), in: Flümann, Gereon et al. (2017): Umkämpfte Begriffe, (Contested Terms), Bonn, pp. 79–101.

Bartov, Omer (2018): Anatomy of a Genocide: The Life and Death of a Town Called Buczacz, New York

Bauer, Yehuda (2001): A History of the Holocaust, A revised edition, Danbury.

Becher, Andrea (2013): Das „Dritte Reich" in Vorstellungen von Grundschul-kindern (The Third Reich in the imagination of kids in elemantary school), in: Gautschi et al. (2013): Shoa und Schule, Lehren und Lernen im 21. Jahrhundert, Chronos (Shoa and School, Teaching and Learning in the 21st century), pp. 19–37.

Becher, Andrea (2018): Die Zeit des Holocaust in Vorstellungen von Grundschulkindern. Perspektiven von Kindern und die Thematisierung von Holocaust und Nationalsozialismus im (Sach)Unterricht der Grundschule (The time of the Holocaust in the imaginations of primary school children. Children's perspectives and the thematization of the Holocaust and National Socialism in elementary school lessons), in: Isabel Enzenbach/Detlef Pech/Christina Klätte (Hg.), Kinder und Zeitgeschichte. Jüdische Geschichte und Gegenwart, Nationalsozialismus und Antisemitismus (Children and contemporary history. Jewish history and present, National Socialism and antisemitism)(101–120), Berlin 2012, 101, http://www.widerstreit-sachunterricht.de/beihefte/beiheft8/pdf, quoted in: Wagensommer, Georg (2020): Empirische Studien zu Nationalsozialismus und Holocaust aus der Perspektive von Kindern und Jugendlichen und darauf aufbauende Möglichkeiten einer Antisemitismus-Prävention (Empirical studies on National Socialism and the Holocaust from the perspective of children and young people and possibilities of antisemitism prevention based on these studies), in: Antisemitismusprävention in der Grundschule, Hamburg.

Becker, Matthias J./ Bechthold–Hengelhaupt, Tilman (2020): Antisemitismus im Internet (Antisemitism on the Internet), in: Grimm et al. (2020): Bildung gegen Antisemitismus (Education against antisemitism), Frankfurt am Main.

Benz, Wolfgang (2008): Was ist Antisemitismus? (What is antisemitism?), Bonn.

Bercuson, David J. (1986): A trust betrayed. The Keegstra Affair, Calgary.

Berendsen, Eva et al. (2017): Natürliche Feind*innen (Natural enemies), in: Mendel, M.; Messerschmidt, A. (et al) (2017): Fragiler Konsens, Antisemitismuskritische Bildung in der Migrationsgesellschaft, (Fragile consensus, Education critical of antisemitism in a migration society), Frankfurt, pp. 223–247.

Berghan, Wilhelm (2020): Demokratiebildung und reflexive Mündigkeit (Democracy and reflective maturity), in: Grimm et al. (2020): Bildung gegen Antisemitismus (Education against antisemitism), Frankfurt.

Bernhardt, Markus (2018): Was? Historisches Lernen in der Schule (What? Learning about history in school) in: Sandkühler et al. (2018): Geschichtsunterricht im 21. Jahrhundert (History lessons in the 21st century), Bonn, pp. 67–75.

Bernstein, Julia (2020): Antisemitismus an Schulen in Deutschland (Antisemitism in German schools), Bonn.

Borries, Bodo von; Firscher, Claudia; Leutner–Ramme, Sibylla; Meyer–Hamme, Johannes (2005): Schulbuchverständnis, Richtlinienbenutzung und Reflexionsprozesse im Geschichtsunterricht (Textbook comprehension, use of guidelines and reflection processes in history lessons), Neuried.

Borries, Bodo von (2008): Historisches Denken Lernen – Welterschließung statt Epochenüberblick (Learning to think historically – exploring the world instead of an overview of eras), Opladen.

Borries, Bodo von (2011): Geschichtslernen und Menschenrechtsbildung (Historical knowledge and human rights building), Schwalbach.

Brodersen, Dammann (2007): Torn Hearts. The history of the Jews in Germany, Bonn.

Brown, Sara E. (2024): The Need for Education about the Holocaust and Genocide in the Twenty-First Century, in: Bachman, Jeffrey S.: Genocide Studies: Pathways Ahead, New York, pp. 14–35.

Brumlik, Micha (2004): Aus Katastrophen lernen? (Learning from disasters) In: Philo und Philo.

Bühl–Gramer, Charlotte (2018): Geschichtsunterricht im 21. Jahrhundert– eine Standortbestimmung (History lessons in the 21st century–an assessment of the current situation) in:

Sandkühler et al. (2018): Geschichtsunterricht im 21. Jahrhundert (History lessons in the 21st century), Bonn, pp. 31–41.

Burkhardt, Hannes (2023): Geschichtsdeutungen über die Zeit des Nationalsozialismus in den Social Media (Historical interpretations of the National Socialist era in social media), in: Homberg et al. (2023): Deutungskämpfe–die „zweite Geschichte" des Nationalsozialismus (Interpretation battles–the "second history" of National Socialism), Frankfurt, pp. 263–287.

Büttner, Ursula (2008): Weimar–die überforderte Republik (Weimar–overstrained republic), Bonn.

Calmbach, Marc (2017): Wie ticken Jugendliche 2016? Lebenswelten von Jugendlichen im Alter von 14–17 Jahren in Deutschland (What makes young people tick in 2016? Lifeworlds of young people aged 14–17 in Germany,), Wiesbaden.

Can, M. (2013): Überlegungen zur pädagogischen Auseinandersetzung mit der Shoa in der deutschen Migrationsgesellschaft (Reflections on the pedagogical confrontation with the Shoah in the German migration society), in: Jikeli, Georg (2013): Umstrittene Geschichte. Ansichten zum Holocaust unter Muslimen im internationalen Vergleich, Frankfurt/Main.

Charnysh, Volha (2023): Remembering past atrocities: Good or bad for attitudes toward minorities?, in: Kopstein, J. et al. (2023): Holocaust: Politics, Violence, Memory. The new Social Science of the Holocaust, London, pp. 245–266.

Cohen, Erik et al. (2010?): Shoah Education in Israeli State Schools: An Educational Research 2007–2009, School of Education, Bar Ilan University, Israel.

Cohen, Haim (1977): The Trial and Death of Jesus, New York.

Confino, Alon (2014): A World Without Jews, New York.

Cowan, P. et al. (2007): Does addressing prejudice and discrimination through Holocaust education produce better citizens? Educational Review, 59/2, pp. 115–130.

Cowan, P. et al. (2011): We saw inhumanity close-up, Journal of Curriculum Studies, 42/2, pp. 163–184.

Dangelmeier, Nadja (2021): „Vielfalt anerkennen, Vielfalt einbeziehen (Recognizing diversity, including diversity)–Lernen über die NS–Herrschaft in diversen Gruppen", in: Erziehung und Unterricht, Österreichische Pädagogische Zeitschrift, LehrerInnenbildung NEU, 5-6, Jahrgang 171, Wien, pp. 490–498.

Dvir, Boaz (2024): How to Get Holocaust Education Right, in: https://time.com/6974378/holocaust-remembrance-education-essay/, 16.07.2024.

Eberle, Annette (2015): Was bedeutet Pädagogik nach Auschwitz heute? (The meaning of Holocaust Education today) In: Matthes, Eva; Meilhammer, Maximiliane (2015): Holocaust Education im 21. Jahrhundert, London, pp. 150–165.

Eckmann, Monique / Österberg Oscar (2017): Research in Germany, in: Eckmann, Monique (2017): Research in teaching and learning about the Holocaust, in: holocaustremembrance. com, 12.10.2024.

Elukin, Jonathan (2020): Antisemitism, in: Hilton, Laura; Patt, Avinoam (2020): Understanding and teaching the Holocaust, Madison, pp. 19–32.

Falter, Jürgen W. (1991): Hitlers Wähler (Hitler's voters), München.

Fechler, Bernd (2006): Antisemitismus im globalisierten Klassenzimmer (Anti-Semitism in the globalized classroom), in: Fechler, Bernd; Kößler, Gottfried; Messerschmidt, Astrid; Schäuble, Barbara (2006): Neue Judenfeindschaft? pp. 187–201, Frankfurt.

Friedländer, Saul et al. 2022: Ein Verbrechen ohne Namen (A crime without name), Munich.

Friedmann, Michel (2024): 07. Oktober 2023, Judenhass (7 October 2023, Jew hatred), Berlin.

Gerson, D. (2013): Von der Leichtigkeit des Einfühlens in die Opfer und von der Schwierigkeit des Verstehens der Täter. Zur Problematik der fehlenden „Täterperspektive" beim Gedenken an den Holocaust, (About the ease of empathizing with the victims and the difficulty of understanding the perpetrators. On the problem of the missing "perpetrator perspective" when commemorating the Holocaust), in: Gautschi et al. (2013), Shoah und Schule (Shoah and School), pp. 137–152.

Galtung, Johan (1982): Strukturelle Gewalt (Structural violence). Beiträge zur Friedens- und Konfliktforschung, Reinbek.

Galtung, Johan (1998): Frieden mit friedlichen Mitteln (Peace by peaceful means). Frieden und Konflikt, Entwicklung und Kultur, Opladen.

Gautschi, Peter (1999): Geschichte lehren (Teaching history), Zürich.

Gautschi, Peter (2008): Der Beitrag des Geschichtsunterrichts zur Entwicklung von Einstellungen (The contribution of history teaching to the development of attitudes) in: Bauer, Jan–Patrick; Meyer–Hamme, Johannes; Körber, Andreas (2008): Geschichtslernen–Innovation und Reflexion (Learning History– Innovation and Reflection), Kenzingen, pp. 289–307.

Gautschi, Peter et al (2013): Shoa und Schule, Lehren und Lernen im 21. Jahrhundert, Chronos (Shoa and School, Teaching and Learning in the 21st century).

Gautschi, Peter; Lücke, Martin (2018): Historisches Lernen im Digitalen Klassenzimmer (Historisches Lernen in the digital classroom), in: Sandkühler et al. (2018): Geschichtsunterricht im 21. Jahrhundert (History lessons in the 21st century), Bonn, pp. 465–487.

Glickman, Yaacov; Bardikoff, Alan (1982): The treatment of the Holocaust in Canadian history and social science textbooks, Toronto.

Goldenhagen, Daniel (1996): Hitler's willing executioners, New York.

Gordon, Stacy et al (2004): The Effects of Holocaust Education on Students' Level of Antisemitism, in: Educational Research Quarterly, Vol. 27, No 3. March 2004, pp. 58–71.

Götz, Maya (2018): Was Kinder vom Zweiten Weltkrieg wissen (What kids know about Second World War), Televizion, 31, quoted in: Wagensommer, Georg (2020): Empirische Studien zu Nationalsozialismus und Holocaust aus der Perspektive von Kindern und Jugendlichen und darauf aufbauende Möglichkeiten einer Antisemitismus-Prävention (Empirical studies on National Socialism and the Holocaust from the perspective of children and young people and possibilities of antisemitism prevention based on these studies), in: Antisemitismusprävention in der Grundschule, Hamburg.

Graumann, Madita (2024): Werte, Gemeinschaft, Musik (Values, community, music: Does Taylor Swift have what the church no longer has?), NTV, in: https://www.n-tv.de/panorama/Taylor-Swift-und-ihre-Fans-Swifties-sind-ein-Phaenomen-mit-religioesen-Strukturen-article25127518.html, 31.08.2024.

Graziano, Manlio (2017): Holy Wars and Holy Alliance, The Return of Religion to the Global Political Stage, New York.

Grenz, Dagmar (2013): Kinder–und Jugendliteratur zum Thema Nationalsozialismus und Holocaust in der (Deutsch-) Lehrerausbildung (Children's and youth literature on the subject of National Socialism and the Holocaust in (German) teacher training), in: Rathenow et al. (2013): Handbuch Nationalsozialismus und Holocaust, Schwalmbach, pp. 331–348.

Grünberg, Arnon (2024): Westliche Gegner des Antisemitismus besuchen die ermordeten Juden im Museum, mit den lebenden dagegen haben sie ein Problem (Western opponents of antisemitism visit the murdered Jews in the museum, but they have a problem with the living ones), Neue Züricher Zeitung, 2024.

Gryglewski, E. (2010): Teaching about the Holocaust in multicultural societies: Appreciating the learner, Intercultural Education, 21 (Suppl. 1), pp. 41–49.

Heinz, Hanspeter (2020): An allem sind die Juden Schuld, (The Jews are to blame for everything), Hamburg.

Helbling, Marc; Traunmüller, Richard (2024): Wie tickt Deutschland?: Antisemitismus, Antizionismus und pro-palästinensische Einstellungen in Deutschland (What makes Germany tick?: Anti-Semitism, anti-Zionism and pro-Palestinian attitudes in Germany), in: https://www.uni-mannheim.de/newsroom/presse/pressemitteilungen/2024/oktober/gip-antisemitismus/, 30.12.2024.

Hilton, Laura; Patt, Avinoam (2020): Understanding and teaching the Holocaust, Madison.

Hollenbach, Michael (2020): Klischee mit Kippa (Cliché with Kippa), in: Deutschlandfunk, Das Judentum in Schulbüchern, https://www.deutschlandfunk.de/das-judentum-in-schulbuechern-klischee-mit-kippa-100.html, 13.07.2022.

Hollstein, Olivier et al. (2002): Nationalsozialismus im Geschichtsunterricht. Beobachtungen unterrichtlicher Kommunikation (National Socialism in history lessons. Observations of classroom communication).

Horn, Dara (2023): Is Holocaust Education Making Anti-Semitism Worse? In: https://www.theatlantic.com/magazine/archive/2023/05/holocaust-student-education-jewish-anti-semitism/673488/, 26.09.2024.

Haug, Verena (2017): Antisemitismuskritische Bildungsarbeit in Gedenkstätten (Educational work critical of antisemitism in memorial sites), in: Mendel, M.; Messerschmidt, A. et al. (2017): Fragiler Konsens, Antisemitismuskritische Bildung in der Migrationsgesellschaft, (Fragile consensus, Education critical of antisemitism in a migration society), Frankfurt, pp. 155–169.

Heyl, Matthias (1995): Erziehung nach Auschwitz, 50 Jahre danach (Education after Auschwitz, 50 yeas later), in: Hamburg macht Schule,Nr. III/ 1995, pp. 26–28.

Heyl, Matthias (1997a): Erziehung nach Auschwitz–eine Bestandsaufnahme. Deutschland, Niederlande, Israel, USA (Education after Auschwitz–a survey. Germany, Netherlands, Israel, USA), Hamburg.

Heyl, Matthias (1997b): Holocaust Education in (West) Germany–Now and then, in: Schreier, Helmut et al. (1997): Never Again! The Holocausts' Challenge for Educators, Hamburg, pp. 165–180.

Heyl, Matthias (2017): Die nationalsozialistischen Massenverbrechen (The National Socialist Massmurder), in: Mendel, M.; Messerschmidt, A. et al. (2017): Fragiler Konsens, Antisemitismuskritische Bildung in der Migrationsgesellschaft, (Fragile consensus, Education critical of antisemitism in a migration society), Frankfurt, pp. 133–154.

Hutchins, E. (1996): Cognition in the wild, The MIT Press.

Jacobmeyer, Wolfgang (1998): Das Schulgeschichtsbuch (The school history textbook), in: Geschichte, Politik und ihre Didaktik, 26, pp. 26–35.

Jakubowicz-Mount, Tanna (2005): In a Spirit of Reconciliation, in: Ambrosewicz-Jacobs, J. et al. (2005): Why Should We Teach About the Holocaust? Cracow, pp. 46–52.

Jedward, Jack (2010): Measuring Holocaust knowledge and its impact: A Canadian case study, Springer.

Jeismann, Karl–Ernst (2000): Geschichte und Bildung (History and Education). Beiträge zur Geschichtsdidaktik und zur Bildungsforschung, Paderborn.

John, Anke (2018): Wie? Der Blick auf die Unterrichtsgestaltung (How? A view on lesson design), in: Sandkühler et al. (2018): Geschichtsunterricht im 21. Jahrhundert (History lessons in the 21st century), Bonn, pp. 265–274.

Jourová, Vera (2018): Statement on antisemitism, in: https://ec.europa.eu/newsroom/just/items/640113/en, 19.07.2024.

Kalmijn, Matthijs (2915): The Children of Intermarriage in Four European Countries, Annals of American Academy of Political and Social Science 662, November 2015, pp. 246–278.

Kaplan, Edward H. (2024): Radicalized faculty are the greater danger lurking behind campus protests – opinion, Jerusalem Post, in: https://www.jpost.com/opinion/article-803732#:~:-text=Radicalized%20academic%20faculty%20are%20danger-

ous%20in%20pro-Palestinian%20protests,greater%20dan-
ger%20by%20far.%20By%20EDWARD%20H.%20KAPLAN,
07.10.2024.

Kistenmacher, Olaf (2017): Schuldabwehr–Antisemitismus
als Herausforderung (Guilt defense–antisemitism as a challenge), in: Mendel, M.; Messerschmidt, A. et al. (2017): Fragiler
Konsens, Antisemitismuskritische Bildung in der Migrationsgesellschaft, (Fragile consensus, Education critical of antisemitism in a migration society), Frankfurt, pp. 203–221.

Klein-Halevi, Yossi (2024): The war against the Jewish Story, in:
https://blogs.timesofisrael.com/the-war-against-the-jewish-
story/, 14.10.2024.

Klein-Halevi, Yossi (2024): The end of the post-Holocaust era,
in: https://blogs.timesofisrael.com/the-end-of-the-post-holo-
caust-era/, 16.10.2024.

Knigge, Volkhard (2016): Das radikal Böse ist das, was nicht
hätte passieren dürfen (Radical evil is what should not have
happened), in: Aus Politik und Zeitgeschichte, Unannehmbare
Geschichte begreifen (Understanding unacceptable history),
66. Jahrgang · 3–4/2016, pp. 3–9.

Kößler, Gottfried (2006): Antisemitismus als Thema im schulischen Kontext (Anti-Semitism as a topic in the school context), in: Fechler, Bernd; Kößler, Gottfried; Messerschmidt,
Astrid; Schäuble, Barbara (2006): Neue Judenfeinschaft? (New
Jew hatred?) Frankfurt.

Krajewski, Stanislaw (2005): Teach Everywhere, and Especially in Poland! In: Ambrosewicz–Jacobs, J. et al. (2005): Why Should We Teach About the Holocaust? Cracow, pp. 37–42.

Kranz, Dani (2024): Da fehlt doch was…(Something is missing…), in: Jüdische Allgemeine, https://www.juedische-allgemeine.de/kultur/da-fehlt-doch-was/, 17.12.2024.

Kriesten, Jasmin (2020): Antisemitismus-Prävention als Aufgabe der Lehramtsaus- und fortbildung – auch für Grundschullehrkräfte, in: Antisemitismusprävention in der Grundschule, Hamburg.

Krzemiñski, Ireneusz (2005): In Light of Later History, in: Ambrosewicz–Jacobs, J. et al. (2005): Why Should We Teach About the Holocaust? Cracow, pp. 26–33.

Kuchler, Christian (2013): Den Opfern eine Stimme geben (To give voice to the victims), in: Gautschi, Peter et al. (2013): Shoa und Schule, Lehren und Lernen im 21. Jahrhundert, Chronos (Shoa and School, Teaching and Learning in the 21st century), pp. 171–191.

Kühner, Angela (2009): NS–Erinnerung und Migrationsgemeinschaft (NS-Remembrance and Immigration society), in: Einsichten und Perspektiven (Insights and Perspectives), Bayerische Zeitschrift für Politik und Geschichte, München.

Künzel, Ruth (2020): Das Thema Nationalsozialismus im Geschichtsunterricht: Jugendliche zwischen Abwehrhaltung und Interesse? (The topic of National Socialism in history lessons: Young people between defensiveness and interest?),

Köln, in: https://www.fachportal-paedagogik.de/literatur/vollanzeige.html?FId=3422584, 12.12.2024.

Kottmann, Nils (2024): AJC ruft „globalen Ausnahmezustand für das jüdische Volk" aus (AJC declares "global state of emergency for the Jewish people"), Jüdische Allgemeine, in: https://www.juedische-allgemeine.de/juedische-welt/ajc-ruft-globalen-ausnahmezustand-fuer-das-juedische-volk-aus/, 31.08.2024.

Kottmann, Nils (2024): Mangel an historischem Verständnis (Lack of historical understanding), in: https://www.juedische-allgemeine.de/kultur/mangel-an-historischem-verstaendnis/, 07.10.2024.

Kößler, Gottfried (2006): Antisemitismus als Thema im schulischen Kontext (Antisemitism a topic in schools), in: Fechler, Bernd; Kößler, Gottfried; Messerschmidt, Astrid; Schäuble, Barbara (2006): Neue Judenfeinschaft? (New hostility towards Jews?) Frankfurt, pp. 172–187.

Lapin, Andrew (2024): Third of non-Jewish college students hostile to Jews or Israel, Brandeis U study finds, in: Jerusalem Post (2024): https://www.jpost.com/diaspora/antisemitism/article-815999, 26.11.2024.

Laznik, Jacob (2024): How did antisemitism become the new mainstream, what can be done?–Interview, in: Jerusalem Post, in: https://www.jpost.com/diaspora/antisemitism/article-804455, 31.08.2024.

Levi Julian, Hanna (2024): Report: Dramatic Rise in Global Antisemitism After October 7, Jewish Press, in: https://www.jewishpress.com/news/jewish-news/antisemitism-news/

report-dramatic-rise-in-global-antisemitism-after-october-7/2024/01/31/ , 22.05.2024.

Lobo, Sasha (2024): Antisemitismus für Anfänger (Antisemitism for Beginners), DER SPIEGEL, in: https://www.spiegel.de/netzwelt/antisemitismus-erkennen-fuer-anfaenger-wie-man-hass-gegen-juden-enttarnt-a-7752e35c-52df-4646-9222-bfcd206040ed, 28.05.2024.

Lorenz, Friederike et al. (2021): German Teachers Learning about the Shoah in Israel, Wuppertal.

Lower, Wendy (2012): Holocaust Studien im Internationalen Kontext, in: Brenner, Michael; Strnad, Maximilian (2012): Der Holocaust in der deutschsprachigen Geschichtswissenschaft, Göttingen, pp. 42–57.

Mach, Zdzislaw (2005): The Memory of the Holocaust and Education for Europe, in: Ambrosewicz-Jacobs, J. et al. (2005): Why Should We Teach About the Holocaust? Cracow, pp. 22–26.

Mägdefrau, Jutta/Michler, Andreas (2018): Wo ist das Kind in der Geschichtsunterrichtsforschung? (Where is the child in analysis about history lessons?), in: Sandkühler et al. (2018): Geschichtsunterricht im 21. Jahrhundert (History lessons in the 21st century), Bonn, pp. 143–165.

Manca, Stefania et al. (2023): Participating in professional development programmes or learning in the wild? Understanding the learning ecologies of Holocaust educators, British Educational Research Journal, 16.10.2023.

Marks, Stephan (2007): Scham–die tabuisierende Emotion (Shame–the tabooing emotion), Düsseldorf.

Mathis Christian; Urech, Natalie (2013): „... da hat man sie in Häuser eingesperrt und Gas reingetan" („... one locked them in houses and put gas into") in: Gautschi et al. (2013): Shoa und Schule, Lehren und Lernen im 21. Jahrhundert, Chronos (Shoa and School, Teaching and Learning in the 21st century), pp. 37–55.

Mendel, Meron; Messerschmidt, Astrid (2017): Fragiler Konsens, Antisemitismuskritische Bildung in der Migrationsgesellschaft, (Fragile consensus, Education critical of antisemitism in a migration society), Frankfurt.

Mendel, Meron, Uhlig, Tom (2021): Globaler Antisemitismus und die Universalisierung der Shoah. Konstellationen der politischen Bildungsarbeit In: Zeitschrift für Pädagogik und Theologie, 2021; 73(2), pp. 190–201, based on Andreas Zick/ Jonas Rees/Michael Papendick/Franziska Wäschle, Multidimensionaler Erinnerungsmonitor. Studie III. Bielefeld (Institut für interdisziplinäre Konflikt- und Gewaltforschung) 2020, 7 (online abrufbar unter: https://www.stiftung-evz.de/ fileadmin/user_upload/ EVZ_Uploads/Publikationen/Studien/EVZ_Studie_MEMO_2020_dt_Endfassung.pdf

Meseth, Wolfgang et al. (2004): Schule und Nationalsozialismus. Ansprüche und Grenzen des Geschichtsunterrichts (School and National Socialism. The demands and limits of history lessons), Frankfurt am Main.

Meseth, W. (2012): Education after Auschwitz in a United Germany, in: European Education, 44(3), pp. 13–38.

Messerschmidt, Astrid (2016): Geschichtsbewusstsein ohne Identitätsbesetzungen Kritische Gedenkstättenpädagogik in der Migrationsgesellschaft (Historical awareness without identity occupations Critical memorial pedagogy in the migration society), in: https://www.bpb.de/shop/zeitschriften/apuz/218720/geschichtsbewusstsein-ohne-identitaetsbesetzungen/, 13.12.2024.

Meyer–Hamme, Johannes (2018): Was heißt "historisches Lernen"? Eine Begriffsbestimmung (What does "historical learning" mean? A definition), in: Sandkühler et al. (2018): Geschichtsunterricht im 21. Jahrhundert (History lessons in the 21st century), Bonn, pp. 75–92.

Michalski, Bohdan (2005): Let's teach all of it from the Start, in: Ambrosewicz–Jacobs, J. et al. (2005): Why Should We Teach About the Holocaust? Cracow, pp. 33–37.

Milchman, Alan; Rosenberg, Alan (1997): The Holocaust: The Question of Uniqueness, in: Schreier, Helmut et al. (1997): Never Again! The Holocaust's Challenge for Educators, Hamburg, pp. 88–109.

Möller, Rainer (2015): Was geht uns heute Auschwitz an? (Why should we care about Auschwitz today?) In: https://comenius.de/2015/12/04/was_geht_uns_heute_auschwitz_an_2015/, 24.09.2024

Mock, K. (2000): Holocaust and Hope, in: De Coste et al. (2000): The Holocaust's Ghost, Edmonton.

Mohammed, Omar (2024): Why discussing antisemitism is dangerous for Arab intellectuals, Times of Israel, in: https://blogs.

timesofisrael.com/why-discussing-antisemitism-is-dangerous-for-arab-intellectuals/, 27.11.2024.

Moisan/ Hirsch (2015): Holocaust Education in Quebec: Teachers' Positioning and Practices, Enseigner l'Holocauste au Québec : postures et pratiques d'enseignants, in: McGill Journal of Education, Revue des sciences de l'éducation de McGill, Volume 50, Number 2-3, Spring–Fall 2015, pp. 247–268.

Monteath, P. (2013): Holocaust remembrance in the German Democratic Republic—and beyond, in: Himka J./Michlic J. (2013) Bringing the dark past to light: The reception of the Holocaust in Post-Communist Europe, pp. 223– 260.

Müller, Tim B. (2014): Nach dem Ersten Weltkrieg, Lebensversuche moderner Demokratien, (After the First World War–life experiemences of modern democracies) Bonn.

Müller, Stephan (2020): Antisemitismusprävention als Bildungserfahrung (Preventing anti-Semitism as an educational experience), in: Grimm et al. (2020): Bildung gegen Antisemitismus (Education against antisemitism), Frankfurt am Main.

Nägel, Verena et al. (2017): Die universitäre Lehre über den Holocaust in Deutschland (Academic teaching about the Holocaust in Germany), Berlin.

Nägel, Verena/Stegmaier, Sanna (2019): AR und VR in der historisch-politischen Bildung zum Nationalsozialismus und Holocaust – (Interaktives) Lernen oder emotionale Überwältigung? (AR and VR in historical-political education on National Socialism and the Holocaust – (interactive) learning or emotional overwhelming?) In: https://www.bpb.de/lernen/

digitale-bildung/werkstatt/298168/ar-und-vr-in-der-historisch-politischen-bildung-zum-nationalsozialismus-und-holocaust-interaktives-lernen-oder-emotionale-ueberwaeltigung/, 13.12.2024.

Novik, Peter (1999): The Holocaust in American Life, Boston.

Novis–Deutsch et al. (2023): Sites of tension: Shifts in Holocaust memory in relation to antisemitism and political contestation in Europe.

Otto, Marcus (2018): Inklusion/Exklusion und die Anrufung von Subjekten (Inclusion/exclusion and the invocation of subjekts), in: Sandkühler et al. (2018): Geschichtsunterricht im 21. Jahrhundert (History lessons in the 21st century), Bonn, pp. 209–225.

Paxton, R. J. (2002): The Influence of Author Visibility on High School Students Solving a Historical Problem, Cognition, and Instruction, 20(2), pp. 197–248, in: http://www.jstor.org/stable/3233874, 09.12.2024.

Pearce, A.; Foster, S.; Pettigrew, A. (2020): Antisemitism and Holocaust education, in: Pearce, A.; Foster, S.; Pettigrew, A. (2020): Holocaust Education, UCL Press, pp. 150–171.

Pistone at al. (2023): Teaching and learning about the Holocaust, in: https://www.tandfonline.com/doi/full/10.1080/17504902.2023.2245282#abstract06.08.2024.

Pittinsky, Todd: Why 'Jew hate' shouldn't replace 'antisemitism', Times of Israel, in: https://blogs.timesofisrael.com/why-jew-hate-shouldnt-replace-antisemitism/ 16.07.2024

Radvan, Heike (2017): Die Bedeutung von Kommunikation im Umgang mit Antisemitismus (The meaning of communication in dealing with antisemitism), in: Mendel, Meron; Messerschmidt, Astrid (2017): Fragiler Konsens, Antisemitismuskritische Bildung in der Migrationsgesellschaft, (Fragile consensus. Education critical of antisemitism in a migration society), Frankfurt, pp.43–58.

Rathenow, Hanns – Fred; Wenzel, Birgit; Weber, Norbert H. (2013): Gegen das Verschwinden der Vergangenheit (Against the disappearance of the past), in: Rathenow et al. (2013): Handbuch Nationalsozialismus und Holocaust (Manual National Socialism and Holocaust), Schwalmbach, pp. 9–15.

Rajal, Elke (2020): Möglichkeiten und Grenzen antisemitismuskritischer Pädagogik (Possibilities and limits of pedagogy critical of anti-Semitism), in: Grimm et al. (2020): Bildung gegen Antisemitismus (Education against antisemitism), Frankfurt am Main.

Rajal, Elke (2023): Countering antisemitism through Holocaust education. A comparative perspective on Scotland and Austria, in: https://www.tandfonline.com/doi/full/10.1080/0013 1911.2024.2325068#abstract, 06.08.2024.

Rensmann, Lars (2024): Globalisierter Antisemitismus: Neue Wege der politik- und sozialwissenschaftlichen Forschung zu Judenfeindschaft im globalen und digitalen Zeitalter (Globalized antisemitism: new directions in political and social science research on hostility towards Jews in the global and digital age), in: Gustenau et al. (2024): Antisemitismus auf dem Vormarsch (antisemitism on the rise), Baden–Baden, pp. 43–88.

Rosenbaum, Alan (2024): Who's afraid of the big bad Jew? Exploring the root of antisemitism, Jerusalem Post, in: https://www.jpost.com/diaspora/antisemitism/article-829121, 27.11.2024.

Rumbell, Olivia (2024): New AI campaign aims to get mandatory Holocaust education in Canadian schools, National Post, in: https://nationalpost.com/news/canada/ai-campaign-mandatory-holocaust-education-canadian-schools#:~:-text=New%20AI%20campaign%20seeks%20mandatory%20Holocaust%20education%20in,we%20combat%20the%20scourge%20of%20antisemitism%20and%20denialism%27, 16.10.2024.

Rüssen, Jörn (1994): Historisches Lernen (Historical Learning). Grundlagen und Paradigmen, Wien.

Salzborn, Samuel (2017): Geschichte (History), in: Flümann, Gereon et al. (2017): Umkämpfte Begriffe, (Contested Terms), Bonn, pp. 319–334.

Salzborn, Samuel/ Kurth, Alexandra (2019): Antisemitismus in der Schule (Antisemitism in school), Berlin.

Sandkühler, Thomas/Lenkeit, Guido (2018): Exklusion durch historische Bildung? (Exclusion through historical education?) in: Sandkühler et al. (2018): Geschichtsunterricht im 21. Jahrhundert (History lessons in the 21st century), Bonn, pp. 225–255.

Scharples, Caroline (2016): Postwar Germany and the Holocaust, London.

Schäuble, Barbara; Thoma, Hanne (2006): Ergebnisse des Europäischen Workshops „Antisemitismus eine Herausforderung für die (politische) Bildungsarbeit" (Results of the European workshop "Anti-Semitism a challenge for (political) educational work"), in: Fechler, Bernd; Kößler, Gottfried; Messerschmidt, Astrid; Schäuble, Barbara (2006): Neue Judenfeinschaft? Frankfurt, pp. 233–245.

Scherr, Albert/ Schäuble, Barbara (2017): Ich habe nicht gegen Juden, aber... (I have nothing against Jews, but...), in: https://archive.org/details/amadeu-antonio-stiftung-ich-habe-nichts-gegen-juden-ausgangsbedingungen-und-pers, 3011.2024.

Schmoll, Melanie Carina (2018): „Holo...What?! Teaching the Holocaust against all obstacles", unpublished paper, Hamburg.

Schmoll, Melanie Carina (2024): Misinformation about Israel and Antisemitic Views in School Textbooks? The Case of Germany, Münster, 2024.

Schreier, Helmut et al. (1997): Never Again! The Holocaust's Challenge for Educators, Hamburg.

Schu, Anke (2017): Inter-Generationelle Narrative Muslimischer Jugendlicher (Inter-generational narratives of Muslim youths), in: Mendel, M.; Messerschmidt, A. et al. (2017): Fragiler Konsens, Antisemitismuskritische Bildung in der Migrationsgesellschaft, (Fragile consensus, Education critical of antisemitism in a migration society), Frankfurt, pp. 77–100.

Schubert, A. (2020): Israelbezogener Antisemitismus–eine Herausforderung für die Bildungsarbeit (Israel related antisemitism), in: Grimm et al. (2020): Bildung gegen Antisemitismus (Education against antisemitism), Frankfurt am Main.

Schwarz–Friesel, Monika; Reinharz, Jehuda (2013): Die Sprache der Judenfeindschaft im 21. Jahrhundert (The language of hostility towards Jews in the 21st century), Berlin.

Schwarz–Friesel, Monika; Reinharz, Jehuda (2017): Inside the antisemitic mind, New York.

Sharansky Natan (2004): 3D Test of Anti-Semitism: Demonization, Double Standards, Delegitimization, Jewish Political Studies Review 16:3-4 (Fall 2004), in: https://jcpa.org/article/3d-test-of-anti-semitism-demonization-double-standards-delegitimization/, 10.12.2024.

Short, Geoffrey (1991): Combatting anti-Semitism: A dilemma for anti-racist education. British Journal of Educational Studies, 39/1, pp. 33–44.

Short, Geoffrey; Reed, Carole Ann (2004): Issues in Holocaust Education, Bodmin.

Sigel, Robert (2015): Die International Holocaust Remembrance Alliance, in: Matthes, Eva; Meilhammer, Elisabeth (2015): Holocaust Education im 21. Jahrhundert, Kempten.

Sigel, Robert (?): Holocaust Education—ein neues Unterrichtsfach? (Holocaust Education–a new subject?) In: http://www.gedenkstaettenpaedagogik-bayern.de/holocaust_education.php (31.05.2018).

Simmel, Ernst (1946/ 2002): Antisemitismus und Massen-Psychopathologie (Antisemitism and mass psychopathology), in: Simmel, Ernst et al. (1946/2002): Antisemitismus, Frankfurt, pp. 58–100.

Smith, T. (2005): The Holocaust and its implications: A seven-nation comparative study, AJC.

Spiegel, Miriam Victory (2013): Begegnungen zwischen Holocaust–Überlebenden und Schweizer Schülerinnen und Schülern (Meetings between Holocaust survivors and pupils from Switzerland), in: Gautschi, Peter et al. (2013): Shoa und Schule, Lehren und Lernen im 21. Jahrhundert, Chronos (Shoa and School, Teaching and Learning in the 21st century), pp. 101–117.

Starr, Michael (2024): Touro president: These are three reasons that antisemitism spread on campus–interview, Jerusalem Post, in: https://www.jpost.com/diaspora/antisemitism/article-811386, 07.10.2024.

Steinbacher, Sybille (2022): Über Holocaustvergleiche und Kontinuitäten kolonialer Gewalt (On Holocaust comparisons and continuities of colonial violence), in: Friedländer, Saul et al. (2022): Ein Verbrechen ohne Namen (A Crime without a name), München, pp. 53–69.

Stefaniak, A. et al. (2016): Contact with a multicultural past: A prejudice-reducing intervention, International Journal of Intercultural Relations, 50, pp. 60–65.

Subotic, Jelena (2023): The International Relations of Holocaust Memory, in: Kopstein, Jeffrey et al. (2023): Holocaust: Politics,

Violence, Memory. The New Social Science of the Holocaust, London, pp. 283–297.

Tobin, Jonathan S. (2024): Yom HaShoah after Oct. 7: How Holocaust Education Failed, in: Jewish Press, https://www.jewishpress.com/indepth/columns/jonathan-tobin/yom-hashoah-after-oct-7-how-holocaust-education-failed/2024/05/07/, 26.09.2024.

Tomaszewski, Jerzy (2005): Why…; in: Ambrosewicz–Jacobs, J. et al. (2005): Why Should We Teach About the Holocaust? Cracow, pp. 17–21.

Totten, S. (1999): Should there be Holocaust education for K-4 students? The answer is no. Social Sciences and the Young Learner, 12(1), pp. 36–39.

Urech, Urs (2013): Vom Ort des Grauens ins Schulzimmer („From the place of horror to the class room"), in: Gautschi, Peter et al. (2013): Shoa und Schule, Lehren und Lernen im 21. Jahrhundert, Chronos (Shoa and School, Teaching and Learning in the 21st century), pp. 127–137.

Verstandig, Yonatan (2024): Words to Action: How the ADL is fighting antisemitism with education, Jerusalem Post, in: https://www.jpost.com/diaspora/antisemitism/article-824727, 26.11.2024.

Wagensommer, Georg (2020): Empirische Studien zu Nationalsozialismus und Holocaust aus der Perspektive von Kindern und Jugendlichen und darauf aufbauende Möglichkeiten einer Antisemitismus-Prävention (Empirical studies on National Socialism and the Holocaust from the perspective of children and young people and possibilities of antisemitism prevention based on these studies), in: Antisemitismusprävention in der Grundschule, Hamburg.

Weber, Philippe (2018): Dialogisches Erzählen im Geschichtsunterricht (Dialogic storytelling in history lessons), in: Sandkühler et al. (2018): Geschichtsunterricht im 21. Jahrhundert (History lessons in the 21st century), Bonn, pp. 313–352.

Welzer, Harald (1997): „Was wir für böse Menschen sind!" Der Nationalsozialismus im Gespräch zwischen den Generationen ("What evil people we are!" National Socialism in conversation between the generations), Tübingen.

Welzer, Harald (2002): „Opa war kein Nazi". Nationalsozialismus und Holocaust im Familiengedächtnis ("Grandpa wasn't a Nazi". National Socialism and the Holocaust in family memory), Frankfurt am Main.

Wenzel, Birgit (2013): Die Darstellung von Nationalsozialismus und Holocaust in deutschen Geschichtsbüchern (The Portrayal of the Holocaust and National Socialism in German history books), in: Rathenow et al. (2013): Handbuch Nationalsozialismus und Holocaust, Schwalbach, pp. 167–186.

Wiesel, Elie (1979): President's Commission on the Holocaust, Washington DC, http://www.ushmm.org/research/library/faq/languages/en/06/01/commission/ 10.06.2024.

Wilson, P. (2015): The UK supports education and projects that address anti- Semitism and all other forms of hatred: Statement by Ambassador Peter Wilson of the UK Mission to the UN, to the General Assembly Informal Meeting on Anti–Semitism, in: https:// www. gov.uk/ government/ speeches/ the- uk-supports- education- and- projects- that- address- anti-semitism- and- all- other- forms- of- hatred, 19.07.2024.

Winter, Sebastian (2017): (Un-) Ausgesprochen: Antisemitische Artikulation ((Un-) Spoken: Antisemitic articulation), in: Mendel, M.; Messerschmidt, A. et al. (2017): Fragiler Konsens, Antisemitismuskritische Bildung in der Migrationsgesellschaft, (Fragile consensus, Education critical of antisemitism in a migration society), Frankfurt, pp. 27–42.

Wyman, David S. (1996): The world reacts to the Holocaust, Baltimore.

Zehnpfennig, Barbara (2017): Volk-Nation-Gemeinschaft-Gesellschaft, (People Nation Community Society), in: Flümann, Gereon et al. (2017): Umkämpfte Begriffe, (Contested Terms), Bonn, pp. 213–232.

Zick, Andreas et al. (2015): Die Abwertung des Anderen (The devaluation of the other), Bonn.

Zülsdorf–Kersting, Meik (2007): Sechzig Jahre danach: Jugendliche und der Holocaust (60 years after–Youth and the Holocaust). Berlin.

Zülsdorf–Kerstin, Meik (2013): Wie umgehen mit dem Zivilisationsbruch Holocaust? (How to deal with the rupture of civilisation?), in: Gautschi, Peter et al. (2013): Shoa und Schule, Lehren und Lernen im 21. Jahrhundert, Chronos (Shoa and School, Teaching and Learning in the 21st century), pp. 209–225.

Zunzer, Daniela (2013): „Die Exkursion nach Dachau müssen Sie unbedingt beibehalten" (You have to maintain the excursion to Dachau), in: Gautschi, Peter et al. (2013): Shoa und Schule, Lehren und Lernen im 21. Jahrhundert, Chronos (Shoa and School, Teaching and Learning in the 21st century), pp. 117–127.

Internet sources, without naming authors:

ADL (2020): Survey of U.S. College Students Shows Holocaust Education is Effective in Building Empathy, Tolerance and Open Mindedness, in: https://www.adl.org/resources/press-release/survey-us-college-students-shows-holocaust-education-effective-building, 26.09.2024.

ADL (2023): Task force, J7, in: https://www.adl.org/j7-large-communities-task-force-against-antisemitism, 02.10.2024.

Azrieli Foundation, Canadian Holocaust Knowledge, in: https://azrielifoundation.org/canadian-holocaust-knowledge-and-awareness-study, 30.07.2024.

Bayerische Staatsregierung (2024), Bayerische Informationsstelle für Extremismus, in: https://www.bige.bayern.de/beratung_und_bildung/km/gedenkstaettenpaedagogik/index.html, 16.07.2024.

Bnai Brith (2024): https://www.bnaibrith.ca/league-for-human-rights/ , 10.06.2024.

Bundesministerium des Inneren, Antisemitismus in Deutschland, in: https://www.bmi.bund.de/SharedDocs/

downloads/DE/publikationen/themen/heimat-inte-gration/expertenkreis-antisemitismus/antisemitis-mus-in-deutschland-bericht.html, 19.07.2024.

Bundeszentale für Politische Bildung: Beutelsbacher Konsens, in: https://www.bpb.de/die-bpb/ueber-uns/auftrag/51310/beutelsbacher-konsens/, 30.11.2024.

Calgary Jewish Federation: https://www.jewishcalgary.org/federation-programs/holocaust-and-human-rights-remem-brance-and-education, 25.07.2024.

CBC News, Alberta government released latest draft of new social studies curriculum, French, Janett (2024): CBC, in: https://www.cbc.ca/news/canada/edmonton/alberta-gov-ernment-releases-latest-draft-of-new-social-studies-curricu-lum-1.7144061, 31.08.2024.

CBC News, Holocaust Education to be mandatory in Alberta, Dennis Kovtun, CBC, in: https://www.cbc.ca/news/canada/edmonton/holocaust-education-to-be-mandatory-in-alber-ta-s-new-social-studies-curriculum-1.7025990, 25.07.2024.

CBC News, Guidance for Holocaust education in school cur-riculum promised for next school year, CBC, in: https://www.cbc.ca/news/canada/manitoba/holocaust-educa-tion-in-schools-ndp-announce-1.7196093, 31.08.2024.

Cambrigde Dictionary, to educate: https://dictionary.cam-bridge.org/de/worterbuch/englisch/educate#:~:text=to%20teach%20someone%2C%20especially%20using%20the%20formal%20system,The%20form%20says%20he%20was%20educated%20in%20Africa, 24.07.2024.

Centre for Holocaust Education IOE, UCL's Faculty of Education and Society University College London: What do students know and understand about the Holocaust? Evidence from English secondary schools, 2016, in: https://holocausteducation.org.uk/research/what-do-students-know-and-understand-about-the/, 01.06.2024.

CNN, Antisemitism in Europe: https://cnnpressroom.blogs.cnn.com/2018/11/27/cnn-investigation-anti-semitism-widespread-in-europe-memory-of-holocaust-is-fading/, 30.07.2024.

Colorado General Assembly, https://leg.colorado.gov/bills/hb20-1336, 25.07.2024.

Council of the Israel Academy (2020): Report on the State of Holocaust Studies in Research Universities and Colleges in Israel, approved by the Council of the Israel Academy on December 10, 2019, in: https://www.academy.ac.il/Index3/Entry.aspx?nodeId=842&entryId=21248, 09.12.2024.

Deutscher Bundestag: Aufklärung von Schülerinnen und Schülern über Antisemitismus und den Holocaust Deutscher (Educating pupils about anti-Semitism and the German Holocaust), Bundestag Drucksache 19/7595 19, Wahlperiode 11.02.2019.

Deutscher Bundestag: Die Verankerung des Themas Nationalsozialismus im Schulunterricht in Deutschland, Österreich, Polen und Frankreich, in: Wissenschaftlicher Dienst, Deutscher Bundestag (The anchoring of the topic of National Socialism in school lessons in Germany, Austria, Poland and France, in: Wissenschaftlicher Dienst, Deutscher Bundestag) Aktenzeichen: WD 8 – 3000 – 091/18, 30.07.2024.

Deutsche Welle (DW): Deutschlands Kampf gegen die Holocaust Verharmloser (Germanys fight against of trivalization of the Holocaust), in: https://www.dw.com/de/deutschlands-kampf-gegen-holocaust-verharmloser/a-54196952, 13.07.2022.

Deutsche Welle (DW): Germany records over 300, in: https://www.dw.com/en/germany-records-over-300-increase-in-antisemitic-incidents/a-67569427, 22.05.2024.

Duden, *erziehen*: https://www.duden.de/rechtschreibung/erziehen, 24.07.2024.

Echoes and Reflection (2024): https://echoesandreflections.org/interactive-map/, 16.07.2024.

Encyclopedia Britannica (2024): https://www.britannica.com/story/what-is-the-origin-of-the-term-holocaust, 02.06.2024.

Encyclopedia Britannica (2024): https://www.britannica.com/biography/Herbert-Spencer , 04.06.2024.

Eva's Stories, https://www.instagram.com/eva.stories/, 12.12.2024.

Friends of Simon Wiesenthal Center for Holocaust Studies (2018): Best Practices on Holocaust Education, Toronto.

Friends of Simon Wiesenthal Center (2024), https://www.fswc.ca/tour-for-humanity, 25.07.2024.

Government of Saskatchewan, https://www.saskatchewan.ca/government/news-and-media/2023/november/20/

holocaust-education-to-be-mandatory-in-saskatchewan-classrooms-for-2025-26-school-year, 28.12.2024.

Hamburg: http://www.hamburg.de/contentblob/2373302/20adcd9a929113b7c34d726fbb58be8a/data/geschichte-gym-seki.pdf, 18.06.2018.

Holocaust Education Symposium (2018): The Holocaust Education Symposium in Cooperation with Mount Royal University, Calgary, in: https://www.jewishcalgary.org/holocaust-education-symposium, 19.06.2018.

Institut für Lehrerfortbildung (LI)/ Institute for Teacher Training in Hamburg, Hamburg (2020): Holocaust/Shoa im Unterricht, in: https://li.hamburg.de/fortbildung/faecher-lernbereiche/gesellschaft/geschichte/holocaust-im-unterricht-653788, 12.10.2024.

International Holocaust Remembrance Alliance: https://holocaustremembrance.com/resources/working-definition-antisemitism, 28.05.2024.

International Holocaust Remembrance Alliance: https://ihra.combatantisemitism.org/, 02.06.2024.

Jerusalem Post, Blog on the Pogrom in Amsterdam, November 2024: https://www.jpost.com/israel-news/2024-11-08/live-updates-828163, 27.11.2024.

KMK Ständige Konferenz der Kultusminister der Länder der Bundesrepublik Deutschland/The Standing Conference of the Ministers of Education and Cultural Affairs: Beschluss der KMK vom 11.12.2014: Erinnern für die

Zukunft. Empfehlungen zur Erinnerungskultur als Gegenstand historisch – politischer Bildung in der Schule, in: https://www.kmk.org/fileadmin/Dateien/pdf/PresseUndAktuelles/2014/2014-12-11-Empfehlung_Erinnern_fuer_die_Zukunft.pdf, 08.06.2018. English: Remembering our past for our future, Recommendations for a culture of remembrance to form an object of historical and political education in schools (Resolution adopted by the KMK on 11 December 2014).

KMK Ständige Konferenz der Kultusminister der Länder der Bundesrepublik Deutschland, The Standing Conference of the Ministers of Education and Cultural Affairs, https://www.kmk.org/themen/allgemeinbildende-schulen/weitere-unterrichtsinhalte-und-themen/holocaust-und-nationalsozialismus.html, 24.07.2024.

KMK Ständige Konferenz der Kultusminister der Länder der Bundesrepublik Deutschland, The Standing Conference of the Ministers of Education and Cultural Affairs: "The Education System in the Federal Republic of Germany 2018/2019, A description of the responsibilities, structures and developments in education policy for the exchange of information in Europe", in: https://www.kmk.org/zab/central-office-for-foreign-education/education-system-in-germany.html, 01.05.2023.

LI: https://tis.li-hamburg.de/web/guest/catalog, 18.07.2024.

Ministry of Education, British Columbia, Canada: https://news.gov.bc.ca/releases/2023PREM0077-001688, 25.07.2024.

Ministry of Education, Ontario, Canada: https://www.dcp.edu.gov.on.ca/en/curriculum/elementary-sshg,

Ministry of Education, Ontario, Canada: https://www.dcp.edu.gov.on.ca/en/key-changes-ss-g6, 31.10.2023.

Nordrhein Westfahlen (NRW), Minisitry of Education: https://www.schulentwicklung.nrw.de/lehrplaene/lehrplannavigator-s-i/gymnasium-aufsteigend-ab-2019-20/index.html, 31.07.2022.

North Carolina, Council on the Holocaust: https://www.dpi.nc.gov/districts-schools/classroom-resources/academic-standards/programs-and-initiatives/nc-council-holocaust, 25.07.2024.

North Carolina, Council on the Holocaust: https://ncholocaust-councilworkshops.org/nc-holocaust-curriculum/, 25.07.2024.

OSCE (2017): Understanding Anti-Semitic Hate Crimes and Addressing the Security Needs of Jewish Communities: A Practical Guide, https://www.osce.org/odihr/317166, 30.11.2024.

Province of Alberta (2024): https://www.alberta.ca/teaching-in-alberta, 24.12.2024.

Reuters (2024): https://www.reuters.com/world/middle-east/how-hamas-attack-israel-unfolded-2023-10-07/ , 22.05.2024.

Task Force for International Cooperation on Holocaust Education, Remembrance, and Research Liaison Projects – Baseline Study, Canada, April 2008.

The Center for the Study of Contemporary European Jewry, The Lester and Sally Entin Faculty of Humanities, Tel Aviv University (2023): For a Righteous Cause, Annual Report

2023, in: https://www.eurekalert.org/news-releases/977517 (please follow link to the full report), Tel Aviv.

The New York State Archives Partnership Trust (2024): https://considerthesourceny.org/, 11.12.2024.

UN (2024): News: https://news.un.org/en/story/2024/ 03/1147217, 22.05.2024.

UNESCO (2014): The impact of Holocaust Education: How to assess policies and practices? International Seminar, 27. January 2014, Paris, https://unesdoc.unesco.org/ark:/48223/ pf0000228087, 02.10.2024.

UNESCO (2018): Education about the Holocaust, in: https:// en.unesco.org/themes/holocaust-genocide-education, 09.06.2018.

UNESCO (2018): Global Citizenship, in: https://en.unesco.org/ themes/gced, 09.06.2018.

UNESCO (2024): What you need to know about global citizenship education, in: https://www.unesco.org/en/global-citizenship-peace-education/need-know, 25.05.2024.

University of Hamburg, https://www.lehramt.uni-hamburg. de/studiengaenge/aufbau-der-lehramtsstudiengaenge.html, 18.07.2024.

University of Hamburg: https://www.uni-hamburg.de/campuscenter/bewerbung/bachelor-staatsexamen/fremd-sprachenkenntnisse.html, 18.07.2024.

USHMM: https://encyclopedia.ushmm.org/content/en/article/introduction-to-the-holocaust, 30.05.2024.

USHMM: https://www.ushmm.org/information/press/press-releases/never-again-education-act, 16.07.2024.

USHMM: https://encyclopedia.ushmm.org/content/en/article/the-german-churches-and-the-nazi-state, 07.12.2024.

US Department of State: Guidelines for countering antisemitism, in: https://www.state.gov/global-guidelines-for-countering-antisemitism/, 12.10.2024.

Yad Vashem: Holocaust Introduction: https://www.yadvashem.org/holocaust/about.html#learnmore, 29.05.2024.

Yad Vashem: Nazi Germany: https://www.yadvashem.org/holocaust/about/nazi-germany-1933-39/non-jewish-victims.html, 30.05.2024

Zentralrat der Juden in Deutschland et al (2021): Gemeinsame Empfehlung des Zentralrats der Juden in Deutschland, der Bund-Länder-Kommission der Antisemitismusbeauftragten und der Kultusministerkonferenz zum Umgang mit Antisemitismus in der Schule (Joint recommendation of the Central Council of Jews in Germany, the Federal-Länder Commission of Anti-Semitism Commissioners and the Conference of Education Ministers on dealing with anti-Semitism in schools), in: https://www.zentralratderjuden.de/aktuelle-meldung/artikel/news/gemeinsame-empfehlung/, 10.12.2024.

ZDF: Die Deutschen und der Holocaust, in: https://www.presseportal.de/pm/105413/4780039, 30.07.2024.

ENDNOTES

1 INTRODUCTION

1 Zülsdorf–Kerstin, Meik (2013): Wie umgehen mit dem Zivilisationsbruch Holocaust? (How to deal with the rupture of civilisation?), in: Gautschi, Peter et al. (2013): Shoa und Schule, Lehren und Lernen im 21. Jahrhundert, Chronos (Shoa and School, Teaching and Learning in the 21st century), p. 221.

2 UNESCO (2024): "What you need to know about global citizenship education", in: https://www.unesco.org/en/global-citizenship-peace-education/need-know, 25.05.2024.

3 Friedmann, Michel (2024): 07. Oktober 2023, Judenhass (7 October, 2023, Jew hatred), Berlin, p. 37.

4 Reuters (2024): https://www.reuters.com/world/middle-east/how-hamas-attack-israel-unfolded-2023-10-07/ , 22.05.2024.

5 UN (2024): https://news.un.org/en/story/2024/03/1147217 , 22.05.2024.

6 Levi Julian, Hanna (2024): Report: Dramatic Rise in Global Antisemitism After October 7, https://www.jewishpress.com/news/jewish-news/antisemitism-news/report-dramatic-rise-in-global-antisemitism-after-october-7/2024/01/31/ , 22.05.2024.

7 For more information see: Eckmann, Monique / Österberg Oscar (2017): Research in Germany, in: Eckmann, Monique (2017): Research in teaching and learning about the Holocaust, in: holocaustremembrance.com, 03.06.2018.

8 More information can be found here: Mendel, Meron; Messerschmidt, Astrid (2017): Fragiler Konsens, Antisemitismuskritische Bildung in der Migrationsgesellschaft, (Fragile consensus, Education critical of antisemitism in a migration society), Frankfurt, pp. 14–16.

9   Winter, Sebastian (2017): (Un-) Ausgesprochen: Antisemitische Artikulation ((Un-) Spoken: Antisemitic articulation), in: Mendel, M.; Messerschmidt, A. et al. (2017): Fragiler Konsens, Antisemitismuskritische Bildung in der Migrationsgesellschaft, (Fragile consensus, Education critical of antisemitism in a migration society), Frankfurt, p. 38.

10   Heyl, Matthias (2017): Die nationalsozialistischen Massenverbrechen (The National Socialist Massmurder), in: Mendel, M.; Messerschmidt, A. et al. (2017): Fragiler Konsens, Antisemitismuskritische Bildung in der Migrationsgesellschaft, (Fragile consensus, Education critical of antisemitism in a migration society), Frankfurt, p. 142.

11   For more information: Bundesministerium des Inneren, Antisemitismus in Deutschland, in: https://www.bmi.bund.de/SharedDocs/downloads/DE/publikationen/themen/heimat-integration/expertenkreis-antisemitismus/antisemitismus-in-deutschland-bericht.html, 19.07.2024.

12   Deutsche Welle, DW (2024): https://www.dw.com/en/germany-records-over-300-increase-in-antisemitic-incidents/a-67569427, 22.05.2024.

13   Deutsche Welle, DW (2024): https://www.dw.com/en/germany-records-over-300-increase-in-antisemitic-incidents/a-67569427, 22.05.2024.

14   Friedmann, Michel (2024): 07. Oktober 2023, Judenhass (7 October 2023, Jew hatred), Berlin, pp. 42/43.

15   Kaplan, Edward H. (2024): Radicalized faculty are the greater danger lurking behind campus protests – opinion, in: https://www.jpost.com/opinion/article-803732#:~:text=Radicalized%20academic%20faculty%20are%20dangerous%20in%20pro-Palestinian%20protests,greater%20danger%20by%20far.%20By%20EDWARD%20H.%20KAPLAN, 07.10.2024.

16   Lapin, Andrew (2024): Third of non-Jewish college students hostile to Jews or Israel, Brandeis U study finds, in: Jerusalem Post (2024):

https://www.jpost.com/diaspora/antisemitism/article-815999, 26.11.2024.

17 Kottmann, Nils (2024): AJC ruft „globalen Ausnahmezustand für das jüdische Volk" aus" (AJC declares "global state of emergency for the Jewish people"), in: Jüdische Allgemeine (2024): https://www. juedische-allgemeine.de/juedische-welt/ajc-ruft-globalen-ausnah-mezustand-fuer-das-juedische-volk-aus/, 31.08.2024.

18 Grünberg, Arnon (2024): Westliche Gegner des Antisemitismus be-suchen die ermordeten Juden im Museum, mit den lebenden dage-gen haben sie ein Problem (Western opponents of antisemitism visit the murdered Jews in the museum, but they have a problem with the living ones), Neue Züricher Zeitung, 2024.

19 Tobin, Jonathan S. (2024): Yom HaShoah after Oct. 7: How Holocaust Education Failed, in: Jewish Press (2024): https://www.jewishpress. com/indepth/columns/jonathan-tobin/yom-hashoah-after-oct-7-how-holocaust-education-failed/2024/05/07/, 26.09.2024.

20 More information can be found here: ALD (2024), in: https://www. adl.org/j7-large-communities-task-force-against-antisemitism, 02.10.2024.

21 Klein-Halevi, Yossi (2024): The end of the post-Holocaust era, in: Times of Israel (2024): https://blogs.timesofisrael.com/the-end-of-the-post-holocaust-era/, 16.10.2024.

22 E.g. Pittinsky who wrote "most alarming, the concept of "Jew hate" undermines the fight against antisemitism by—and this was sup-posed to be a point in its favor—making antisemitism just one in-stance of a broader category: hate" (in: Pittinsky, Todd (2024): "Why 'Jew hate' shouldn't replace 'antisemitism'" in: Times of Israel, https://blogs.timesofisrael.com/why-jew-hate-shouldnt-replace-an-tisemitism/ 16.07.2024.).

23 Pearce, A.; Foster, S.; Pettigrew, A. (2020): Antisemitism and Holo-caust education, in: Pearce, A.; Foster, S.; Pettigrew, A. (2020): Holo-caust Education, UCL Press, p. 152.

24 Bernstein, Julia (2020): Antisemitismus an Schulen in Deutschland (Antisemitism in German schools), Bonn, pp. 138/139.

25 Mohammed, Omar (2024): Why discussing antisemitism is dangerous for Arab intellectuals, in: Times of Israel (2024): https://blogs.timesofisrael.com/why-discussing-antisemitism-is-dangerous-for-arab-intellectuals/, 27.11.2024.

26 Bernstein, Julia (2020): Antisemitismus an Schulen in Deutschland (Antisemitism in German schools), Bonn, pp. 138/139.

2. Holocaust Education – A Confusing Term and Concept?

1 Reinhard Kosellek, Nachwort zu Charlotte Beradt, zitiert nach: Wagensommer, Georg (2020): Empirische Studien zu Nationalsozialismus und Holocaust aus der Perspektive von Kindern und Jugendlichen und darauf aufbauende Möglichkeiten einer Antisemitismus-Prävention (Empirical studies on National Socialism and the Holocaust from the perspective of children and young people and possibilities of antisemitism prevention based on these studies), in: Antisemitismusprävention in der Grundschule, Hamburg.

2 Totten 1999 quoted in Jedward, Jack (2010): Measuring Holocaust knowledge and its impact: A Canadian case study, Springer, p. 285.

3 Schreier, Helmut et al. (1997): Never Again! The Holocaust´s Challenge for Educators, Hamburg, pp. 195/ 196.

4 Encyclopedia Britannica: https://www.britannica.com/story/what-is-the-origin-of-the-term-holocaust, 02.06.2024.

5 Yad Vashem: https://www.yadvashem.org/holocaust/about.html#learnmore, 29.05.2024.

6 Milchman, Alan; Rosenberg, Alan (1997): The Holocaust: The Question of Uniqueness, in: Schreier, Helmut et al. (1997): Never Again! The Holocaust´s Challenge for Educators, Hamburg, p. 88–109.

7 USHMM: https://encyclopedia.ushmm.org/content/en/article/introduction-to-the-holocaust, 29.05.2024.

8   USHMM: https://encyclopedia.ushmm.org/content/en/article/in-troduction-to-the-holocaust, 29.05.2024.

9   USHMM: https://encyclopedia.ushmm.org/content/en/article/in-troduction-to-the-holocaust, 29.05.2024.

10   USHMM:: https://encyclopedia.ushmm.org/content/en/article/in-troduction-to-the-holocaust, 30.05.2024.

11   For more information, Yad Vashem: https://www.yadvashem.org/holocaust/about/nazi-germany-1933-39/non-jewish-victims.html, 30.05.2024.

12   Salzborn, Samuel (2017): Geschichte (History), in: Flümann, Gereon et al (2017): Umkämpfte Begriffe, (Contested Terms), Bonn, p. 319.

13   For example: Significant new initiatives in several Eastern-Europe-an countries for teaching the history of the Holocaust and fighting antisemitism can be observed. Cyprus has become a leader in the fight against antisemitism and racism. There is also a growing interest in Holocaust education in several African countries. In the Arab world a growing recognition of the Holocaust alongside with renewed cultivation of Jewish heritage can be mentioned. Addi-tionally, a wave of educational and legislative initiatives in Western Europe, America, and Australia have taken place. For more infor-mation see: The Center for the Study of Contemporary European Jewry, The Lester and Sally Entin Faculty of Humanities (2023): „For a Righteous Cause, Annual Report 2023", Tel Aviv University.

14   For more information see: Eckmann, Monique / Österberg Oscar (2017): Research in Germany, in: Eckmann, Monique (2017): Re-search in teaching and learning about the Holocaust, in: holocaus-tremembrance.com, 03.06.2018.

15   Arendt, Hannah (1963): Eichmann in Jerusalem, New York.

16   For more information: Short, Geoffrey; Reed, Carole Ann (2004): Issues in Holocaust Education, Bodmin, pp. 19–21.

17   Wyman, David S. (1996): The world reacts to the Holocaust, Balti-more, p. 727.

18   For more information: Short, Geoffrey; Reed, Carole Ann (2004):
      Issues in Holocaust Education, Bodmin, pp.22 –25.

19   Wiesel, Elie (1979): Presidents Commission on the Holocaust, Wash-
      ington DC, http://www.ushmm.org/research/library/faq/languag-
      es/en/06/01/commission/ 10.06.2024.

20   For more information see: Bnai Brith (2024): https://www.bnaibrith.
      ca/league-for-human-rights/ 10.06.2024.

21   For more information: Mock, K. (2000): Holocaust and Hope, in: De
      Coste et al. (2000): The Holocaust´s Ghost, Edmonton.

22   For more information: Bercuson, David (1986): A trust betrayed. The
      Keegstra Affair, Calgary.

23   For more information: Glickman, Yaacov; Bardikoff, Alan (1982):
      The treatment of the Holocaust in Canadian history and social sci-
      ence textbooks, Toronto.

24   For more information: Short, Geoffrey; Reed, Carole Ann (2004):
      Issues in Holocaust Education, Bodmin.

25   Echoes and Reflection (2024): https://echoesandreflections.org/in-
      teractive-map/, 16.07.2024.

26   USHMM (2024): https://www.ushmm.org/information/press/
      press-releases/never-again-education-act, 16.07.2024.

27   Dvir, Boaz (2024): How to Get Holocaust Education Right, Times, in:
      https://time.com/6974378/holocaust-remembrance-education-es-
      say/, 16.07.2024.

28   Sigel, Robert (2015): Die International Holocaust Remembrance
      Alliance, in: Matthes, Eva; Meilhammer, Elisabeth (2015): Holocaust
      Education im 21. Jahrhundert, Kempten, p. 61.

29   Heyl, Matthias (1997b): Holocaust Education in (West) Germany–
      Now and then, in: Schreier, Helmut et al. (1997): Never Again! The
      Holocaust´s Challenge for Educators, Hamburg, p. 168.

30   German speaking researchers do have a problem using the term
      and tend to explain why they do or do not use the term Holocaust
      education, e. g. Urech, Eckmann et al. (2013) in: Gautschi, Peter et
      al. (2013): Shoa und Schule, Lehren und Lernen im 21. Jahrhundert,

Chronos (Shoa and School, Teaching and Learning in the 21st century).

31 Kuchler, Christian (2013): Den Opfern eine Stimme geben (To give voice to the victims), in: Gautschi, Peter et al. (2013): Shoa und Schule, Lehren und Lernen im 21. Jahrhundert, Chronos (Shoa and School, Teaching and Learning in the 21st century), p. 175.

32 Bühl-Gramer, Charlotte (2018): Geschichtsunterricht im 21. Jahrhundert–eine Standortbestimmung (History lessons in the 21st century–an assessment of the current situation) in: Sandkühler et al (2018): Geschichtsunterricht im 21. Jahrhundert (History lessons in the 21st century), Bonn, pp. 38/39.

33 Sandkühler, Thomas/ Lenkeit, Guido (2018): Exklusion durch historische Bildung? (Exclusion through historical education?) in: Sandkühler et al. (2018): Geschichtsunterricht im 21. Jahrhundert (History lessons in the 21st century), Bonn, p. 227.

34 Rathenow, Hanns–Fred; Wenzel, Birgit; Weber, Norbert H. (2013): Gegen das Verschwinden der Vergangenheit (Against the disappearance of the past), in: Rathenow et al. (2013): Handbuch Nationalsozialismus und Holocaust (Manual National Socialism and Holocaust), Schwalmbach, p. 10.

35 Hilton, Laura / Patt, Avinoam (2020): Understanding and teaching the Holocaust, Madison, p. 3.

36 Manca, Stefania et al. (2023): Participating in professional development programmes or learning in the wild? Understanding the learning ecologies of Holocaust educators, British Educational Research Journal, 16.10.2023.

37 For more informatioen: Adorno, T. (1967): Erziehung nach Auschwitz (Education after Auschwitz), in: Heydorn, Heinz–Joachim et al. (1967): Zum Bildungsbegriff der Gegenwart (About the term education in present times), Frankfurt/M, 1967, pp. 111–123.

38 Scharples, Caroline (2016): Postwar Germany and the Holocaust, London, p. 156.

39 Pearce, A.; Foster, S.; Pettigrew, A. (2020): Antisemitism and Holo-

caust education, in: Pearce, A.; Foster, S.; Pettigrew, A. (2020): Holocaust Education, UCL Press, p. 154.

40   For more information: Meseth, W. (2012): Education after Auschwitz in a United Germany, in: European Education, 44(3), p. 13–38; Monteath, P. (2013): Holocaust remembrance in the German Democratic Republic—and beyond, in: Himka J. & Michlic J. (2013): Bringing the dark past to light: The reception of the Holocaust in Post-Communist Europe, pp. 223–260.

41   Lorenz, Friederike et al. (2021): German Teachers Learning about the Shoah in Israel, Wuppertal, pp. 7/8.

42   Lorenz, Friederike et al. (2021): German Teachers Learning about the Shoah in Israel, Wuppertal, pp. 7/8.

43   Monteath, P. (2013): Holocaust remembrance in the German Democratic Republic—and beyond, in: Himka J. & Michlic J. (2013): Bringing the dark past to light: The reception of the Holocaust in Post-Communist Europe, pp. 223–260.

44   For a first impression see Eberle, Annette (2015): Was bedeutet Pädagogik nach Auschwitz heute? (The meaning of Holocaust Education today) In: Matthes, Eva; Meilhammer, Maximiliane (2015): Holocaust Education im 21. Jahrhundert, London, p. 150–165

45   Lorenz, Friederike et al. (2021): German Teachers Learning about the Shoah in Israel, Wuppertal, pp. 7/8.

46   Lorenz, Friederike et al. (2021): German Teachers Learning about the Shoah in Israel, Wuppertal, pp. 7/8.

47   For more information: Bayerische Staatsregierung (2024): https://www.bige.bayern.de/beratung_und_bildung/km/gedenkstaetten-paedagogik/index.html, 16.07.2024.

48   Gautschi, Peter (2008): Der Beitrag des Geschichtsunterrichts zur Entwicklung von Einstellungen (The contribution of history teaching to the development of attitudes) in: Bauer, Jan-Patrick; Meyer-Hamme, Johannes; Körber, Andreas (2008): Geschichtslernen–Innovation und Reflexion (Learning History - Innovation and Reflection), pp. 289–307, Kenzingen, p. 294.

49   Jeismann, Karl–Ernst (2000): Geschichte und Bildung (History and Education). Beiträge zur Geschichtsdidaktik und zur Bildungsforschung, Paderborn.

50   Gautschi, Peter; Lücke, Martin (2018): Historisches Lernen im Digitalen Klassenzimmer (Historisches Lernen in the digital classroom), in: Sandkühler et al. (2018): Geschichtsunterricht im 21. Jahrhundert (History lessons in the 21st century), Bonn, p. 472.

51   Borries, Bodo von; Firscher, Claudia; Leutner – Ramme, Sibylla; Meyer – Hamme, Johannes (2005): Schulbuchverständnis, Richtlinienbenutzung und Reflexionsprozesse im Geschichtsunterricht (Textbook comprehension, use of guidelines and reflection processes in history lessons), Neuried, p. 233.

52   Borries, Bodo von (2011): Geschichtslernen und Menschenrechtsbildung (Historical knowledge and human rights building), Schwalbach, p. 12.

53   Borries, Bodo von (2011): Geschichtslernen und Menschenrechtsbildung (Historical knowledge and human rights building), Schwalbach, p. 56.

54   Borries, Bodo von (2011): Geschichtslernen und Menschenrechtsbildung (Historical knowledge and human rights building), Schwalbach, p. 59.

55   Borries, Bodo von (2011): Geschichtslernen und Menschenrechtsbildung (Historical knowledge and human rights building), Schwalbach, p. 288.

56   For more information see: Novis-Deutsch et al. (2023): Sites of tension: Shifts in Holocaust memory in relation to antisemitism and political contestation in Europe.

57   Hilton, Laura/ Patt, Avinoam (2020): Understanding and teaching the Holocaust, Madison, p. 4.

58   Schmoll, Melanie Carina (2018): „Holo...What?! Teaching the Holocaust against all obstacles", unpublished paper, Hamburg.

59   Manca, Stefania et al. (2023): Participating in professional development programmes or learning in the wild? Understanding the

learning ecologies of Holocaust educators, British Educational Research Journal, p. 312, 16.10.2023.

60 Province of Alberta (2024): https://www.alberta.ca/teaching-in-alberta, 24.12.2024.

61 Interwiev with Lori Gale (teacher), July 2018.

62 For more information: Gryglewski, E. (2010): Teaching about the Holocaust in multicultural societies: Appreciating the learner, Intercultural Education, 21 (Suppl. 1), pp. 41–49.

63 Mendel, Meron; Messerschmidt, Astrid (2017): Fragiler Konsens, Antisemitismuskritische Bildung in der Migrationsgesellschaft, (Fragile consensus, Education critical of antisemitism in a migration society), Frankfurt, p. 14.

64 Universität Hamburg (2024): https://www.lehramt.uni-hamburg.de/studiengaenge/aufbau-der-lehramtsstudiengaenge.html, 18.07.2024.

65 Unversität Hamburg (2024): https://www.uni-hamburg.de/campuscenter/bewerbung/bachelor-staatsexamen/fremdsprachenkenntnisse.html, 18.07.2024.

66 Schmoll, Melanie Carina (2018): „Holo...What?! Teaching the Holocaust against all obstacles", unpublished paper, Hamburg.

67 Nägel, Verena et al. (2017): Die universitäre Lehre über den Holocaust in Deutschland (Academic teaching about the Holocaust in Germany), Berlin.

68 Schmoll, Melanie Carina (2018): „Holo...What?! Teaching the Holocaust against all obstacles", unpublished paper, Hamburg; Nägel, Verena et al. (2017): Die universitäre Lehre über den Holocaust in Deutschland (Academic teaching about the Holocaust in Germany), Berlin.

69 Kranz, Dani (2024): Da fehlt doch was...(Something is missing...), in: Jüdische Allgemeine, https://www.juedische-allgemeine.de/kultur/da-fehlt-doch-was/, 17.12.2024.

70 LI Hamburg (2024): https://tis.li-hamburg.de/web/guest/catalog, 18.07.2024.

71 Kriesten, Jasmin (2020): Antisemitismus-Prävention als Aufgabe der Lehramtsaus- und fortbildung – auch für Grundschullehrkräfte, in: Antisemitismusprävention in der Grundschule, Hamburg.

72 Manca, Stefania et al. (2023): Participating in professional development programmes or learning in the wild? Understanding the learning ecologies of Holocaust educators, British Educational Research Journal, p. 310, 16.10.2023.

73 Hutchins, E. (1996): Cognition in the wild, The MIT Press.

74 Manca, Stefania et al. (2023): Participating in professional development programmes or learning in the wild? Understanding the learning ecologies of Holocaust educators, British Educational Research Journal, p. 311, 16.10.2023.

75 Manca, Stefania et al. (2023): Participating in professional development programmes or learning in the wild? Understanding the learning ecologies of Holocaust educators, British Educational Research Journal, p. 311, 16.10.2023.

76 Manca, Stefania et al. (2023): Participating in professional development programmes or learning in the wild? Understanding the learning ecologies of Holocaust educators, British Educational Research Journal, p. 311, 16.10.2023.

77 More information can be found here: UNESCO (2024): https://www.unesco.org/en/articles/importance-teaching-and-learning-about-holocaust, 18.07.2024.

3. Antisemitism or hatred of Jews?

1 Bauer, Yehuda (2001): A History of the Holocaust, A revised edition, Danbury, p. 51.

2 Source: What do students know and understand about the Holocaust? Evidence from English secondary schools, 2016, in: https://holocausteducation.org.uk/research/what-do-students-know-and-understand-about-the/, 01.06.2024.

3 Source: Pearce, A.; Foster, S.; Pettigrew, A. (2020): Antisemitism and

Holocaust education, in: Pearce, A.; Foster, S.; Pettigrew, A. (2020): Holocaust Education, UCL Press, pp. 150–171.

4   IHRA (2024): https://holocaustremembrance.com/resources/working-definition-antisemitism, 28.05.2024.

5   Lobo, Sasha (2024): Antisemitismus für Anfänger (Antisemitism for Beginners),
     in: https://www.spiegel.de/netzwelt/antisemitismus-erkennen-fuer-anfaenger-wie-man-hass-gegen-juden-enttarnt-a-7752e35c-52df-4646-9222-bfcd206040ed, 28.05.2024.

6   Lobo, Sasha (2024): Antisemitismus für Anfänger (Antisemitism for Beginners), in:https://www.spiegel.de/netzwelt/antisemitismus-erkennen-fuer-anfaenger-wie-man-hass-gegen-juden-enttarnt-a-7752e35c-52df-4646-9222-bfcd206040ed, 28.05.2024.

7   IHRA (2024): Working Definition, in: https://holocaustremembrance.com/resources/working-definition-antisemitism 28.05.2024.

8   Jersualem Declaration (2024): https://jerusalemdeclaration.org/, 26.09.2024.

9   Nexusproject (2024): https://nexusproject.us/, 26.09.2024.

10   Statements were made during a panel discussion organized by the City University of New York, Center of Jewish Studies, under the topic: Defintions od Antisemitism: A Conversation on the IHRA, JDA, and Nexus Definition on 19.09.2024.

11   "Among those, 45 countries have done so—including the United States, Canada, Germany, United Kingdom, and France. In the US, 36 state governments have done so, along with 92 city and county governments", in: IHRA (2024): https://ihra.combatantisemitism.org/ , 02.06.2024.

12   For more information see Mendel, Meron; Uhlig Tom (2021): Globaler Antisemitismus und die Universalisierung der Shoah (Global Antisemitism and Universalization of the Shoa), in: Zeitschrift für Pädagogik und Theologie, 73 (2), pp. 190–201.

13   Klein-Halevi, Yossi (2024): The war against the Jewish Story, in:

Times of Israel (2024): https://blogs.timesofisrael.com/the-war-against-the-jewish-story/, 14.10.2024.

14 For more information see Mendel, Meron; Uhlig Tom (2021): Globaler Antisemitismus und die Universalisierung der Shoah (Global Antisemitism and Universalization of the Shoa), in: Zeitschrift für Pädagogik und Theologie, 73 (2), pp. 190–201.

15 Resecularization was already predicted by Manlio Graziano (2017) in: Holy Wars and Holy Alliance, The Return of Religion to the Global Political Stage, New York. But can also be observed, for example, in the context of US superstar Taylor Swift's world tour. Madita Graumann asked in the German web portal NTV in August 2024: Werte, Gemeinschaft, Musik/Values, community, music: Does Taylor Swift have what the church no longer has?", NTV, in : https://www.n-tv.de/panorama/Taylor-Swift-und-ihre-Fans-Swifties-sind-ein-Phaenomen-mit-religioesen-Strukturen-article25127518.html, 31.08.2024.

16 For more information see Mendel, Meron; Uhlig Tom (2021): Globaler Antisemitismus und die Universalisierung der Shoah (Global Antisemitism and Universalization of the Shoa), in: Zeitschrift für Pädagogik und Theologie, 73 (2), pp. 190–201.

17 Simmel, Ernst (1946/2002): Antisemitismus und Massen-Psychopathologie (Antisemitism and mass psychopathology), in: Simmel, Ernst et al. (1946/2002): Antisemitismus, Frankfurt, pp. 58–100.

18 Following Winter, Sebastian (2017): (Un-) Ausgesprochen: Antisemitische Artikulation ((Un-) Spoken: Antisemitic articulation), in: Mendel, M.; Messerschmidt, A. (et al.) (2017): Fragiler Konsens, Antisemitismuskritische Bildung in der Migrationsgesellschaft, (Fragile consensus, Education critical of antisemitism in a migration society), Frankfurt, p. 32.

19 Schwarz-Friesel, M.; Reinharz, J. (2017): Inside the antisemitic mind, New York, p. 29.

20 For more information see Mendel, Meron; Uhlig Tom (2021): Globaler Antisemitismus und die Universalisierung der Sho-

ah (Global Antisemitism and Universalization of the Shoa), in: Zeitschrift für Pädagogik und Theologie, 73 (2), pp. 190–201. One example is the participation of NPD representatives in Hizb ut-Tahir events, the Holocaust denial conferences in Tehran organized by the Islamic Republic of Iran and promoted by Iran-oriented forums in Germany, or the activities of some people from the extreme left. More details also about the Führer concept and the Umma concept can be found here: Backes, Uwe (2017): Demokratie (Democracy), pp. 79–101

21   For more definitions and explanations about the terms: Heinz, Hanspeter (2020): "An allem sind die Juden schuld" (The Jews are to blame for everything), Hamburg.

22   Elukin, Jonathan (2020): Antisemitism, in: Hilton, Laura; Patt, Avinoam (2020): Understanding and teaching the Holocaust, Madison, pp. 19–32.

23   Benz, Wolfgang (2008): Was ist Antisemitismus? (What is antisemitism?), Bonn, p. 26.

24   Maizels, Linda, quoted in Kottmann, Nils (2024): Mangel an historischem Verständnis (Lack of historical understanding), in: https://www.juedische-allgemeine.de/kultur/mangel-an-historischem-verstaendnis/, 07.10.2024.

25   Schwarz-Friesel, M.; Reinharz, J. (2017): Inside the antisemitic mind, New York, p. 62.

26   Schwarz-Friesel, M.; Reinharz, J. (2017): Inside the antisemitic mind, New York, p. 352, footnote 3.

27   Schwarz-Friesel, M.; Reinharz, J. (2017): Inside the antisemitic mind, New York, p. 34.

28   Scholars have not yet definitively defined philo-Semitism. What is clear, however, is that the term emerged in Germany at the end of the 19th century. In other words, at a time when Jew hatred was rampant. In 1880, von Treitschke (German historian and Jew hater) used the term philo-Semitism for the first time in an essay–as a

fighting term to brand left-wing liberals as friends of the Jews. Also known as Jew-baiting.

29 Schwarz-Friesel, M.; Reinharz, J. (2017): Inside the antisemitic mind, New York, pp. 28/29.

30 For more information see: Cohen, Haim (1977): The Trial and Death of Jesus, New York.

31 Benz, Wolfgang (2008): Was ist Antisemitismus? (What is antisemitism?), Bonn, p. 65.

32 Schwarz-Friesel, M.; Reinharz, J. (2017): Inside the antisemitic mind, New York, p. 32.

33 Benz, Wolfgang (2008): Was ist Antisemitismus? (What is antisemitism?), Bonn, p. 82.

34 Synagogues (ancient Greek: assembly) are Jewish places of worship in which communal services are celebrated. However, they also serve as a teaching centre or meeting place for the Jewish community.

35 Bauer, Yehuda (2001): A History of the Holocaust, p. 22.

36 Statement made during a panel discussion, 01.10.2024, title: "Anti-Judaism, Antisemitism, and the Holocaust: The Weight and Consequences", Parkes Institute, United Kingdom.

37 For more information: Bauer, Yehuda (2001): A History of the Holocaust, pp.19–23.

38 Brodersen, Dammann (2007): Torn Hearts. The history of the Jews in Germany, Bonn, p. 42

39 Pogrom comes from the Russian and means devastation or destruction. Pogroms refer to violent actions, attacks, and riots against ethnic, national or religious minorities or political groups, for example.

40 Berendsen, Eva et al. (2017): Natürliche Feind*innen (Natural enemies), in: Mendel, M.; Messerschmidt, A. et al. (2017): Fragiler Konsens, Antisemitismuskritische Bildung in der Migrationsgesellschaft, (Fragile consensus, Education critical of antisemitism in a migration society), Frankfurt, pp. 225/226.

41   Goldenhagen, Daniel (1996): Hitler's willing executioners, New York.

42   More details on this aspect e. g. Bauer, Yehuda (2001): A History of the Holocaust, p. 56.

43   Kalmijn, Matthijs (2915): The Children of Intermarriage in Four European Countries, Annals of American Academy of Political and Social Science 662, November 2015, pp. 246–278.

44   Friedmann, Michel (2024): 07. Oktober 2023, Judenhass (7 October 2023, Jew hatred), Berlin, p. 14.

45   Adorno, Theodor (1959/1997): Theorie der Halbbildung (Theory of semi-education), Bd. 8, Frankfurt, pp. 93–121.

46   For the entire explanation see Winter, Sebastian (2017): (Un-) Ausgesprochen: Antisemitische Artikulation ((Un-)Spoken: Antisemitic articulation), in: Mendel, M.; Messerschmidt, A. (et al.) (2017): Fragiler Konsens, Antisemitismuskritische Bildung in der Migrationsgesellschaft, (Fragile consensus, Education critical of antisemitism in a migration society), Frankfurt, pp. 33–35.

47   Based on: Bauer, Yehuda (2001): A History of the Holocaust, pp. 33–49.

48   Schwarz-Friesel, M.; Reinharz, J. (2017): Inside the antisemitic mind, New York, p. 41.

49   Encyclopedia Britannica (2024): Spencer, Herbert, https://www.britannica.com/biography/Herbert-Spencer, 04.06.2024.

50   Bauer, Yehuda (2001): A History of the Holocaust, p. 50.

51   Bauer, Yehuda (2001): A History of the Holocaust, pp. 49/50.

52   Bauer, Yehuda (2001): A History of the Holocaust, p. 51.

53   Schwarz-Friesel, M.; Reinharz, J. (2017): Inside the antisemitic mind, New York, p. 57.

54   For more information: Yad Vashem (2024): https://www.yadvashem.org/de/holocaust/about/introduction/antisemitism.html , 04.06.2024.

55   Bauer, Yehuda (2001): A History of the Holocaust, p. 63.

56 For more information: Benz, Wolfgang (2008): Was ist Antisemitismus? (What is antisemitism?), Bonn, p. 84.

57 The German National Assembly met before in Berlin. Due to civil war in the capital, the members decided to move to a more quiet and less dangerous Weimar.

58 Büttner, Ursula (2008): Weimar–die überforderte Republik (Weimar–overstrained republic), p. 54.

59 Müller, Tim B. (2014): Nach dem Ersten Weltkrieg, Lebensversuche moderner Demokratien, (After World War 1–life experience of modern democracies) Bonn, p. 34.

60 All numbers taken from Falter, Jürgen W. (1991): Hitlers Wähler (Hitler's voters), München.

61 For more information: Büttner, Ursula (2008): Weimar–die überforderte Republik (Weimar–overstrained republic), pp. 240-242.

62 For more information: Büttner, Ursula (2008): Weimar–die überforderte Republik (Weimar–overstrained republic), p.186.

63 Confino, Alon (2014): A World Without Jews, New York, p. 121.

64 For more information: Büttner, Ursula (2008): Weimar–die überforderte Republik (Weimar–overstrained republic), p.287.

65 For more information: Büttner, Ursula (2008): Weimar–die überforderte Republik (Weimar–overstrained republic), p.291.

66 For more information: Büttner, Ursula (2008): Weimar–die überforderte Republik (Weimar–overstrained republic), p.188.

67 For more information: Büttner, Ursula (2008): Weimar–die überforderte Republik (Weimar–overstrained republic), p.295

68 Confino, Alon (2014): A World Without Jews, New York, p. 6.

69 Confino, Alon (2014): A World Without Jews, New York, pp. 6/7.

70 For more information: Büttner, Ursula (2008): Weimar–die überforderte Republik (Weimar–overstrained republic), p. 294.

71 Schwarz-Friesel, M.; Reinharz, J. (2017): Inside the antisemitic mind, New York, p. 50.

72 For more information: Müller, Tim B. (2014): Nach dem Ersten Welt-

krieg, Lebensversuche moderner Demokratien, (After World War 1–life experience of modern democracies) Bonn, p. 122.

73 For more infomation Confino, Alon (2014): A World Without Jews, New York, pp.78–81.

74 For more information: Müller, Tim B. (2014): Nach dem Ersten Weltkrieg, Lebensversuche moderner Demokratien, (After World War 1–life experience of modern democracies) Bonn, p. 122.

75 For more information: Yad Vashem (2024): https://www.yad-vashem.org/holocaust/about.html#learnmore, 29.05.2024.

76 Schwarz-Friesel, M.; Reinharz, J. (2017): Inside the antisemitic mind, New York, p. 52.

77 Schwarz-Friesel, M.; Reinharz, J. (2017): Inside the antisemitic mind, New York, p. 54.

78 Friedmann, Michel (2024): 07. Oktober 2023, Judenhass (7 October 2023, Jew hatred), Berlin, p. 14.

79 Benz, Wolfgang (2008): Was ist Antisemitismus? (What is antisemitism?), Bonn, p. 23.

80 Benz, Wolfgang (2008): Was ist Antisemitismus? (What is antisemitism?), Bonn, p. 23.

81 Friedmann, Michel (2024): 07. Oktober 2023, Judenhass (7 October 2023, Jew hatred), Berlin, p. 47.

82 Mohammend, Omar (2024), in: Kottmann, Nils (2024): Mangel an historischem Verständnis (Lack of historical understanding), in: https://www.juedische-allgemeine.de/kultur/mangel-an-historischem-verstaendnis/, 07.10.2024.

83 Kistenmacher, Olaf (2017): Schuldabwehr-Antisemitismus als Herausforderung (Guilt defense- antisemitism as a challenge), in: Mendel, M.; Messerschmidt, A. et al. (2017): Fragiler Konsens, Antisemitismuskritische Bildung in der Migrationsgesellschaft, (Fragile consensus, Education critical of antisemitism in a migration society), Frankfurt, p. 212/ 213.

84 Kistenmacher, Olaf (2017): Schuldabwehr-Antisemitismus als Herausforderung (Guilt defense- antisemitism as a challenge), in:

Mendel, M.; Messerschmidt, A. et al. (2017): Fragiler Konsens, Antisemitismuskritische Bildung in der Migrationsgesellschaft, (Fragile consensus, Education critical of antisemitism in a migration society), Frankfurt, p. 214.

85   Allwork, Larissa (2019): Holocaust education and contemporary anti-semitism, in: Policy Papers, https://www.historyandpolicy.org/policy-papers/papers/holocaust-education-and-contemporary-anti-semitism, 02.10.2024.

86   Benz, Wolfgang (2008): Was ist Antisemitismus? (What is antisemitism?), Bonn, p. 57.

87   Salzborn, Samuel (2017): Geschichte (History), in: Flümann, Gereon et al. (2017): Umkämpfte Begriffe, (Contested Terms), Bonn, p. 332.

88   Zehnpfennig, Barbara (2017): Volk-Nation-Gemeinschaft-Gesellschaft, (People Nation Community Society), in: Flümann, Gereon et al. (2017): Umkämpfte Begriffe, (Contested Terms), Bonn, p. 218.

89   More information in Mendel, Meron; Messerschmidt, Astrid (2017): Fragiler Konsens, Antisemitismuskritische Bildung in der Migrationsgesellschaft, (Fragile consensus, Education critical of antisemitism in a migration society), Frankfurt, p. 12.

90   Friedmann, Michel (2024): 07. Oktober 2023, Judenhass (7 October 2023, Jew hatred), Berlin, p. 27.

91   Schwarz-Friesel, M.; Reinharz, J. (2017): Inside the antisemitic mind, New York, p. 63.

92   Rensmann, Lars (2024): Globalisierter Antisemitismus: Neue Wege der politik- und sozialwissenschaftlichen Forschung zu Judenfeindschaft im globalen und digitalen Zeitalter (Globalized antisemitism: new directions in political and social science research on hostility towards Jews in the global and digital age), in: Gustenau et al. (2024): Antisemitismus auf dem Vormarsch (antisemitism on the rise), Baden–Baden, p. 83.

93   Zentralrat der Juden in Deutschland et al. (2021): Gemeinsame Empfehlung des Zentralrats der Juden in Deutschland, der Bund-Länder-Kommission der Antisemitismusbeauftragten und

der Kultusministerkonferenz zum Umgang mit Antisemitismus in der Schule (Joint recommendation of the Central Council of Jews in Germany, the Federal-Länder Commission of Anti-Semitism Commissioners and the Conference of Education Ministers on dealing with anti-Semitism in schools), in: https://www.zentralratderjuden.de/aktuelle-meldung/artikel/news/gemeinsame-empfehlung/, 10.12.2024.

94   Tobin, Jonathan S. (2024): Yom HaShoah after Oct. 7: How Holocaust Education Failed, in: Jewish Press, https://www.jewishpress.com/indepth/columns/jonathan-tobin/yom-hashoah-after-oct-7-how-holocaust-education-failed/2024/05/07/, 26.09.2024.

95   Benz, Wolfgang (2008): Was ist Antisemitismus? (What is antisemitism?), Bonn, p. 25.

96   Adorno, Theodor (1962/1977): Zur Bekämpfung des Antisemitismus heute (On the fight against antisemitism today), in: Gesammelte Schriften, Bd. 20/1, p. 263.

97   Rensmann, Lars (2024): Globalisierter Antisemitismus: Neue Wege der politik- und sozialwissenschaftlichen Forschung zu Judenfeindschaft im globalen und digitalen Zeitalter (Globalized antisemitism: new directions in political and social science research on hostility towards Jews in the global and digital age), in: Gustenau et al. (2024): Antisemitismus auf dem Vormarsch (antisemitism on the rise), Baden–Baden, p. 71.

98   Rosenbaum, Alan (2024): Who's afraid of the big bad Jew? Exploring the root of antisemitism, in: Jerusalem Post, https://www.jpost.com/diaspora/antisemitism/article-829121, 27.11.2024.

4.   Holocaust Education in Practice

1   Source: Deutscher Bundestag: Aufklärung von Schülerinnen und Schülern über Antisemitismus und den Holocaust Deutscher, Bundestag Drucksache 19/7595 19, Wahlperiode 11.02.2019.

2   For more information: https://ec.europa.eu/newsroom/just/
     items/640113/en, 19.07.2024.
3   Rumbell, Olivia (2024): New AI campaign aims to get mandatory
     Holocaust education in Canadian schools, in: https://national-
     post.com/news/canada/ai-campaign-mandatory-holocaust-ed-
     ucation-canadian-schools#:~:text=New%20AI%20campaign%20
     seeks%20mandatory%20Holocaust%20education%20in,we%20
     combat%20the%20scourge%20of%20antisemitism%20and%20de-
     nialism%27, 16.10.2024.
4   Borries, Bodo von (2011): Geschichtslernen und Menschenrechts-
     bildung (Historical knowledge and human rights building), Schwal-
     bach, p. 292.
5   Novik, Peter (1999): The Holocaust in American Life, Boston.
6   Mach, Zdzislaw (2005): The Memory of the Holocaust and Education
     for Europe, in: Ambrosewicz-Jacobs, J. et al. (2005): Why Should We
     Teach About the Holocaust? Cracow, p 23.
7   Allwork, Larissa (2019): Holocaust education and contemporary an-
     ti-semitism, in: Policy Papers, https://www.historyandpolicy.org/
     policy-papers/papers/holocaust-education-and-contemporary-an-
     ti-semitism, 02.10.2024.
8   Krzemiñski, Ireneusz (2005): In Light of Later History, in: Ambrose-
     wicz-Jacobs, J. et al. (2005): Why Should We Teach About the Holo-
     caust? Cracow, p. 32.
9   Krajewski, Stanislaw (2005): Teach Everywhere, and Especially in
     Poland!, in: Ambrosewicz-Jacobs, J. et al. (2005): Why Should We
     Teach About the Holocaust? Cracow, p. 39.
10   Jakubowicz-Mount, Tanna (2005): In a Spirit of Reconciliation, in:
     Ambrosewicz-Jacobs, J. et al. (2005): Why Should We Teach About
     the Holocaust? Cracow, p. 59.
11   Mach, Zdzislaw (2005): The Memory of the Holocaust and Education
     for Europe, in: Ambrosewicz-Jacobs, J. et al. (2005): Why Should We
     Teach About the Holocaust? Cracow, pp. 24/25.
12   Knigge, Volkhard (2016): Das radikal Böse ist das, was nicht hätte

passieren dürfen." (Radical evil is what should not have happened), in: APuZ, Aus Politik und Zeitgeschichte, Unannehmbare Geschichte begreifen (Understanding unacceptable history), in : APuZ, Aus Politik und Zeitgeschichte, 66. Jahrgang · 3–4/2016, p. 4.

13   Jakubowicz-Mount, Tanna (2005): In a Spirit of Reconciliation, in: Ambrosewicz-Jacobs, J. et al (2005): Why Should We Teach About the Holocaust? Cracow, p. 50.

14   Pearce, A.; Foster, S.; Pettigrew, A. (2020): Antisemitism and Holocaust education, in: Pearce, A.; Foster, S.; Pettigrew, A. (2020): Holocaust Education, UCL Press, p. 152.

15   Gautschi, Peter (2008): Der Beitrag des Geschichtsunterrichts zur Entwicklung von Einstellungen (The contribution of history teaching to the development of attitudes) in: Bauer, Jan-Patrick; Meyer-Hamme, Johannes; Körber, Andreas (2008): Geschichtslernen – Innovation und Reflexion (Learning History - Innovation and Reflection), pp. 289–307, Kenzingen, p. 304.

16   Johan Galtung (1982): Strukturelle Gewalt (Structural violence). Beiträge zur Friedens- und Konfliktforschung, Reinbeck; Galtung, Johan (1998): Frieden mit friedlichen Mitteln (Peace by peaceful means). Frieden und Konflikt, Entwicklung und Kultur, Opladen.

17   Friedmann, Michel (2024): 07. Oktober 2023, Judenhass (7 October 2023, Jew hatred), Berlin, p. 69.

18   Jakubowicz-Mount, Tanna (2005): In a Spirit of Reconciliation, in: Ambrosewicz-Jacobs, J. et al. (2005): Why Should We Teach About the Holocaust? Cracow, p. 50.

19   Jakubowicz-Mount, Tanna (2005): In a Spirit of Reconciliation, in: Ambrosewicz-Jacobs, J. et al. (2005): Why Should We Teach About the Holocaust? Cracow, p. 49.

20   Krajewski, Stanislaw (2005): Teach Everywhere, and Especially in Poland!, in: Ambrosewicz-Jacobs, J. et al. (2005): Why Should We Teach About the Holocaust? Cracow, pp. 37/38.

21   Mach, Zdzislaw (2005): The Memory of the Holocaust and Education

for Europe, in: Ambrosewicz-Jacobs, J. et al. (2005): Why Should We Teach About the Holocaust? Cracow, p. 24/ 25.

22 Charnysh, Volha (2023): Remembering past atrocities: Good or bad for attitudes toward minorities?, in: Kopstein, J. et al. (2023): Holocaust: Politics, Violence, Memory. The new Social Science of the Holocaust, London, p. 248.

23 Tomaszewski, Jerzy (2005): Why...; in: Ambrosewicz-Jacobs, J. et al. (2005): Why Should We Teach About the Holocaust? Cracow, p. 21.

24 To educate, in: Cambridge Dictionary, https://dictionary.cambridge. org/de/worterbuch/englisch/educate#:~:text=to%20teach%20 someone%2C%20especially%20using%20the%20formal%20system,The%20form%20says%20he%20was%20educated%20in%20 Africa, 24.07.2024.

25 Erziehen, in: Duden, https://www.duden.de/rechtschreibung/erziehen, 24.07.2024.

26 Charnysh, Volha (2023): Remembering past atrocities: Good or bad for attitudes toward minorities?, in: Kopstein, J. et al. (2023): Holocaust: Politics, Violence, Memory. The new Social Science of the Holocaust, London, p. 248.

27 Colorado General Assembly, in: https://leg.colorado.gov/bills/hb20-1336, 25.07.2024.

28 NC Council on the Holocaust, in: https://www.dpi.nc.gov/districts-schools/classroom-resources/academic-standards/programs-and-initiatives/nc-council-holocaust, 25.07.2024.

29 NC Council on the Holocaust, in: https://ncholocaustcouncilworkshops.org/nc-holocaust-curriculum/, 25.07.2024.

30 Task Force for International Cooperation on Holocaust Education, Remembrance, and Research, Liaison Projects - Baseline Study on Canada, April 2008.

31 For more information, Ministry of Education Ontario, in: https:// www.dcp.edu.gov.on.ca/en/curriculum/elementary-sshg, https:// www.dcp.edu.gov.on.ca/en/key-changes-ss-g6, 31.10.2023.

32 For more information: CBC News, in: https://www.cbc.ca/news/

canada/edmonton/holocaust-education-to-be-mandatory-in-al-berta-s-new-social-studies-curriculum-1.7025990, 25.07.2024.// French, Janett (2024): Alberta government released latest draft of new social studies curriculum, in: https://www.cbc.ca/news/cana-da/edmonton/alberta-government-releases-latest-draft-of-new-so-cial-studies-curriculum-1.7144061, 31.08.2024.

33 For more information: https://news.gov.bc.ca/releases/2023PREM-0077-001688, 25.07.2024.

34 For more information: https://www.cbc.ca/news/canada/mani-toba/holocaust-education-in-schools-ndp-announce-1.7196093, 31.08.2024

35 Government of Saskatchewan, in: https://www.saskatchewan. ca/government/news-and-media/2023/november/20/holocaust-education-to-be-mandatory-in-saskatchewan-classrooms-for-2025-26-school-year, 28.12.2024.

36 In the province of Alberta/ Canada for example the books used in grade 11/12 are called "Exploring Nationalism", "Understanding Nationalism" and "Perspectives on ideology", as well as "Under-standing of Ideologies"; in grade 11: „Exploring nationalism" and „Understanding nationalism" by McGraw-Hill Ryerson, „Perspec-tives on ideology" by Alberta Education; in grade 12 „Perspectives on ideology" and „Understandings of ideologies" by Alberta Educa-tion and „Understanding of ideologies" by Oxford University Press.

37 For more information: Calgary Jewish Federation, in: https:// www.jewishcalgary.org/federation-programs/holocaust-and-hu-man-rights-remembrance-and-education, 25.07.2024.

38 For more information: FOSWC, in: https://www.fswc.ca/ tour-for-humanity, 25.07.2024.

39 Namely for example the New Israel Fund Canada, JNF Canada or Jewish Federations of Canada.

40 In 2015 Moisan/ Hirsch published a study on Holocaust Education in state schools in the Canadian province of Quebec. In 2018 the „Friends of Simon Wiesenthal Center for Holocaust Studies" pre-

sented a study on „Best Practices on Holocaust Education" which is a collection of findings, insights, and tips from educators in Canada.

41   Wagensommer, Georg (2020): Empirische Studien zu Nationalsozialismus und Holocaust aus der Perspektive von Kindern und Jugendlichen und darauf aufbauende Möglichkeiten einer Antisemitismus-Prävention (Empirical studies on National Socialism and the Holocaust from the perspective of children and young people and possibilities of antisemitism prevention based on these studies), in: Antisemitismusprävention in der Grundschule, Hamburg, provides an overview.

42   In addition to Germany and North America, this also applies to Israel for example. Here the extensive research activity in the field is neither balanced nor deep-reaching. For more information see: Council of the Israel Academy (2020): Report on the State of Holocaust Studies in Research Universities and Colleges in Israel, approved by the Council of the Israel Academy on December 10, 2019, in: https://www.academy.ac.il/Index3/Entry.aspx?nodeId=842&entryId=21248, 09.12.2024.
       Much research was conducted, when it comes to the outcome of Holocaust education, but not about the content (Allwork, Larissa (2019): Holocaust education and contemporary anti-semitism, in: Policy Papers, https://www.historyandpolicy.org/policy-papers/papers/holocaust-education-and-contemporary-anti-semitism, 02.10.2024).

43   KMK, in: https://www.kmk.org/themen/allgemeinbildende-schulen/weitere-unterrichtsinhalte-und-themen/holocaust-und-nationalsozialismus.html, 24.07.2024.

44   KMK, Erinnern für die Zukunft. Empfehlungen zur Erinnerungskultur als Gegenstand historisch – politischer Bildung in der Schule (Remembering our past for our future, Recommendations for a culture of remembrance to form an object of historical and political education in schools), in: https://www.kmk.org/fileadmin/Dateien/pdf/PresseUndAktuelles/2014/2014-12-11-Empfehlung_Erinnern_fuer_die_Zukunft.pdf, 08.06.2018.

45   Further information: University of Hamburg, in: http://www. hamburg.de/contentblob/2373302/20adcd9a929113b7c34d726fbb-58be8a/data/geschichte-gym-seki.pdf, 18.06.2018.

46   For more information: University of Hamburg, in: http://www. hamburg.de/contentblob/1475202/84d318c8718980ee54d18b-3d65ece106/data/geschichte-gyo.pdf, 18.06.2018.

47   Kernlehrpläne NRW, in: https://www.schulentwicklung.nrw. de/lehrplaene/lehrplannavigator-s-i/gymnasium-aufstei-gend-ab-2019-20/index.html, 31.07.2022.

48   KMK, "The Education System in the Federal Republic of Germany 2018/2019, A description of the responsibilities, structures and developments in education policy for the exchange of information in Europe", in: https://www.kmk.org/zab/central-office-for-for-eign-education/education-system-in-germany.html, 01.05.2023.

49   The exceptions are Bavaria and starting in 2025 Saarland.

50   Sandkühler, Thomas/ Lenkeit, Guido (2018): Exklusion durch his-torische Bildung? (Exclusion through historical education?) in: in: Sandkühler et al. (2018): Geschichtsunterricht im 21. Jahrhundert (History lessons in the 21st century), Bonn, p. 247.

51   For more information about German history class textbooks see: Schmoll, Melanie Carina (2024): Misinformation about Israel and Antisemitic Views in School Textbooks? The Case of Germany, Mün-ster, 2024.

52   Hollenbach, Michael (2020): Klischee mit Kippa (Cliche with Kippa), in: Deutschlandfunk, Das Judentum in Schulbüchern, https://www. deutschlandfunk.de/das-judentum-in-schulbuechern-klischee-mit-kippa-100.html, 13.07.2022.

53   Jacobmeyer, Wolfgang (1998): Das Schulgeschichtsbuch (The school history textbook), in: Geschichte, Politik und ihre Didaktik, 26, p. 26.

54   Source: https://li.hamburg.de/fortbildung/faecher-lernbere-iche/gesellschaft/geschichte/holocaust-im-unterricht-653788, 12.10.2024.

55 Eckmann, Monique / Österberg Oscar (2017): Research in Germany, in: Eckmann, Monique (2017): Research in teaching and learning about the Holocaust, in: holocaustremembrance.com, 12.10.2024.

56 Gautschi, Peter; Lücke, Martin (2018): Historisches Lernen im Digitalen Klassenzimmer (Historisches Lernen in the digital classroom), in: Sandkühler et al. (2018): Geschichtsunterricht im 21. Jahrhundert (History lessons in the 21st century), Bonn, p. 466.

57 Möller, Rainer (2015): Was geht uns heute Auschwitz an? (Why should we care about Auschwitz today?) In: https://comenius.de/2015/12/04/was_geht_uns_heute_auschwitz_an_2015/, 24.09.2024

58 Allwork, Larissa (2019): Holocaust education and contemporary anti-semitism, in: Policy Papers, https://www.historyandpolicy.org/policy-papers/papers/holocaust-education-and-contemporary-anti-semitism, 02.10.2024.

59 Bernhardt, Markus (2018): Was? Historisches Lernen in der Schule (What? Learning about history in school) in: Sandkühler et al. (2018): Geschichtsunterricht im 21. Jahrhundert (History lessons in the 21st century), Bonn, pp. 67–69.

60 Alavi, Bettina/ Barsch, Sebastian (2018): Geschichtsunterricht zwischen Subjektorientierung und Standardisierung (History lessons between subject orientation and standardization), in: Sandkühler et al. (2018): Geschichtsunterricht im 21. Jahrhundert (History lessons in the 21st century), Bonn, pp. 189 –209.

61 „It would seem that they (the students) are saturated with information and explanation about it" (Schreier 1997: 195). See also: Becher, Andrea (2013): Das „Dritte Reich" in Vorstellungen von Grundschulkindern (The Third Reich in the imagination of kids in elemantary school), in: Gautschi et al. (2013): Shoa und Schule, Lehren und Lernen im 21. Jahrhundert, Chronos (Shoa and School, Teaching and Learning in the 21st century), p. 19–37; Mathis Christian; Urech, Natalie (2013): „... da hat man sie in Häuser eingesperrt und Gas reingetan" („... one locked them in houses and put gas into") in: Gautschi et al. (2013): Shoa und Schule, Lehren und Lernen im

21. Jahrhundert, Chronos (Shoa and School, Teaching and Learning in the 21st century), pp. 37–55; Jedward, Jack (2010): Measuring Holocaust knowledge and its impact: A Canadian case study, Springer; Smith, T. (2005): The Holocaust and its implications: A seven-nation comparative study, AJC.

62   Azrieli Foundation, Canadian Holocaust Knowledge, in: https://azrielifoundation.org/canadian-holocaust-knowledge-and-aware-ness-study, 30.07.2024.

63   Hollstein, Olivier et al. (2002): Nationalsozialismus im Geschichtsunterricht. Beobachtungen unterrichtlicher Kommunikation (National Socialism in history lessons. Observations of classroom communication); Meseth, Wolfgang et al. (2004): Schule und Nationalsozialismus. Ansprüche und Grenzen des Geschichtsunterrichts (School and National Socialism. The demands and limits of history lessons), Frankfurt am Main; Zülsdorf – Kersting, Meik (2007): Sechzig Jahre danach: Jugendliche und der Holocaust (60 years after–Youth and the Holocaust), Berlin.

64   CNN, in: https://cnnpressroom.blogs.cnn.com/2018/11/27/cnn-in-vestigation-anti-semitism-widespread-in-europe-memory-of-holo-caust-is-fading/, 30.07.2024.

65   ZDF, in: https://www.presseportal.de/pm/105413/4780039, 30.07.2024.

66   Deutscher Bundestag, in: Die Verankerung des Themas Nationalsozialismus im Schulunterricht in Deutschland, Österreich, Polen und Frankreich, Die Verankerung des Themas Nationalsozialismus im Schulunterricht in Deutschland, Österreich, Polen und Frankreich (The anchoring of the topic of National Socialism in school lessons in Germany, Austria, Poland and France), in: Wissenschaftlicher Dienst, Deutscher Bundestag) Aktenzeichen: WD 8 - 3000 - 091/18, 30.07.2024.

67   Götz, Maya (2018): Was Kinder vom Zweiten Weltkrieg wissen (What kids know about Second World War), Televizion, 31, quoted in: Wagensommer, Georg (2020): Empirische Studien zu National-

sozialismus und Holocaust aus der Perspektive von Kindern und Jugendlichen und darauf aufbauende Möglichkeiten einer Antisemitismus-Prävention (Empirical studies on National Socialism and the Holocaust from the perspective of children and young people and possibilities of antisemitism prevention based on these studies), in: Antisemitismusprävention in der Grundschule, Hamburg.

68 Zülsdorf – Kersting, Meik (2007): Sechzig Jahre danach: Jugendliche und der Holocaust (60 years after–Youth and the Holocaust). Berlin.

69 For example, it is not inherently a sign for hatred of Jews to support Palestinian rights, but how many young people know what exactly is meant when they chant From the river to the sea? It means that Israel must be destroyed in order for a Palestinian state to exist. This is one of the cases where Jew hatred goes unrecognized and can take root. For more, see: Mohammed, Omar (2024), in: Kottmann, Nils (2024): Mangel an historischem Verständnis (Lack of historical understanding), in: https://www.juedische-allgemeine.de/kultur/mangel-an-historischem-verstaendnis/, 07.10.2024.

70 Heyl, Matthias (1997b): Holocaust Education in (West) Germany–Now and then, in: Schreier, Helmut et al. (1997): Never Again! The Holocaust´s Challenge for Educators, Hamburg, p. 169.

71 Bernstein, Julia (2020): Antisemitismus an Schulen in Deutschland (Antisemitism in German schools), Bonn, p. 361.

72 Winter, Sebastian (2017): (Un-) Ausgesprochen: Antisemitische Artikulation ((Un-) Spoken: Antisemitic articulation), in: Mendel, M.; Messerschmidt, A. et al. (2017): Fragiler Konsens, Antisemitismuskritische Bildung in der Migrationsgesellschaft, (Fragile consensus, Education critical of antisemitism in a migration society), Frankfurt, p. 32/33.

73 Wagensommer, Georg (2020): Empirische Studien zu Nationalsozialismus und Holocaust aus der Perspektive von Kindern und Jugendlichen und darauf aufbauende Möglichkeiten einer Antisemitismus-Prävention (Empirical studies on National Socialism and the Holocaust from the perspective of children and young people

and possibilities of antisemitism prevention based on these studies), in: Antisemitismusprävention in der Grundschule, Hamburg.

74 Knigge, Volkhard (2016): Das radikal Böse ist das, was nicht hätte passieren dürfen." (Radical evil is what should not have happened), in: APuZ, Aus Politik und Zeitgeschichte, Unannehmbare Geschichte begreifen (Understanding unacceptable history), 66. Jahrgang · 3–4/2016, p. 4.

75 Heyl, Matthias (1997a): Erziehung nach Auschwitz–eine Bestandsaufnahme. Deutschland, Niederlande, Israel, USA (Education after Auschwitz–a survey. Germany, Netherlands, Israel, USA), Hamburg, p. 143.

76 Borries, Bodo von (2011): Geschichtslernen und Menschenrechtsbildung (Historical knowledge and human rights building), Schwalbach, p. 283.

77 Lorenz, Friederike et al. (2021): German Teachers Learning about the Shoah in Israel, Wuppertal, p. 12

78 Schu, Anke (2017): Inter-Generationelle Narrative Muslimischer Jugendlicher (Inter-generational narratives of Muslim youths), in: Mendel, M.; Messerschmidt, A. et al. (2017): Fragiler Konsens, Antisemitismuskritische Bildung in der Migrationsgesellschaft, (Fragile consensus, Education critical of antisemitism in a migration society), Frankfurt, p. 93–96.

79 Winter, Sebastian (2017): (Un-) Ausgesprochen: Antisemitische Artikulation ((Un-) Spoken: Antisemitic articulation), in: Mendel, M.; Messerschmidt, A. et al. (2017): Fragiler Konsens, Antisemitismuskritische Bildung in der Migrationsgesellschaft, (Fragile consensus, Education critical of antisemitism in a migration society), Frankfurt, p. 28/29.

80 Kistenmacher, Olaf (2017): Schuldabwehr-Antisemitismus als Herausforderung (Guilt defense- antisemitism as a challenge), in: Mendel, M.; Messerschmidt, A. et al. (2017): Fragiler Konsens, Antisemitismuskritische Bildung in der Migrationsgesellschaft, (Fragile

consensus, Education critical of antisemitism in a migration society), Frankfurt, p. 216/217.

81 Borries, Bodo von; Firscher, Claudia; Leutner–Ramme, Sibylla; Meyer–Hamme, Johannes (2005): Schulbuchverständnis (Textbook comprehension, use of guidelines and reflection processes in history lessons), Richtlinienbenutzung und Reflexionsprozesse im Geschichtsunterricht, Neuried, p. 25.

82 Sandkühler, Thomas/ Lenkeit, Guido (2018): Exklusion durch historische Bildung? (Exclusion through historical education?) in: in: Sandkühler et al (2018): Geschichtsunterricht im 21. Jahrhundert (History lessons in the 21st century), Bonn, p. 248.

83 Radtke quoted in Zülsdorf – Kerstin, Meik (2013): Wie umgehen mit dem Zivilisationsbruch Holocaust? (How to deal with the rupture of civilisation?), in: Gautschi, Peter et al. (2013): Shoa und Schule, Lehren und Lernen im 21. Jahrhundert, Chronos (Shoa and School, Teaching and Learning in the 21st century), pp. 223.

84 Zülsdorf – Kersting, Meik (2007): Sechzig Jahre danach: Jugendliche und der Holocaust (60 years after–Youth and the Holocaust), Berlin, p. 85.

85 Winter, Sebastian (2017): (Un-) Ausgesprochen: Antisemitische Artikulation ((Un-) Spoken: Antisemitic articulation), in: Mendel, M.; Messerschmidt, A. et al. (2017): Fragiler Konsens, Antisemitismuskritische Bildung in der Migrationsgesellschaft, (Fragile consensus, Education critical of antisemitism in a migration society), Frankfurt, p. 28.

86 Helbling, Marc; Traunmüller, Richard (2024): „Wie tickt Deutschland?“: Antisemitismus, Antizionismus und pro-palästinensische Einstellungen in Deutschland ("What makes Germany tick?": Anti-Semitism, anti-Zionism and pro-Palestinian attitudes in Germany), in: https://www.uni-mannheim.de/newsroom/presse/pressemitteilungen/2024/oktober/gip-antisemitismus/, 30.12.2024.

87 Kößler, Gottfried (2006): Antisemitismus als Thema im schulischen

Kontext (Anti-Semitism as a topic in the school context), in: Fechler, Bernd; Kößler, Gottfried; Messerschmidt, Astrid; Schäuble, Barbara (2006): Neue Judenfeinschaft? (New Jew hatred?) Frankfurt, p. 174.

88 Borries, Bodo von; Firscher, Claudia; Leutner – Ramme, Sibylla; Meyer–Hamme, Johannes (2005): Schulbuchverständnis, Richtlinienbenutzung und Reflexionsprozesse im Geschichtsunterricht ((Textbook comprehension, use of guidelines and reflection processes in history lessons),), Neuried, p. 301.

89 Schmoll, Melanie Carina (2018): „Holo...What?! Teaching the Holocaust against all obstacles", unpublished paper, Hamburg.

5. Holocaust Education to Change Minds?

1 Knigge, Volkhard (2016): Das radikal Böse ist das, was nicht hätte passieren dürfen." (Radical evil is what should not have happened), in: APuZ, Aus Politik und Zeitgeschichte, Unannehmbare Geschichte begreifen (Understanding unacceptable history), 66. Jahrgang, 3–4/2016, p. 4.

2 Grenz, Dagmar (2013): Kinder–und Jugendliteratur zum Thema Nationalsozialismus und Holocaust in der (Deutsch-) Lehrerausbildung, in: Rathenow et al. (2013): Handbuch Nationalsozialismus und Holocaust, Schwalmbach, p. 337.

3 Welzer, Harald (1997): „Was wir für böse Menschen sind!" Der Nationalsozialismus im Gespräch zwischen den Generationen ("What evil people we are!" National Socialism in conversation between the generations), Tübingen; Welzer, Harald (2002): „Opa war kein Nazi". Nationalsozialismus und Holocaust im Familiengedächtnis ("Grandpa wasn't a Nazi". National Socialism and the Holocaust in family memory), Frankfurt am Main.

4 Wagensommer 2003 quoted in Zülsdorf–Kersting, Meik (2007): Sechzig Jahre danach: Jugendliche und der Holocaust (60 years after–Young people and the Holocaust), Berlin, p. 113.

5 Borries, Bodo von (2011): Geschichtslernen und Menschenrechts-

bildung (Historical knowledge and human rights building), Schwalbach, p. 276.

6   Möller, Rainer (2015): Was geht uns heute Auschwitz an? (Why should we care about Auschwitz today?) In: https://comenius.de/2015/12/04/was_geht_uns_heute_auschwitz_an_2015/, 24.09.2024

7   Bernstein, Julia (2020): Antisemitismus an Schulen in Deutschland (Antisemitism in German schools), Bonn, p. 314/ WJC 2019.

8   Moré 2009, in Bernstein, Julia (2020): Antisemitismus an Schulen in Deutschland (Antisemitism in German schools), Bonn, p. 462.

9   Borries, Bodo von (2011): Geschichtslernen und Menschenrechtsbildung (Historical knowledge and human rights building), Schwalbach, p. 280.

10 Charnysh, Volha (2023): Remembering past atrocities: Good or bad for attitudes toward minorities? In: Kopstein, J. et al. (2023): Holocaust: Politics, Violence, Memory. The new Social Science of the Holocaust, London, p. 245.

11 Marks, Stephan (2007): Scham–die tabuisierende Emotion (Shame–the tabooing emotion), Düsseldorf.

12 Bernstein, Julia (2020): Antisemitismus an Schulen in Deutschland (Antisemitism in German schools), Bonn, p. 320.

13 Welzer, Harald (1997): „Was wir für böse Menschen sind!" Der Nationalsozialismus im Gespräch zwischen den Generationen ("What evil people we are!" National Socialism in conversation between the generations), Tübingen; Welzer, Harald (2002): „Opa war kein Nazi". Nationalsozialismus und Holocaust im Familiengedächtnis ("Grandpa was not a Nazi". National Socialism and the Holocaust in family memory), Frankfurt am Main.

14 Borries, Bodo von (2011): Geschichtslernen und Menschenrechtsbildung (Historical knowledge and human rights building), Schwalbach, p. 294.

15 Friedmann, Michel (2024): 07. Oktober 2023, Judenhass (7 October 2023, Jew hatred), Berlin, pp. 63/64.

16   Lorenz, Friederike et al. (2021): German Teachers Learning about the Shoah in Israel, Wuppertal, p. 11.

17   Wagensommer, Georg (2020): Empirische Studien zu National-sozialismus und Holocaust aus der Perspektive von Kindern und Jugendlichen und darauf aufbauende Möglichkeiten einer Antisem-itismus-Prävention (Empirical studies on National Socialism and the Holocaust from the perspective of children and young people and possibilities of antisemitism prevention based on these studies), in: Antisemitismusprävention in der Grundschule, Hamburg.

18   Borries, Bodo von (2011): Geschichtslernen und Menschenrechts-bildung (Historical knowledge and human rights building), Schwal-bach, p. 294; similar Nägel, who says there seems to be a distinctive need to give German history a positive turn and to find positive ways to identify with (Nägel, Verena et al. (2017): Die universitäre Lehre über den Holocaust in Deutschland (Academic teaching about the Holocaust in Germany), Berlin, p. 90).

19   Wagensommer, Georg (2020): Empirische Studien zu National-sozialismus und Holocaust aus der Perspektive von Kindern und Jugendlichen und darauf aufbauende Möglichkeiten einer Antisem-itismus-Prävention (Empirical studies on National Socialism and the Holocaust from the perspective of children and young people and possibilities of antisemitism prevention based on these studies), in: Antisemitismusprävention in der Grundschule, Hamburg.

20   Becher, Andrea (2018): Die Zeit des Holocaust in Vorstellungen von Grundschulkindern. Perspektiven von Kindern und die Thematisi-erung von Holocaust und Nationalsozialismus im (Sach)Unterricht der Grundschule (The time of the Holocaust in the imaginations of primary school children. Children's perspectives and the themati-zation of the Holocaust and National Socialism in elementary school lessons), in: Isabel Enzenbach/Detlef Pech/Christina Klätte (Hg.), Kinder und Zeitgeschichte. Jüdische Geschichte und Gegenwart, Nationalsozialismus und Antisemitismus (Children and contem-porary history. Jewish history and present, National Socialism and

antisemitism)(101–120), Berlin 2012, 101, http://www.widerstreit-sachunterricht.de/beihefte/beiheft8/pdf, quoted in: Wagensommer, Georg (2020): Empirische Studien zu Nationalsozialismus und Holocaust aus der Perspektive von Kindern und Jugendlichen und darauf aufbauende Möglichkeiten einer Antisemitismus-Prävention (Empirical studies on National Socialism and the Holocaust from the perspective of children and young people and possibilities of antisemitism prevention based on these studies), in: Antisemitismusprävention in der Grundschule, Hamburg.

21   UNESCO (2014): The impact of Holocaust Education: How to assess policies and practices? International Seminar, 27. January 2014, Paris, https://unesdoc.unesco.org/ark:/48223/pf0000228087, 02.10.2024.

22   Lorenz, Friederike et al (2021): German Teachers Learning about the Shoah in Israel, Wuppertal, p. 16.

23   Borries, Bodo von (2011): Geschichtslernen und Menschenrechtsbildung (Historical knowledge and human rights building), Schwalbach, p. 299.

24   Friedmann, Michel (2024): 07. Oktober 2023, Judenhass (7 October 2023, Jew hatred), Berlin, p. 50.

25   Confino, Alon (2014): A World Without Jews, New York, p. 243.

26   Tobin, Jonathan S. (2024): Yom HaShoah after Oct. 7: How Holocaust Education Failed, in: Jewish Press, https://www.jewishpress.com/indepth/columns/jonathan-tobin/yom-hashoah-after-oct-7-how-holocaust-education-failed/2024/05/07/, 26.09.2024.

27   Rensmann, Lars (2024): Globalisierter Antisemitismus: Neue Wege der politik- und sozialwissenschaftlichen Forschung zu Judenfeindschaft im globalen und digitalen Zeitalter (Globalized antisemitism: new directions in political and social science research on hostility towards Jews in the global and digital age), in: Gustenau et al. (2024): Antisemitismus auf dem Vormarsch (antisemitism on the rise), Baden–Baden, p. 45.

28   Mohammed, Omar (2024), in: Kottmann, Nils (2024): Mangel an

historischem Verständnis (Lack of historical understanding), in: https://www.juedische-allgemeine.de/kultur/mangel-an-histor-ischem-verstaendnis/, 07.10.2024.

29 Kadish, Alan (2024), in: Starr, Michael (2024): Touro president: These are three reasons that antisemitism spread on campus–in-terview, in: https://www.jpost.com/diaspora/antisemitism/arti-cle-811386, 07.10.2024.

30 Steinbacher, Sybille (2022): Über Holocaustvergleiche und Konti-nuitäten kolonialer Gewalt (On Holocaust comparisons and conti-nuities of colonial violence), in: Friedländer, Saul et al. (2022): Ein Verbrechen ohne Namen (A Crime without a name), München, pp. 53–69.

31 Elukin, Jonathan (2020): Antisemitism, in: Hilton, Laura/ Patt, Avi-noam (2020): Understanding and teaching the Holocaust, Madison, p. 30.

32 Mohammed, Omar (2024), in: Kottmann, Nils (2024): Mangel an historischem Verständnis (Lack of historical understanding), in: https://www.juedische-allgemeine.de/kultur/mangel-an-histor-ischem-verstaendnis/, 07.10.2024.

33 Rajal, Elke (2023): Countering antisemitism through Holocaust education. A comparative perspective on Scotland and Austria, in: https://www.tandfonline.com/doi/full/10.1080/00131911.2024.23 25068#abstract, 06.08.2024.

34 Kistenmacher, Olaf (2017): Schuldabwehr-Antisemitismus als Herausforderung (Guilt defense- antisemitism as a challenge), in: Mendel, M.; Messerschmidt, A. et al. (2017): Fragiler Konsens, Anti-semitismuskritische Bildung in der Migrationsgesellschaft, (Fragile consensus, Education critical of antisemitism in a migration socie-ty), Frankfurt, pp. 208/209.

35 Horn, Dara (2023): Is Holocaust Education Making Anti-Semitism Worse? In: https://www.theatlantic.com/magazine/archive/2023/05/holocaust-student-education-jewish-anti-semitism/673488/, 26.09.2024.

36 Wilson, P. (2015): The UK supports education and projects that address anti- Semitism and all other forms of hatred: Statement by Ambassador Peter Wilson of the UK Mission to the UN, to the General Assembly Informal Meeting on Anti- Semitism, in: https:// www. gov.uk/ government/ speeches/ the- uk- supports- education- and- projects- that- address- anti-semitism- and- all- other- forms- of- hatred, 19.07.2024.

37 Charnysh, Volha (2023): Remembering past atrocities: Good or bad for attitudes toward minorities? In: Kopstein, J. et al. (2023): Holocaust: Politics, Violence, Memory. The new Social Science of the Holocaust, London, p. 245.

38 Borries, Bodo von; Firscher, Claudia; Leutner–Ramme, Sibylla; Meyer–Hamme, Johannes (2005): Schulbuchverständnis, Richtlinienbenutzung und Reflexionsprozesse im Geschichtsunterricht (Textbook comprehension, use of guidelines and reflection processes in history lessons), Neuried, p. 301.

39 Schreier, Helmut et al. (1997): Never Again! The Holocaust´s Challenge for Educators, Hamburg, p. 195.

40 Borries, Bodo von (2011): Geschichtslernen und Menschenrechtsbildung (Historical knowledge and human rights building), Schwalbach, p. 298.

41 Lower, Wendy (2012): Holocaust Studien im Internationalen Kontext, in: Brenner, Michael; Strnad, Maximilian (2012): Der Holocaust in der deutschsprachigen Geschichtswissenschaft, Göttingen, p. 53.

42 Manca, Stefania et al. (2023): Participating in professional development programmes or learning in the wild? Understanding the learning ecologies of Holocaust educators, British Educational Research Journal, p. 310, 16.10.2023.

43 Kistenmacher, Olaf (2017): Schuldabwehr-Antisemitismus als Herausforderung (Guilt defense- antisemitism as a challenge), in: Mendel, M.; Messerschmidt, A. et al (2017): Fragiler Konsens, Antisemitismuskritische Bildung in der Migrationsgesellschaft, (Fragile

consensus, Education critical of antisemitism in a migration society), Frankfurt, p. 210.

44 Eckmann, Monique/Österberg Oscar (2017): Research in Germany, in: Eckmann, Monique (2017): Research in teaching and learning about the Holocaust, in: holocaustremembrance.com, 12.10.2024.

45 Schmoll, Melanie Carina (2018): „Holo…What?! Teaching the Holocaust against all obstacles", unpublished paper, Hamburg.

46 This seems to be not only an issue in Canada or Germany, but also in most of the other countries. For more details: UNESCO (2014): The impact of Holocaust Education: How to assess policies and practices? International Seminar, 27. January 2014, Paris, https://unesdoc.unesco.org/ark:/48223/pf0000228087, 02.10.2024.

47 Borries, Bodo von (2011): Geschichtslernen und Menschenrechtsbildung (Historical knowledge and human rights building), Schwalbach, pp. 291/292.

48 Kühner, Angela (2009): NS–Erinnerung und Migrationsgemeinschaft (NS–Remembrance and Immigration society), in: Einsichten und Perspektiven (Insights and Perspectives), Bayerische Zeitschrift für Politik und Geschichte, München.

49 Zunzer, Daniela (2013): „Die Exkursion nach Dachau müssen Sie unbedingt beibehalten" (You have to maintain the excursion to Dachau), in: Gautschi, Peter et al. (2013): Shoa und Schule, Lehren und Lernen im 21. Jahrhundert, Chronos (Shoa and School, Teaching and Learning in the 21st century), p. 124.

50 Bernstein, Julia (2020): Antisemitismus an Schulen in Deutschland (Antisemitism in German schools), Bonn, p. 334.

51 Zülsdorf–Kersting, Meik (2007): Sechzig Jahre danach: Jugendliche und der Holocaust (60 years after–Youth and the Holocaust), Berlin, p. 114.

52 Gerson, D. (2013): Von der Leichtigkeit des Einfühlens in die Opfer und von der Schwierigkeit des Verstehens der Täter. Zur Problematik der fehlenden „Täterperspektive" beim Gedenken an den Holocaust, (About the ease of empathizing with the victims and the

difficulty of understanding the perpetrators. On the problem of the missing "perpetrator perspective" when commemorating the Holocaust), in: Gautschi et al. (2013), Shoah und Schule (Shoah and School), p. 147.

53 Rajal, Elke (2023): Countering antisemitism through Holocaust education. A comparative perspective on Scotland and Austria, in: https://www.tandfonline.com/doi/full/10.1080/00131911.2024.23 25068#abstract, 06.08.2024.

54 For more information: https://encyclopedia.ushmm.org/content/en/article/the-german-churches-and-the-nazi-state, 07.12.2024.

55 Borries, Bodo von (2008): Historisches Denken Lernen – Welter-schließung statt Epochenüberblick (Learning to think historically - exploring the world instead of an overview of eras), Opladen.

56 Dangelmeier, Nadja (2021): „Vielfalt anerkennen, Vielfalt einbez-iehen (Recognizing diversity, including diversity)–Lernen über die NS–Herrschaft in diversen Gruppen", in: Erziehung und Unterricht, Österreichische Pädagogische Zeitschrift, LehrerInnenbildung NEU, 5-6, Jahrgang 171, 490 – 498, Wien; M. Can (2013): Überlegun-gen zur pädagogischen Auseinandersetzung mit der Shoa in der deutschen Migrationsgesellschaft (Reflections on the pedagogical confrontation with the Shoah in the German migration society), in: Jikeli, Georg (2013): Umstrittene Geschichte. Ansichten zum Hol-ocaust unter Muslimen im internationalen Vergleich, Frankfurt/Main.

57 Short, Geoffrey (1991): Combatting anti-Semitism: A dilemma for anti-racist education. British Journal of Educational Studies, 39/1, pp. 33–44.

58 Fechler, Bernd (2006): Antisemitismus im globalisierten Klassen-zimmer (Anti-Semitism in the globalized classroom), in: Fechler, Bernd; Kößler, Gottfried; Messerschmidt, Astrid; Schäuble, Barbara (2006): Neue Judenfeindschaft? Frankfurt, p. 199; similar: Schäuble, Barbara; Thoma, Hanne (2006): Ergebnisse des Europäischen Work-shops „Antisemitismus eine Herausforderung für die (politische)

Bildungsarbeit" (Results of the European workshop "Anti-Semitism a challenge for (political) educational work"), in: Fechler, Bernd; Kößler, Gottfried; Messerschmidt, Astrid; Schäuble, Barbara (2006): Neue Judenfeinschaft? Frankfurt, p. 237.

59 Bernstein, Julia (2020): Antisemitismus an Schulen in Deutschland (Antisemitism in German schools), Bonn, p. 153.

60 Similar Bernstein, Julia (2020): Antisemitismus an Schulen in Deutschland (Antisemitism in German schools), Bonn, pp. 334/ 335.

61 Schmoll, Melanie Carina (2018): „Holo...What?! Teaching the Holocaust against all obstacles", unpublished paper, Hamburg.

62 Schmoll, Melanie Carina (2018): „Holo...What?! Teaching the Holocaust against all obstacles", unpublished paper, Hamburg; similar Bernstein, Julia (2020): Antisemitismus an Schulen in Deutschland (Antisemitism in German schools), Bonn, pp. 332/333.

63 Kistenmacher, Olaf (2017): Schuldabwehr-Antisemitismus als Herausforderung (Guilt defense- antisemitism as a challenge), in: Mendel, M.; Messerschmidt, A. et al. (2017): Fragiler Konsens, Antisemitismuskritische Bildung in der Migrationsgesellschaft, (Fragile consensus, Education critical of antisemitism in a migration society), Frankfurt, p. 217.

64 Borries, Bodo von (2011): Geschichtslernen und Menschenrechtsbildung (Historical knowledge and human rights building), Schwalbach, p. 59.

65 Borries, Bodo von (2011): Geschichtslernen und Menschenrechtsbildung (Historical knowledge and human rights building), Schwalbach, p. 62.

66 Lorenz, Friederike et al. (2021): German Teachers Learning about the Shoah in Israel, Wuppertal, p. 10.

67 Schmoll, Melanie Carina (2024): Misinformation about Israel and Antisemitic Views in School Textbooks? The Case of Germany, Münster, 2024.

68 Bernstein, Julia (2020): Antisemitismus an Schulen in Deutschland (Antisemitism in German schools), Bonn, pp. 456/ 457.

69 Möller, Rainer (2015): Was geht uns heute Auschwitz an? (Why should we care about Auschwitz today?) In: https://comenius.de/2015/12/04/was_geht_uns_heute_auschwitz_an_2015/, 24.09.2024.

70 Council of the Israel Academy (2020): Report on the State of Holocaust Studies in Research Universities and Colleges in Israel, approved by the Council of the Israel Academy on December 10, 2019, in: https://www.academy.ac.il/Index3/Entry.aspx?nodeId=842&entryId=21248, 09.12.2024.

71 For more information see: Meyer–Hamme, Johannes (2018): Was heißt "historisches Lernen? Eine Begriffsbestimmung (What does "historical learning" mean? A definition), in: Sandkühler et al. (2018): Geschichtsunterricht im 21. Jahrhundert (History lessons in the 21st century), Bonn, pp. 75–92.

72 Berghan, Wilhelm (2004): Demokratiebildung und reflexive Mündigkeit (Democracy and reflective maturity), in: Grimm et al. (2024): Bildung gegen Antisemitismus (Education against antisemitism), p. 76.

73 Borries, Bodo von (2011): Geschichtslernen und Menschenrechtsbildung (Historical knowledge and human rights building), Schwalbach, p. 56.

74 Borries, Bodo von (2011): Geschichtslernen und Menschenrechtsbildung (Historical knowledge and human rights building), Schwalbach, p. 58.

75 Borries, Bodo von (2011): Geschichtslernen und Menschenrechtsbildung (Historical knowledge and human rights building), Schwalbach, p. 12.

76 Kistenmacher, Olaf (2017): Schuldabwehr-Antisemitismus als Herausforderung (Guilt defense- antisemitism as a challenge), in: Mendel, M.; Messerschmidt, A. et al. (2017): Fragiler Konsens, Antisemitismuskritische Bildung in der Migrationsgesellschaft, (Fragile consensus, Education critical of antisemitism in a migration society), Frankfurt, p. 218.

77 For more information see: Mägdefrau, Jutta/Michler, Andreas

(2018): Wo ist das Kind in der Geschichtsunterrichtsforschung? (Where is the child in analysis about history lessons?), in: Sandkühler et al. (2018): Geschichtsunterricht im 21. Jahrhundert (History lessons in the 21st century), Bonn, pp. 143–165.

78 John, Anke (2018): Wie? Der Blick auf die Unterrichtsgestaltung (How? A view on lesson design), in: Sandkühler et al. (2018): Geschichtsunterricht im 21. Jahrhundert (History lessons in the 21st century), Bonn, pp. 270–272.

79 For more details, see: Pistone at al. (2023): Teaching and learning about the Holocaust, in: https://www.tandfonline.com/doi/full/10.1080/17504902.2023.2245282#abstract, 06.08.2024.

80 Stefaniak, A. et al. (2016): Contact with a multicultural past: A prejudice-reducing intervention, International Journal of Intercultural Relations, 50, pp. 60–65; Cowan, P. et al. (2007): Does addressing prejudice and discrimination through Holocaust education produce better citizens? Educational Review, 59/2, pp. 115–130.

81 Schäuble, Barbara; Thoma, Hanne (2006): Ergebnisse des Europäischen Workshops „Antisemitismus eine Herausforderung für die (politische) Bildungsarbeit", in: Fechler, Bernd; Kößler, Gottfried; Messerschmidt, Astrid; Schäuble, Barbara (2006): Neue Judenfeindschaft? Frankfurt, pp. 233–245.

82 ADL (2020): Survey of U.S. College Students Shows Holocaust Education is Effective in Building Empathy, Tolerance and Open Mindedness, in: https://www.adl.org/resources/press-release/survey-us-college-students-shows-holocaust-education-effective-building, 26.09.2024.

83 Gautschi, Peter (2008): Der Beitrag des Geschichtsunterrichts zur Entwicklung von Einstellungen (The contribution of history teaching to the development of attitudes) in: Bauer, Jan–Patrick; Meyer–Hamme, Johannes; Körber, Andreas (2008): Geschichtslernen–Innovation und Reflexion (Learning History–Innovation and Reflection), Kenzingen, p. 289.

84 Gordon, Stacy et al. (2004): The Effects of Holocaust Education on

Students' Level of Antisemitism, in: Educational Research Quarterly, Vol. 27, No 3. March 2004, pp. 58–71.

85 For more information: Cowan, P. et al. (2011): We saw inhumanity close up, Journal of Curriculum Studies, 42/2, pp. 163–184.

86 Wagensommer 2003, quoted in: Zülsdorf–Kersting, Meik (2007): Sechzig Jahre danach: Jugendliche und der Holocaust (60 years after–Young people and the Holocaust). Berlin, p. 113.

87 Lorenz, Friederike et al. (2021): German Teachers Learning about the Shoah in Israel, Wuppertal.–
This arrogant attitude even goes so far that that Germany speaks of a responsibility with regard to Israel, which unfortunately all too often translates into an attitude that was probably not intended in this way to begin with. Israel is not a child for which Germany should assume any kind of responsibility. Israeli society and the government are well able to make their own assessments and take action. Germany is responsible for ensuring that the Holocaust is not repeated. Germany is not the supposedly better-knowing, superior parent that has to look after little, immature Israel.

88 For more information: Bundesministerium des Inneren, Antisemitismus in Deutschland, in: https://www.bmi.bund.de/SharedDocs/downloads/DE/publikationen/themen/heimat-integration/expertenkreis-antisemitismus/antisemitismus-in-deutschland-bericht.html, 19.07.2024.

89 It must be mentioned, that at present all training courses for teachers e.g. in Germany are equally weighted. Teachers are overwhelmed by the need to attend, internalize, and ultimately apply all the desired courses in the classroom, so they often react with resistance and rejection to the offers. In: Bernstein, Julia (2020): Antisemitismus an Schulen in Deutschland (Antisemitism in German schools), Bonn, p. 389.

90 Cohen, Erik et al. (2010?): Shoah Education in Israeli State Schools: An Educational Research 2007–2009, School of Education, Bar Ilan University, Israel.

91 Subotic, Jelena (2023): The International Relations of Holocaust Memory, in: Kopstein, Jeffrey et al. (2023): Holocaust: Politics, Violence, Memory. The New Social Science of the Holocaust, London, pp. 283–297.

92 The D–test helps to distinguish legitimate criticism of Israel from hatred of Jews. The first D is the test of demonization. When the Jewish state is being demonized; when Israel's actions are blown out of all sensible proportion; when comparisons are made between Israelis and National Socialists and between Palestinian refugee camps and Auschwitz–this is hatred of Jews, not legitimate criticism of Israel. The second D is the test of double standards. When criticism of Israel is applied selectively; when Israel is singled out by the United Nations for human rights abuses while the behavior of known and major abusers, such as China, Iran, Cuba, and Syria, is ignored; when Israel's Magen David Adom, alone among the world's ambulance services, is denied admission to the International Red Cross–this is hatred of Jews. The third D is the test of delegitimization: when Israel's fundamental right to exist is denied –alone among all peoples in the world–this too is hatred of Jews. The fourth D is the test of de-realization. This means that the portrayal of Israel is very distorted and differs greatly from the factual reality. The first three D's are ultimately a consequence of this false image (Schwarz–Friesel, Monika; Reinharz, Jehuda (2013): Die Sprache der Judenfeindschaft im 21. Jahrhundert (The language of hostility towards Jews in the 21st century), Berlin, p. 249).

93 ADL (2020): Survey of U.S. College Students Shows Holocaust Education is Effective in Building Empathy, Tolerance and Open Mindedness, in: https://www.adl.org/resources/press-release/survey-us-college-students-shows-holocaust-education-effective-building, 26.09.2024.

6. The Future of Holocaust Education

1   Even if Brown and others support the idea of a cross-curricular approach to teach the topic, because it is most impactful of the Holocaust, interdisciplinary and across subjects, studies underline this approach is not as impactful in Germany, for example, as it might be in the US (Brown, Sara E. (2024): The Need for Education about the Holocaust and Genocide in the Twenty-First Century, in: Bachman, Jeffrey S.(2024): Genocide Studies: Pathways Ahead, New York, pp. 14–35).

2   Bernhardt, Markus (2018): Was? Historisches Lernen in der Schule (What? Learning about history in school) in: Sandkühler et al. (2018): Geschichtsunterricht im 21. Jahrhundert (History lessons in the 21st century), Bonn, pp. 67–69.

3   Bühl–Gramer, Charlotte (2018): Geschichtsunterricht im 21. Jahrhundert–eine Standortbestimmung (History lessons in the 21st century–an assessment of the current situation) in: Sandkühler et al. (2018): Geschichtsunterricht im 21. Jahrhundert (History lessons in the 21st century), Bonn, pp. 38/39.

4   Schmoll, Melanie Carina (2024): Misinformation about Israel and Antisemitic Views in School Textbooks? The Case of Germany, Münster, 2025, p. 50.

5   Grünberg, Arnon (2024): Westliche Gegner des Antisemitismus besuchen die ermordeten Juden im Museum, mit den lebenden dagegen haben sie ein Problem (Western opponents of antisemitism visit the murdered Jews in the museum, but they have a problem with the living ones), Neue Züricher Zeitung, 2024.

6   For example, in the US or Israel. For more information about the US: The New York State Archives Partnership Trust, https://considerthesourceny.org/; for Isarel: Cohen, Erik et al. (2010?): Shoah Education in Israeli State Schools: An Educational Research 2007–2009, School of Education, Bar Ilan University, Israel.

7   Schmoll, Melanie Carina (2024): Misinformation about Israel and

Antisemitic Views in School Textbooks? The Case of Germany, Münster, 2024, p. 50.

8   Bernstein, Julia (2020): Antisemitismus an Schulen in Deutschland (Antisemitism in German schools), Bonn, pp. 456/457.

9   Paxton, R. J. (2002): The Influence of Author Visibility on High School Students Solving a Historical Problem, Cognition, and Instruction, 20(2), pp. 197–248, in: http://www.jstor.org/stable/3233874, 09.12.2024.

10   Nägel, Verena/Stegmaier, Sanna (2019): AR und VR in der historisch-politischen Bildung zum Nationalsozialismus und Holocaust – (Interaktives) Lernen oder emotionale Überwältigung? (AR and VR in historical-political education on National Socialism and the Holocaust - (interactive) learning or emotional overwhelming?) In: https://www.bpb.de/lernen/digitale-bildung/werkstatt/298168/ar-und-vr-in-der-historisch-politischen-bildung-zum-nationalsozialismus-und-holocaust-interaktives-lernen-oder-emotionale-ueberwaeltigung/, 13.12.2024.

11   For example, Call of Duty WWII.

12   For example, Eva´s Stories, in: https://www.instagram.com/eva.stories/, 12.12.2024. An Instagram page that showed the reality of a Jewish girl's life in Germany during the National Socialist regime. There are now several similar projects, including on Sophie Scholl and Anne Frank.

13   Rumbell, Olivia (2024): New AI campaign aims to get mandatory Holocaust education in Canadian schools, National Post, May 2024, in: https://nationalpost.com/news/canada/ai-campaign-mandatory-holocaust-education-canadian-schools, 26.11.2024. Overall, it is clear that AR/VR offerings are negotiated differently in different national cultures of remembrance and therefore need to be adapted or supplemented locally. In the USA, where empathy is a central component of Holocaust education, there are fewer reservations about the use of immersive and affective applications. In Germany, on the other hand, the applications must be measured against the

Beutelsbacher Consensus (Nägel, Verena/Stegmaier, Sanna (2019): AR und VR in der historisch-politischen Bildung zum Nationalsozialismus und Holocaust - (Interaktives) Lernen oder emotionale Überwältigung? (AR and VR in historical-political education on National Socialism and the Holocaust - (interactive) learning or emotional overwhelming?) In: https://www.bpb.de/lernen/digitale-bildung/werkstatt/298168/ar-und-vr-in-der-historisch-politischen-bildung-zum-nationalsozialismus-und-holocaust-interaktives-lernen-oder-emotionale-ueberwaeltigung/, 13.12.2024).

14   Burkhardt, Hannes (2023): Geschichtsdeutungen über die Zeit des Nationalsozialismus in den Social Media (Historical interpretations of the National Socialist era in social media), in: Homberg et al. (2023): Deutungskämpfe–die „zweite Geschichte" des Nationalsozialismus (Interpretation battles–the "second history" of National Socialism), Frankfurt, pp. 263–287.

15   Haug, Verena (2017): Antisemitismuskritische Bildungsarbeit in Gedenkstätten (Educational work critical of antisemitism in memorial sites), in: Mendel, M.; Messerschmidt, A. et al (2017): Fragiler Konsens, Antisemitismuskritische Bildung in der Migrationsgesellschaft, (Fragile consensus, Education critical of antisemitism in a migration society), Frankfurt, p. 158.

16   Grünberg, Arnon (2024): Westliche Gegner des Antisemitismus besuchen die ermordeten Juden im Museum, mit den lebenden dagegen haben sie ein Problem (Western opponents of antisemitism visit the murdered Jews in the museum, but they have a problem with the living ones), Neue Züricher Zeitung, 2024.

17   For more details see: Haug, Verena (2017): Antisemitismuskritische Bildungsarbeit in Gedenkstätten (Educational work critical of antisemitism in memorial sites), in: Mendel, M.; Messerschmidt, A. et al. (2017): Fragiler Konsens, Antisemitismuskritische Bildung in der Migrationsgesellschaft, (Fragile consensus, Education critical of antisemitism in a migration society), Frankfurt, pp. 155–169.

18 Bartov, Omer (2018): Anatomy of a Genocide: The Life and Death of a Town Called Buczacz, New York

19 Brown, Sara E. (2024): The Need for Education about the Holocaust and Genocide in the Twenty-First Century, in: Bachman, Jeffrey S.: Genocide Studies: Pathways Ahead, New York, pp. 14–35

20 Bernstein, Julia (2020): Antisemitismus an Schulen in Deutschland (Antisemitism in German schools), Bonn, p. 455.

21 Nägel, Verena/Stegmaier, Sanna (2019): AR und VR in der historisch–politischen Bildung zum Nationalsozialismus und Holocaust– (Interaktives) Lernen oder emotionale Überwältigung? (AR and VR in historical–political education on National Socialism and the Holocaust - (interactive) learning or emotional overwhelming?) In: https://www.bpb.de/lernen/digitale-bildung/werkstatt/298168/ar-und-vr-in-der-historisch-politischen-bildung-zum-nationalsozialismus-und-holocaust-interaktives-lernen-oder-emotionale-ueberwaeltigung/, 13.12.2024.

22 Bernstein, Julia (2020): Antisemitismus an Schulen in Deutschland (Antisemitism in German schools), Bonn, p. 415.

23 Thanks to the unique refugee status, which is hereditary.

24 Kistenmacher, Olaf (2017): Schuldabwehr–Antisemitismus als Herausforderung (Guilt defense–antisemitism as a challenge), in: Mendel, M.; Messerschmidt, A. et al. (2017): Fragiler Konsens, Antisemitismuskritische Bildung in der Migrationsgesellschaft, (Fragile consensus, Education critical of antisemitism in a migration society), Frankfurt, p. 217.

25 Kistenmacher, Olaf (2017): Schuldabwehr-Antisemitismus als Herausforderung (Guilt defense- antisemitism as a challenge), in: Mendel, M.; Messerschmidt, A. et al. (2017): Fragiler Konsens, Antisemitismuskritische Bildung in der Migrationsgesellschaft, (Fragile consensus, Education critical of antisemitism in a migration society), Frankfurt, p. 210.

26 Schubert, A. (2020): Israelbezogener Antisemitismus–eine Herausforderung für die Bildungsarbeit (Israel related antisemitism),

in: Grimm et al. (2020): Bildung gegen Antisemitismus (Education against antisemitism), p. 164.

27 Schmoll, Melanie Carina (2018): „Holo…What?! Teaching the Holocaust against all obstacles", unpublished paper, Hamburg.

28 Kranz, Dani (2024): Da fehlt doch was…(Something is missing…), in: Jüdische Allgemeine, https://www.juedische-allgemeine.de/kultur/da-fehlt-doch-was/, 17.12.2024.

29 Allwork, Larissa (2019): Holocaust education and contemporary anti-Semitism, in: Policy Papers, https://www.historyandpolicy.org/policy-papers/papers/holocaust-education-and-contemporary-anti-semitism, 02.10.2024.

30 Kranz, Dani (2024): Da fehlt doch was…(Something is missing…), in: Jüdische Allgemeine, https://www.juedische-allgemeine.de/kultur/da-fehlt-doch-was/, 17.12.2024.

31 More suggestions can be found here: Council of the Israel Academy (2020): Report on the State of Holocaust Studies in Research Universities and Colleges in Israel, approved by the Council of the Israel Academy on December 10, 2019, in: https://www.academy.ac.il/Index3/Entry.aspx?nodeId=842&entryId=21248, 09.12.2024.

32 Bernstein, Julia (2020): Antisemitismus an Schulen in Deutschland (Antisemitism in German schools), Bonn, p. 389.

33 So-called Beutelsbacher Konsens, information only available in German: https://www.bpb.de/die-bpb/ueber-uns/auftrag/51310/beutelsbacher-konsens/, 30.11.2024.

34 Salzborn, Samuel/Kurth, Alexandra (2019): Antisemitismus in der Schule (Antisemitism in school), Berlin, p. 23.

35 For more information see: Mägdefrau, Jutta/Michler, Andreas (2018): Wo ist das Kind in der Geschichtsunterrichtsforschung? (Where is the child in analysis about history lessons?), in: Sandkühler et al. (2018): Geschichtsunterricht im 21. Jahrhundert (History lessons in the 21st century), Bonn, pp. 143–165.

36 John, Anke (2018): Wie? Der Blick auf die Unterrichtsgestaltung (How? A view on lesson design), in: Sandkühler et al. (2018):

Geschichtsunterricht im 21. Jahrhundert (History lessons in the 21st century), Bonn, p. 272.

37   Allwork, Larissa (2019): Holocaust education and contemporary anti-Semitism, in: Policy Papers, https://www.historyandpolicy.org/policy-papers/papers/holocaust-education-and-contemporary-anti-semitism, 02.10.2024.

38   Calmbach, Marc (2017): Wie ticken Jugendliche 2016? Lebenswelten von Jugendlichen im Alter von 14–17 Jahren in Deutschland (What makes young people tick in 2016? Lifeworlds of young people aged 14–17 in Germany,), Wiesbaden.

39   Allwork, Larissa (2019): Holocaust education and contemporary anti-Semitism, in: Policy Papers, https://www.historyandpolicy.org/policy-papers/papers/holocaust-education-and-contemporary-anti-semitism, 02.10.2024.

40   Weber, Philippe (2018): Dialogisches Erzählen im Geschichtsunterricht (Dialogic storytelling in history lessons), in: Sandkühler et al. (2018): Geschichtsunterricht im 21. Jahrhundert (History lessons in the 21st century), Bonn, pp. 320/321.

41   Gautschi, Peter (1999): Geschichte lehren (Teaching history), Zürich, pp. 49/50.

42   Weber, Philippe (2018): Dialogisches Erzählen im Geschichtsunterricht (Dialogic storytelling in history lessons), in: Sandkühler et al. (2018): Geschichtsunterricht im 21. Jahrhundert (History lessons in the 21st century), Bonn, p. 322.

43   Sandkühler, Thomas/Lenkeit, Guido (2018): Exklusion durch historische ..?, (Exclusion through historical education?) in: Sandkühler et al. (2018): Geschichtsunterricht im 21. Jahrhundert (History lessons in the 21st century), Bonn, p. 246.

44   Sandkühler, Thomas/Lenkeit, Guido (2018): Exklusion durch historische Bildung? (Exclusion through historical education?) in: Sandkühler et al. (2018): Geschichtsunterricht im 21. Jahrhundert (History lessons in the 21st century), Bonn, p. 247.

45   Dvir, Boaz (2024): How to Get Holocaust Education Right, in: Times,

https://time.com/6974378/holocaust-remembrance-education-es-say/, 26.09.2024.

46 For more information: Borries, Bodo von (2011): Geschichtslernen und Menschenrechtsbildung (Historical knowledge and human rights building). Schwalbach.

47 Find out more here: https://www.stolpersteine.eu/en/home/, 01.01.2025.

7. Turning Education into an Experience

1 Michalski, Bohdan (2005): Let's teach all of it from the Start, in: Ambrosewicz-Jacobs, J. et al. (2005): Why Should We Teach About the Holocaust? Cracow, p. 35.

2 Mendel, Meron; Messerschmidt, Astrid (2017): Fragiler Konsens, Antisemitismuskritische Bildung in der Migrationsgesellschaft, (Fragile consensus. Education critical of antisemitism in a migration society), Frankfurt, p. 13.

3 Laznik, Jacob (2024): How did antisemitism become the new mainstream, what can be done?–Interview, in: Jerusalem Post, in: https://www.jpost.com/diaspora/antisemitism/article-804455, 31.08.2024.

4 Source: Laznik, Jacob (2024): How did antisemitism become the new mainstream, what can be done?–Interview, in: Jerusalem Post, in: https://www.jpost.com/diaspora/antisemitism/article-804455, 31.08.2024.

5 Müller, Stephan (2020): Antisemitismusprävention als Bildungserfahrung (Preventing anti-Semitism as an educational experience), in: Grimm et al. (2020): Bildung gegen Antisemitismus (Education against antisemitism), pp. 225/226.

6 Radvan, Heike (2017): Die Bedeutung von Kommunikation im Umgang mit Antisemitismus (The meaning of communication in dealing with antisemitism), in: Mendel, Meron; Messerschmidt, Astrid (2017): Fragiler Konsens, Antisemitismuskritische Bildung in

der Migrationsgesellschaft, (Fragile consensus. Education critical of antisemitism in a migration society), Frankfurt, p. 52/53.

7   See Chapter 5 for more explanation on simplification.

8   Bernstein, Julia (2020): Antisemitismus an Schulen in Deutschland (Antisemitism in German schools), Bonn, pp. 409–413.

9   Bernstein, Julia (2020): Antisemitismus an Schulen in Deutschland (Antisemitism in German schools), Bonn, p. 455.

10 Lorenz, Friederike et al. (2021): German Teachers Learning about the Shoah in Israel, Wuppertal, p. 17.

11 Becker, Matthias J./ Bechthold–Hengelhaupt, Tilman (2020): Antisemitismus im Internet (Antisemitism in the Internet), in: Grimm et al. (2020): Bildung gegen Antisemitismus (Education against antisemitism), pp. 93–95.

12 Pearce, A.; Foster, S.; Pettigrew, A. (2020): Antisemitism and Holocaust education, in: Pearce, A.; Foster, S.; Pettigrew, A. (2020): Holocaust Education, UCL Press, p. 163.

13 UNESCO (2014): The impact of Holocaust Education: How to assess policies and practices? International Seminar, 27. January 2014, Paris, https://unesdoc.unesco.org/ark:/48223/pf0000228087, 02.10.2024.

14 Rajal, Elke (2020): Möglichkeiten und Grenzen antisemitismuskritischer Pädagogik (Possibilities and limits of pedagogy critical of anti-Semitism), in: Grimm et al. (2020): Bildung gegen Antisemitismus (Education against antisemitism), pp. 186–188.

15 Mor, Aharon (2024): A global war on antisemitism must start now– opinion, October 2024, Jerusalem Post, in: https://www.jpost.com/opinion/article-825033, 26.11.2024.

16 US Department of State (2024): Guidelines for countering antisemitism, https://www.state.gov/global-guidelines-for-countering-anti-semitism/, 12.10.2024

17 Bernstein, Julia (2020): Antisemitismus an Schulen in Deutschland (Antisemitism in German schools), Bonn, p. 387.

18 OSCE (2017): Understanding Anti-Semitic Hate Crimes and Ad-

dressing the Security Needs of Jewish Communities: A Practical Guide, https://www.osce.org/odihr/317166, 30.11.2024.

19   Bernstein, Julia (2020): Antisemitismus an Schulen in Deutschland (Antisemitism in German schools), Bonn, p. 389.

20   Mor, Aharon (2024): A global war on antisemitism must start now– opinion, October 2024, Jerusalem Post, in: https://www.jpost.com/ opinion/article-825033, 26.11.2024.

21   Scherr, Albert/Schäuble, Barbara (2017): „Ich habe nicht gegen Juden, aber...“ (I have nothing against Jews, but...), in: https://ar- chive.org/details/amadeu-antonio-stiftung-ich-habe-nichts-gegen- juden-ausgangsbedingungen-und-pers, 3011.2024.

22   And as the events on the night of November 7, 2024 in Amsterdam have shown, the fate of Jews was in the hands of Israel. Since it was Israel that took action and employed an emergency rescue mission to save Jewish people from an anew pogrom (More details can be found here: https://www.jpost.com/israel-news/2024-11-08/live-up- dates-828163, 27.11.2024.).

8.   Conclusion

1   Pearce, A.; Foster, S.; Pettigrew, A. (2020): Antisemitism and Holo- caust education, in: Pearce, A.; Foster, S.; Pettigrew, A. (2020): Holo- caust Education, UCL Press, p. 163.

2   Verstandig, Yonatan (2024): Words to Action: How the ADL is fight- ing antisemitism with education, Jerusalem Post, October 2024, in: https://www.jpost.com/diaspora/antisemitism/article-824727, 26.11.2024.

3   Kistenmacher, Olaf (2017): Schuldabwehr–Antisemitismus als Herausforderung (Guilt defense–antisemitism as a challenge), in: Mendel, M.; Messerschmidt, A. et al. (2017): Fragiler Konsens, Anti- semitismuskritische Bildung in der Migrationsgesellschaft, (Fragile consensus, Education critical of antisemitism in a migration socie- ty), Frankfurt, p. 209.

4   Dangelmeier, Nadja (2021): „Vielfalt anerkennen, Vielfalt einbez-
     iehen (Recognizing diversity, including diversity)–Lernen über die
     NS–Herrschaft in diversen Gruppen", in: Erziehung und Unterricht,
     Österreichische Pädagogische Zeitschrift, LehrerInnenbildung
     NEU, 5-6, Jahrgang 171, Wien, p. 491.

Bibliography

1   For a better understanding German titles were translated by Mela-
     nie Carina Schmoll.